Men and Women in Interaction

Men and Women in Interaction

Reconsidering the Differences

Elizabeth Aries

New York   Oxford

OXFORD UNIVERSITY PRESS

1996

Oxford University Press

Oxford   New York
Athens   Auckland   Bangkok   Bombay
Calcutta   Cape Town   Dar es Salaam   Delhi
Florence   Hong Kong   Istanbul   Karachi
Kuala Lumpur   Madras   Madrid   Melbourne
Mexico City   Nairobi   Paris   Singapore
Taipei   Tokyo   Toronto

and associated companies in
Berlin   Ibadan

Copyright (c) 1996 by Oxford University Press, Inc.

Published by Oxford University Press, Inc.
198 Madison Avenue, New York, New York   10016

Oxford is a registered trademark of Oxford University Press

Library of Congress Cataloging-in-Publication Data
Aries, Elizabeth.
   Men and women in interaction : reconsidering the differences /
Elizabeth Aries.
      p.   cm.
   Includes bibliographical references and index.
   ISBN 0-19-509469-7; ISBN 0-19-510358-0 (pbk.)
   1. Interpersonal communication.   2. Sex differences (Psychology)
3. Stereotype (Psychology)   4. Feminist psychology.   I. Title.
BF637.C45A79   1996 95-9300
305.3—dc20

9 8 7 6 5 4 3 2 1
Printed in the United States of America
on acid-free paper

To my husband,

   Richard Berman,

and my children,

   Joshua and *Anna*

between a statement and a question (e.g., "You're coming at noon, aren't you?). However, speakers may also use tag questions to express solidarity and facilitate interaction. Many researchers have concluded that men express dominance and women express tentativeness in their speech. But they have based these conclusions on incorrect assumptions about the meaning of the behaviors under consideration.

Finally, to what extent do stereotypes shape our perceptions and evaluations of speakers? We immediately recognize participants in interaction as male or female, and this knowledge leads us to form expectations about what participants are like and how they will behave based on their gender. We bend our perceptions in the direction of stereotyped expectations, overlooking things that are not expected and seeing things that are not there. We perceive men and women who display identical behavior differently in accordance with gender stereotypes, and we respond to and evaluate them differently.

My aim in writing this book is to make people more skeptical of the popularized beliefs about gender differences in the interaction styles of men and women. Also, I want to bring into focus the individual and situational variability in behavior that is revealed by research on gender and interaction. Men and women are capable of displaying both masculine and feminine styles of interaction, and the style they display depends on their status, role, gender identity, and interaction goals, as well as on a variety of other situational variables. Stereotyped beliefs have the power to become self-fulfilling prophecies for behavior. The stronger our belief in gender differences, the more firmly we will keep current gender arrangements in place, arrangements that afford greater opportunities and privileges to men.

March 1995   E. A.
Amherst, Massachusetts

Acknowledgments

I want to thank those who first stimulated my interest in the study of gender and interaction. As a graduate student in the Department of Social Relations at Harvard University I worked under the direction of Robert Freed Bales and Stephen Cohen. Their intellectual curiosity, insight, and abiding fascination with the study of interpersonal behavior served as an inspiration to me. I am sincerely appreciative of all the encouragement and support they gave me in pursuing my early work in the field.

Particular thanks goes to my friend and colleague Rose Olver. Rose has been an intellectual companion throughout my career, and I have turned to her throughout the writing of this book to discuss and debate ideas and to have her read and critique drafts of chapters. Rose has always been there for me in innumerable ways, and her wisdom, insight, knowledge, generosity, and confidence in and support of me have been invaluable in my evolution in the field. I want to thank Nancy Aries and Elliott Sclar for taking the time to critique chapters of this book, for their insightful suggestions for revisions, and for their enthusiasm about the ideas. Finally, deep appreciation goes to Rhoda Unger for her insightful critique of the book. Since the 1970s Rhoda Unger and other feminist psychologists have been arguing that gender differences are small effects, that status effects have been confused with the effects of gender, that gender differences appear inconsistently, and that gender stereotypes influence the perception and evaluation of speakers. My own thinking has been deeply influenced by Rhoda's work and that of other feminist scholars of gender, and I am indebted to Rhoda and all those like her whose research and thinking about gender have shaped my analysis of the research on gender and communication.

This book could not have been written without the help of the reference librarians at Amherst College. I thank them for all their help in tracking down and acquiring the many articles and books I needed to obtain from other libraries. I am grateful to Faye Crosby, Ronnie Janoff-Bulman, and Susan Fiske for their helpful advice about book publishing, and for their encouragement throughout this project. My sincere appeciation goes to Joan Bossert at Oxford University Press for her belief in and excitement about this book, and for her help in seeing it through to production.

Special thanks goes to my husband, Richard Berman (Luke), and my children, Joshua and Anna, who are the emotional bedrock of my life, and whose lives fill mine with meaning and joy. Luke has been my best friend throughout our 21 years of marriage. He read every chapter of this book meticulously with an eye to its improvement and encouraged me in every way during the writing of this book. His belief in and support of me has never wavered. Josh and Anna helped me keep this book in perspective, drawing me continually into the whirl of their lives, their schools, and their activities.

Contents

Men and Women in Interaction

1

The Elusive Truth About Women and Men

The popular press and scholarly journals are filled with accounts of differences between men and women, in their verbal, mathematical, and perceptual abilities, their personalities, and their patterns of communication. One of the areas of particular interest to the general public is verbal interaction, as evidenced by the popularity of two recent bestsellers: Deborah Tannen's *You Just Don't Understand: Women and Men in Conversation*[1] and John Gray's *Men Are from Mars, Women Are from Venus.*[2] A very clear and polarized depiction of men and women has emerged from these works. Deborah Tannen has argued that men and women approach conversation with a distinct set of rules and interpretations of talk. Men focus on status and independence; women focus on intimacy and connection—a difference that makes communication between the sexes problematic. John Gray goes even further in his claims: "Not only do men and women communicate differently but they think, feel, perceive, react, respond, love, need, and appreciate differently. They almost seem to be from different planets, speaking different languages."[3]

Deborah Tannen's book relies heavily on anecdotal accounts, John Gray's book on participants' reports in relationship seminars. Neither systematically addresses the large body of interdisciplinary research on gender and communication that has been produced over the past 25 years by scholars in psychology, sociology, anthropology, linguistics, and communication studies. However, recent textbooks reviewing this literature more comprehensively also conclude, like Tannen, that men and women communicate differently. In *Gendered Lives,*[4] for example, Julia Wood claims that communication for

3

women is a way to establish and maintain relationships. Women work to sustain conversation, are responsive and supportive, and value equality. Their talk is personal. Talk for men is oriented toward solving problems and maintaining dominance and assertiveness. Men are less responsive; their talk is more abstract and less personal. In my 1987 review of the research on gender and communication, I too concluded that men were more dominant, directive, and hierarchical, and women more supportive, facilitative, cooperative, personal, and egalitarian in conversation.[5]

Why write another book on gender differences in verbal communication when so much is known about the contrasting styles of male and female interaction?[6] I write this book because there are other ways to interpret the research data that have led to the prevailing characterizations of men and women. When we take a different perspective on the data, we can reach a different understanding of men and women in interaction. I am far from the first person to question popular conceptualizations of men and women in interaction or the data that have led to them. I have been influenced by a great many voices in books, scholarly journals, and edited volumes of researchers of communication,[7] and by voices of feminist psychologists[8]— offering critiques that are just beginning to dampen scholarly if not popular enthusiasm for polarized conceptions about gender differences in verbal communication.

These voices have gained support from certain proponents of postmodern philosophy.[9] Although postmodern thinking cannot be characterized by a homogeneous set of ideas, postmodernists do have in common a skepticism about "truth." Rachel Hare-Mustin and Jeanne Marecek maintain that "Rather than passively observing reality, we actively construct the meanings that frame and organize our perceptions and experience. Thus, our understanding of reality is a representation, that is, a 're-presentation,' not a replica, of what is 'out there.' "[10] When applied to the subject of gender and communication, these ideas challenge the assumption that the contemporary and popular conceptualization of gender differences necessarily represents "the truth" about males and females, and they suggest that there is no real "truth," only what we make of our observations. What we take to be the "truth" is not an objective reading of "the facts" but a reading of "the facts" in light of our cultural assumptions.[11] There may be other truths embedded in our research studies.

Deconstructionists such as Jacques Derrida have questioned our tendency to define the world in terms of oppositions like male/female—to define each term in the pair in opposition to the other, as what it is not, and to see one member of the pair as more valuable than the other.[12] For example, we hold men to be dominant, women to be submissive, and we value dominance over submission. Such oppositions are parsimonious and avoid the ambiguities that are much more difficult for us to tolerate—for example, the fact that men and women exhibit both dominant and submissive behavior.

Let me apply these ideas to a now classic study drawn from the research literature. Fred Strodtbeck and Richard Mann studied interaction in mixed-sex jury deliberations and concluded that "the data suggests that men *pro-act*, that is, they initiate relatively long bursts of acts directed at the solution of the task problem, and women tend more to *react* to the contributions of others."[13] This characterization of men as proactive and women as reactive has been widely cited over the years. Yet there are other "truths" that we can find in the same data.[14] In fact, women devoted close to two thirds of their interaction to task behavior (63.5%), whereas men devoted 15% more of their interaction to task behavior than women. Thus, both men and women assumed a task orientation, and the authors report that there were many instances in which women devoted more of their acts to task behavior than men did. We could choose to highlight the considerable overlap in the behavior of men and women rather than the differences between them. The gender differences found by Strodtbeck and Mann as reported over time have led to polarized characterizations of men and women in interaction, but the actual data show less distinction between the behavior of men and women.

My encounter with postmodern thinking has led me to question further my own understanding of the research literature and to approach research studies with a new openness to the possibility that the "facts" might permit multiple interpretations. I began to recognize the extent to which my understanding of gender differences in verbal communication was based on the way I had chosen to interpret the evidence.

In my 1987 review of the research literature, I searched for evidence of different male and female styles of communication and was impressed by the fact that across a diverse set of individuals, interaction contexts, and research methodologies the same statistically significant gender differences arose.[15] I did not consider the magnitude of the gender differences; they are not large. Although I cautioned that the differences between the communication styles of men and women are not universal and that we have not given sufficient attention to the situational context of interaction in influencing the manifestation of gender differences, I was more impressed by the appearance of gender differences in numerous studies than by the fact that they did not appear in many contexts. Why have we constructed polarized conceptions of men and women when the similarities between them outweigh these differences?

Criteria for the Interpretation of Research Evidence

Statistical Significance

When researchers compare the behavior of men and women, they use a number of interrelated criteria to evaluate and interpret the findings. The conclusions they draw depend on the criteria they use to assess the differences. One criterion that has been widely used to determine whether the behavior of men and women differs is the statistical significance of the results.[16] A statistically "significant" finding can result even when there is a very small average difference between men and women and considerable overlap between the distributions of men and women. A statistically significant difference is not necessarily a sizable or meaningful difference. The larger the sample size, the smaller the difference that is needed to be statistically significant. With very large samples, extremely small differences will be significant.

Effect Size

An additional piece of information that researchers can use to assess the findings is the magnitude of the difference between the behavior of men and women—that is, the degree to which gender differences are manifested.[17] The magnitude of the difference, or effect size, can also be conceptualized by looking at how much overlap there is between the distribution for men and the distribution for women. The greater the overlap between the distributions for men and women, the smaller the effect size. Small but statistically significant differences are often misrepresented to give the impression of mutually exclusive differences rather than considerable overlap between men and women.[18] For example, we could find that only 20% of the scores for men and women overlap, or that 80% of the scores do. In both cases the results may be statistically significant (and therefore of interest for publication), but in the latter case there is much more similarity than difference between the sexes.

But a change has occurred over time in the way the research

community has come to assess research findings. Many now agree that we need to pay greater attention to effect sizes—to how large the difference between the sexes is. The statistically significant findings that have led to our characterizations of men and women are based on many effects that are quite small in magnitude.

Percentage of Variance Explained

A statistical standard related to effect size that many have accepted for determining the meaningfulness of gender differences is the percentage of variance in behavior that can be accounted for by knowledge of a person's sex. For example, when comparing men and women on the expression of task behavior in a group, researchers can examine the average scores for each sex on task behavior, or they can look at the correlation or degree of relationship between gender and task behavior. If men consistently show high rates of task behavior and women consistently show low rates of task behavior, a strong relationship exists between gender and task behavior, and the correlation will be high. If men and women both show a great deal of variability in the expression of task behavior, the correlation will be low. By squaring the correlation, we can calculate the percentage of variance in task behavior that can be predicted by knowledge of a person's gender. If the correlation is high, gender will help us make a good prediction about how much task behavior a person will show in a group.

Turning to the research evidence, we find that generally less than 10% of the variance in social behavior is accounted for by gender, and typically less than 5%.[19] Thus, when we know the gender of a person we have relatively little ability to predict behavior in verbal interaction. In some situations socioeconomic status, age, and ethnicity are more salient predictors of interaction and speech than gender.[20]

Meta-analysis

The magnitude of the difference between the sexes (or effect size) has become an important criterion for assessing the results not only of a single study, but also of studies in whole domains of research. Meta-analysis is a popular statistical method that enables a reviewer to aggregate all research findings on gender for a particular domain of behavior (e.g., leadership). The reviewer combines effect sizes found in individual studies in order to assess the overall magnitude of the effect size across all the studies.[21] For example, if 50 studies have been done looking at gender differences in who emerges as the leader in an initially leaderless group, a meta-analysis would look at the size of the effect found in each individual study and combine the individual effect sizes into an overall measure across all research studies of the effect of gender on leadership emergence.

Meta-analysis is a powerful tool because it can reduce complex research findings from multiple studies to simple numerical assessments. Meta-analysis enables a reviewer to get around the subjective biases inherent in narrative literature reviews, which often highlight impressive results from single studies rather than assessing results from all studies equally. Meta-analysis creates the illusion of objectivity and "truth," but we must view its results with some caution. Findings of gender differences are easier to locate in reviews of the literature for many variables than findings of no difference, producing a tendency for effect sizes to be overestimated in meta-analyses.[22] In many areas, research on gender is methodologically flawed, and an aggregation of methodologically flawed studies cannot yield meaningful results.

How do we interpret the overall effect size produced by a meta-analysis? An effect size of zero (as measured by Jacob Cohen's d[23]) is marked by 100% overlap in the distributions of males and females, a small effect is marked by an 85% overlap in the distributions of males and females, a moderate effect by a 67% overlap, and a relatively large effect by a 53% overlap of the distributions. Cohen suggests that in the course of normal experience it takes an effect of medium size to be "large enough to be visible to the naked eye."[24] In meta-analyses that have been carried out in various domains of research on social behavior, the following pattern emerges: a few studies find large gender differences, most find small ones, and a few find gender differences in the opposite direction to expectation.[25] Effects are primarily small to moderate. Thus, the behavior of 67% to 85% of the men and women in research studies is comparable, and many effects are not large enough to be noticeable in the course of normal experience.

Depending on the perspective we take, these effect sizes can impress us as strong or weak evidence for the importance of gender. Some scholars suggest that we can interpret effect sizes by placing them in a comparative perspective: effect sizes found for gender are indeed meaningful if they are comparable in magnitude to effects found in other domains of psychological research.[26] How do gender differences compare in magnitude to other effects found in psychological research? Although some large effect sizes have been found, most psychological effects are small to moderate and comparable to those found for gender differences in social behavior. From this perspective, either gender differences appear quite meaningful, or the robustness of many psychological findings is called into question.

How do effect sizes found for gender differences in communication compare in magnitude to other types of gender differences? Researchers have found gender to have large effects for some physical abilities (e.g., throw velocity, distance, and accuracy),[27] sexual behaviors,[28] nonverbal behaviors,[29] and visual-spatial perception.[30] By comparison, gender differences in verbal communication are much smaller in magnitude and can appear to be less important or meaningful. But it is also the case that effect sizes for gender differences in verbal communication are comparable in magnitude to gender differences in the realm of helping behavior, empathy, and verbal and math abilities.[31] From this viewpoint, gender differences in verbal behavior appear more meaningful.

The comparative perspective does not yield any absolute criteria, however, for assessing the importance of the findings; such judgments are not value free.[32] As Rhoda Unger argues, "Sex, for example, is comparable in importance to other psychological variables. It is not, however, particularly important in comparison to all the independent variables that influence any particular human behavior."[33]

Some argue that even if an effect size is small, the effect can still be quite important.[34] However, small differences may not even be noticeable to the participants in an interaction. For example, William Kenkel had married couples discuss how they would spend a $300 gift they received.[35] Objective observers counted how frequently each person spoke and how many suggestions and ideas each proposed. After the discussion, less than half of the individuals judged accurately who had done more of the talking, and only 17 of the 50 judged acccurately who had given the most suggestions and ideas. The actual gender differences that occurred were not recognized by the participants.

Replicability of Results

Another criterion that can be used to interpret findings is the replicability of results. There is a bias in research toward single studies rather than replications of studies,[36] even though we have greater confidence in findings that have been replicated in many studies than in results based on a single study. There are many examples of widely cited findings of gender differences that have never been

replicated. The policy in many journals to publish statistically significant findings means that replication studies that find no gender
differences may be considered by journal editors as unworthy of
publication.[37]

An interesting example of the problem of the replicability of
results can be taken from the literature on gender differences in
speech. Anthony Mulac and his colleagues took speech samples from
men and women and coded 35 different language variables to see if
they could identify naturally occurring gender differences in language.[38] Based on a weighted combination of 20 of the variables,
Mulac and his colleagues found that their transcripts could be
reclassified by sex with 100% accuracy using a procedure called discriminant analysis. This finding, taken by itself, provides impressive
evidence for gender differences in speech. In follow-up studies by
Mulac and his colleagues, some combination of these language features were found to predict speaker sex with great accuracy as
well.[39] However, a different set of variables marked the speech of
men and women from one study to another. For some language variables, findings in the direction of one sex were contradicted by
findings in the direction of the opposite sex in other studies.[40] For
example, fillers (e.g., "okay," "like," "well") were found among the
predictors of speech for women in one study[41] but were found
among the predictors of speech for men in another study.[42] In other
words, Mulac and his colleagues noted that differences in the speech
of women and men vary with time and place.

The gender differences that researchers find in speech are not
consistent from study to study. When we look at the accuracy of prediction in a single study, we can find strong evidence for gender differences in language. When we look across a pattern of studies, the
data yield a different interpretation. There does not seem to be a
large, overriding set of language features that distinguish the speech
of men and women.

Some findings of gender difference have gained widespread public attention; for example, Matina Horner's research on fear of success in women[43] and Carol Gilligan's research on gender differences
in morality.[44] Follow-up research has either failed to replicate or
served to greatly qualify the original findings.[45] Although the original studies attracted public attention, the critiques and questions
raised by scholars about the validity of those findings did not reach
the public. Research comes to the attention of the public when it is
seen to have widespread interest and appeal, not when it compli-
cates or undermines what we hold to be true. We live in a climate

today in which findings of gender difference make headlines, while findings of gender similarities are not newsworthy.

Group Representatives

In every study we find variability in behavior from one man to another, and from one woman to another. The behavior of individuals at opposite ends of the distribution may be quite different. Which men and women are we referring to when we say that men and women differ? We tend to take the behavior of men and women at one end of the distribution for members of their sex to characterize the group. For example, in an interview study of adolescent friendship, girls were found to share more personal information with same-sex friends about family, interpersonal relationships, doubts, and fears than boys were—a gender difference that has been found in many other studies.[46] A closer look at the data revealed that the difference was produced by a third of the males who characterized their same-sex friendships by an absence of intimacy, a guardedness or defensiveness. Because a minority of the adolescent males were unable to reveal their true feelings to a friend does not mean that adolescent males in general cannot do this, yet the friendships of adolescent males are characterized as lacking in intimacy.

Multiple Criteria, Multiple Truths

In sum, there are many ways to assign meaning to the results of empirical research on gender differences in interaction. Our interpretation of research results depends on the criteria we use for assessing differences. If we place emphasis on statistical significance, on single studies without replication, on the behavior of individuals with extreme scores, we find many gender differences. If we place emphasis on the magnitude of results, on the replicability of results, or on the percentage of variance in behavior accounted for by sex, gender differences appear to be more minimal and much more variable in their appearance. We can see that no criterion is ultimately "objective." Knowledge of all these criteria demonstrates that there may be different perspectives on the "truth" about gender differences.

Assessing the Research Literature

Moving beyond questions of the criteria we use to interpret research results, we find that many gender differences in verbal interaction that appear to be well founded are open to reinterpretation for three major reasons: we have confounded gender with status and role; we have examined behavior devoid of its situational context; and we have inaccurately assigned meaning to many of the behaviors we have studied. An examination of each of these issues raises questions about many of the conclusions that have been drawn from the research literature about gender differences in verbal interaction.

Status and Role

Let me begin with the issue of the confounding of gender with other variables. For decades, feminists have been arguing that gender varies with status and social roles in our society, that the differences between men and women that we have attributed to gender might be better accounted for by status differences.[47] Gender differences mirror status differences, with men and high-status individuals showing similar patterns of behavior. For example, Barbara Eakins and R. Gene Eakins studied seven mixed-sex university faculty meetings and found that men spoke more than women.[48] However, speaking time also followed a hierarchy of status based on rank and length of time in the department. Did gender or status produce the differences in speaking time?

Gender varies with social roles and experience. We have a division of labor that allocates different work and responsibilities to men and women. Many gender differences in social behavior may be better attributed to differences in the social roles played by men and women. Women tend to interact in more contexts that elicit supportive, cooperative behavior, men in contexts that elicit dominant, directive behavior. In order to determine whether differences are due to gender or to social role, we must compare men and women in the same social roles.

Research by Cathryn Johnson shows that when men and women are assigned to a managerial role and given the same formal legitimate authority, they are quite similar in their patterns of conversation.[49] The demands of the managerial role provide the overriding influence on behavior. Research by Barbara Risman shows single fathers who have sole responsibility for raising children to be more similar to mothers, single or married, than to married fathers.[50]

Thus, the role demands of being a manager or being a primary caretaker of young children may call for the enactment of certain behaviors regardless of a person's gender.

The presence or absence and choice of control groups determine the nature of the conclusions that researchers will reach.[51] They will reach different conclusions if they compare men to women than if the same comparison is done controlling for social role or status. Researchers of gender differences in other realms of behavior who have begun to control for status and role differences no longer find the gender differences that had emerged in earlier research.

For example, recent research by Rosalind Barnett and her colleagues on job experience and psychological distress demonstrates the necessity of controlling for social role in examining gender differences. Poor job quality has been found to be more crucial to mental health and psychological distress for men than for women—a finding consistent with the assumption that work is more emotionally relevant to men than to women. Barnett and her colleagues studied a sample of dual-earner couples where both spouses were employed full time.[52] They controlled for occupational prestige, individual level of education, and salary of men and women and found no gender differences in the relationship between job experiences and psychological distress. They argue that previously assumed gender differences were an artifact of men and women being segregated in different social roles.

Many of the gender differences we experience in the course of our daily lives may be accounted for by differences in status and social role. Based on her study of single fathers who had primary responsibility for children under the age of 13, Risman concluded that "divorced, widowed, and even married fathers are capable of providing the nurturance that young children require despite their gendered socialization. Only when situational contexts change, will parenting behavior among men become more similar to the parenting behavior of women."[53]

Situational Context

A second problem that has clouded our understanding of gender and interaction is that we have not paid sufficient attention to the situational context of the interaction—to the characteristics of the participants (age, race, class, ethnicity, sexual orientation), their relationship to one another, the length of the encounter, the task, and the interaction setting. Gender differences tend to be variable in magnitude depending on the situational context. We need to pay careful attention to the features of the participants and the encounter that may create or mitigate the appearance of gender differences. Many feminist social psychologists have argued that studies of gender differences must explore situational differences because the inclusion of situational variables provides alternative explanations of the findings.[54]

Let us consider the laboratory studies that make up the majority of our studies of verbal interaction. The vast majority of research subjects for these studies are white, middle class, ages 18 to 22, and have never been married. They are late adolescents at a developmental stage of their lives where dating and forming intimate relationships are of concern. They enter experiments as strangers. The experimenter has thus created a situation in which subjects may be concerned about the impression they are making and about making themselves desirable,[55] which may heighten displays of gendered behavior in mixed-sex groups.[56]

We make claims about men and women based on studies of people of a certain age, race, class, and sexual orientation. What we universalize as gender differences in communication—as characterizations of all men and women—may only describe communication patterns for white, middle-class males and females of a certain age. Gender is shaped by our race, class, or culture. Women do not form a homogeneous social group, nor do men. While Gilligan promoted the idea that men and women have different conceptions of self and morality,[57] Carol Stack's data on migrant blacks returning from the urban Northeast to the rural South suggest that these men and women do not fit Gilligan's description as differing in their vocabulary of rights and morality.[58] Our prevailing wisdom about gender differences overlooks the heterogeneity of women and men and may characterize only certain privileged groups of men and women.

There are other aspects to the social context of the interactions we study that may influence the degree to which gender differences emerge in interaction. The appearance of gender differences in interaction depends on the task given to groups, the sex of the participants in an interaction, and the intimacy of their relationships. For example, men are more likely to emerge as leaders in initial encounters, but they are not more likely to be leaders in groups that meet over many sessions. Men show more task orientation and women more focus on relationship in groups of strangers, but this difference has not been found in family groups.[59] Conversation styles that appear in all-male and all-female groups differ from those found in mixed-sex groups. Thus, we need to pay careful attention to the situational context in which we study interaction, because contextual variables play a key role in determining the magnitude of the gender differences we find in our studies. What we experience to be gender differences may be attributed to certain contextual variables: the degree of identification participants have with particular demographic characteristics such as race or ethnicity, the length of their acquaintance, the length of their interaction in the experiment, and the roles and tasks they are assigned.

Assignment of Meaning to Behavior

A third problem in the literature is the assignment of meaning to the behaviors we study. Interruptions, for example, have been taken by many researchers to be mechanisms of power and dominance in conversation. To interrupt is to usurp the turn space of another, to violate the current speaker's right to a turn. Researchers have seen interruptions as a behavioral measure they could use to demonstrate how male dominance pervades our day-to-day interactions. Interruptions, however, may serve many functions. They may be collaborative— used to show support, understanding, and agreement. Interruptions of this type do not involve a vying for turns. We cannot simply add together all instances of interruptions without regard to their function and then assume we have created a measure of dominance.

To take another example, tag questions lie midway between an outright statement and a question (e.g., "John is coming, isn't he?"). Robin Lakoff claimed that women use tag questions to express uncertainty and hesitancy, and many researchers accepted her claim and set out to demonstrate that women, in fact, show greater hesitancy in speech than men.[60] Tag questions, however, can serve a variety of functions; they may be used to express solidarity, to facilitate the addressee's contribution to the conversation, and to encourage that person to join in.[61] Thus, it is not meaningful to add together all tag questions without regard to their function. The literature on gender and language is quite problematic due to inaccurate assignment of meaning to language variables, meanings that support stereotypes of men and women.

When these three issues—the problems of overlooking confounding variables, of examining gender differences devoid of situational context, and of inaccurately assigning meaning to behaviors— are used to reassess the literature, and the magnitude of gender differences is taken into consideration, a new understanding of gender and interaction emerges. What we begin to see are not global differences between men and women. If men and women had different interaction styles, we would find larger effects that were more consistent from one situational context to the next.

Instead, we find contexts in which men and women both display feminine behavior, contexts in which they both display masculine behavior, and contexts in which the behavior of men and women is differentiated by gender. As Janis Bohan suggests, "Thus, none of us is feminine or is masculine or fails to be either of those. In particular contexts, people do feminine; in others, they do masculine."[62] Autonomy and dependence, activity and passivity, dominance and submissiveness are not characteristics of men and women, respectively; they are, as Muriel Dimen puts it, "different moments of the self."[63] We have grown accustomed to thinking about styles, traits, and behaviors as having a gender, to thinking of dominance as masculine and expressivity as feminine. We need to question the assumption that behaviors have a gender. The behaviors we label as feminine or masculine are displayed by both men and women; they are not sex specific. In addition, the behaviors labeled masculine or feminine differ across cultural groups. Allen Harris found, for example, that African-American subjects saw masculine characteristics as no more desirable for a man than a woman.[64]

To explain the data, we need an understanding of the ways gender operates that goes beyond the notion of men and women possessing two contrasting interaction styles. We need to move away from a conceptualization of gender as an attribute or style internalized by individuals, to an understanding of gender as something people do in social interaction[65]—as the performance of gender-related behaviors in certain contexts. We need an understanding of gender to help us explain why gender differences are so variable in their appearance and why the effect of gender is so much stronger in some situational contexts than in others.

Understanding Gender

The Construction of Gender

Sex is a major social variable in our society. We assign importance to distinctions between male and female. In spite of recent changes in society, we still have a division of labor by sex that assigns different work and responsibilities to men and women and a social structure that accords greater power and dominance to men. Male dominance is built into the familial, economic, political, and legal structures of society. From genital anatomy at birth we categorize children as male or female, and we put into operation a set of differential expectations and differential adult-child interactions.[66] By the age of 2, children develop gender identity, or the ability to classify themselves as male or female. By the age of 2 or 3, children can classify toys, roles, and people by gender, and they have acquired extensive knowledge of sex-appropriate behavior:[67]

> It is the imposition of a gender-based classification on social reality, the sorting of persons, attributes, behaviors, and other things on the basis of the polarized definitions of masculinity and femininity that prevail in the culture, rather than on the basis of other dimensions that could serve equally well.[68]

In a society in which we polarize social reality so readily along gender lines, children follow suit. Children will evaluate behavior in terms of whether it is gender appropriate according to cultural definitions and will reject behaviors that are inappropriate for their own gender.[69] Children will monitor and judge both their own behavior and that of others according to cultural definitions of masculinity and femininity. They are pressured to disown thoughts, acts, and self-conceptions that are not congruent with their gender.[70]

This is not to say that there is one homogeneous definition of gender that each of us internalizes. Because we live in a heterogeneous society, we are exposed to variations in definitions of gender that are influenced by our race, class, or ethnicity.[71] Exposure to role models and family values that differ from mainstream definitions of masculinity and femininity will lead to the internalization of broader definitions of how to be a male or a female. In addition, we creatively construct our own internal representations of gender; that is, each of us will internalize the culture in our own idiosyncratic way.[72] But each of us carries a clear sense of our own gender identity—an identification with members of our social group or sex,[73] a knowledge of where our sex stands in power and status in relation to the opposite sex, expectations for the behavior of members of each sex, and knowledge of the consequences of deviating from requirements for members of our sex.

Gender Stereotypes

Beliefs about men and women have a reality and power of their own. Gender stereotypes control us by providing prescriptions for behavior; they guide our interactions by telling us how we ought to behave to be socially acceptable members of our sex. Stereotypes are reinforced by sanctions for deviating from sex role requirements (social rejection, discrimination). When deviation from sex role norms is permitted and even rewarded, men and women perform behaviors considered to be more characteristic of the opposite sex. When deviation has serious consequences, men and women are more likely to perform gender stereotypic behavior.

Gender is one of the primary categories we use to understand the world around us.[74] When we enter into any conversation, based on discernible visible cues we recognize that each participant we are interacting with is a *man* or a *woman*. Immediately, stereotypes come into play that affect the impression we form. As Kathleen Grady argued years ago, sex differences may reside in the eye of the beholder rather than in individuals themselves.[75] When research subjects have been asked to give their impression of what male and female speakers are like, having heard them read the identical prose passage, they see the male speakers as more masculine, arrogant, dominant, and aggressive and the female speakers as more feminine, friendly, and sincere.[76] In other words, with absolutely no knowledge of speakers other than their gender, observers attribute masculine and feminine characteristics to speakers in accordance with traditional stereotypes of males and females.

Even if the sex of an individual is not known, we tend to infer it from stereotyped notions about the behavior of men and women. Bertram John and Lori Sussman had subjects read a story in which one protagonist took the initiative, but the sex of the protagonists was not identified.[77] When asked to record the sex of the protagonists, 89% of the subjects described the person who took the initiative as male. Stereotypes lead us to see what we expect to see. As Florence Geis puts it, "We are more likely to see what we expect to see, sometimes even if it is not actually there, and not to see or reinterpret what we do not expect even if it is there."[78]

Beliefs about gender form the basis for differential responses to others as well.[79] The expectations we hold based on the gender of our conversational partners may be communicated through our actions to become self-fulfilling prophecies. For example, in a task group composed of men and women, research has shown that if no direct information is given about the differential competency of group members on a gender-neutral task, participants will rely on external status characteristics such as sex to form expectations, and men will be assumed to have greater performance ability than women.[80] Men will be given more opportunities to participate, and their task contributions will be given greater weight. Thus, we tend to form expectations and to evaluate the behavior of other participants in a conversation as members of a particular gender category, judging them on the basis of gender and responding to them in ways that make our expectations become reality.

Research has also shown, however, that if we change these culturally based expectations by telling group members before they begin work on a task that women are more competent at the task than men, then the women have more influence, are more competent, and engage in equal amounts of task behavior with men.[81] This research also shows how difficult it is to overcome traditional expectations. It was necessary for women to be shown to have greater task competency than men for women to gain equality with men, but even with superior task ability, women did not gain the advantage over men.

The Fundamental Attribution Error

We have a pervasive tendency to attribute the cause of behavior to personal dispositions rather than to the situational context—to see gendered behavior to stem from internalized male and female styles rather than from normative pressure within a situation to perform a certain type of behavior. This tendency has been labeled the "fundamental attribution error."[82] For example, if we see a male executive act in a dominant or aggressive fashion, we are more likely to attribute that behavior to the fact that he is a dominant, aggressive person than to the fact that successful enactment of the executive role requires such behavior. Because men and women are assigned to different social roles, their behavior is shaped by normative expectations for the performance of those roles.

It is also the case that men and women can behave differently without having internalized different interaction styles. The enactment of gender stereotypic behavior may be accounted for by several different factors: the normative expectations people face in a particular setting; the cultural norms in effect about how men and women should behave toward each other, who should be in charge, who should be taken care of, and who should make decisions;[83] and the consequences for deviating from expectations. If we see men assume leadership in mixed groups, we are likely to assume that they took the lead because they are more dominant and forceful. But research shows men who are low in dominance assume leadership over women who are high in dominance.[84] Sex role norms for who should be in charge can cause men and women to act in ways that actually go against their personality dispositions.

Variability in the Performance of Gender

Gender, then, is much more complex than the acquisition of internalized stable patterns of behavior. We must account for the confounding of gender with social roles and status and for the fact that in particular contexts a man or a woman may display either feminine or masculine behavior. People do not behave consistently from one situation to another.[85] There are multiple aspects to the self, and people display them differently depending on the participants in an interaction or the demands of the situational context.

The behavior of a male or a female lawyer in the courtroom is likely to be dominant and forceful and quite discrepant from the nurturant, expressive behavior that person may show interacting with young children at home. The same woman may be quite dominant in her role as mother but show little assertiveness in her role as wife. The behavior we associate with gender may be performed by members of either sex depending on the demands of the situation. We may act in stereotypic ways because of the way we are treated, our wish to present a valued social identity, and the demands of the situational context.[86]

Implications for Social Change

The particular beliefs we hold about gender have important implications for whether and how we work to achieve greater equality between women and men.[87] A view of gender differences that locates gender in individual personalities suggests that if we as individuals were only to change our personalities, gender inequalities would be reduced, and we could live fuller lives less restricted by gender role stereotypic traits. This view of gender has led to a mental health movement that has attempted to change men and women—to make women more assertive, less submissive, less afraid of success, and to change men to make them more expressive and interpersonally oriented.

The danger of our prevailing emphasis on polarized descriptions of the communication styles of men and women is in its failure to recognize the extent to which these gender differences are produced and maintained by forces outside the individual, by contextual-situational variables. This conceptualization creates the illusion that individual change will be sufficient to achieve equality between men and women. To take a case example reported by Susan Fiske, Ann Hopkins, an aggressive, ambitious woman at the Price Waterhouse accounting firm, was successful in bringing in millions of dollars in accounts but was denied partnership. She was judged to lack interpersonal skills that a supporter told her could be corrected "by walking, talking, and dressing more femininely."[88] Ann Hopkins filed a sex discrimination suit, took it all the way to the Supreme Court, and won. She displayed the masculine traits necessary to be successful at the job, but in so doing she failed to fulfill the requirements for femininity. Thus, gender stereotypes impeded her success and led to the perpetuation of inequalities.

A view of gender differences that recognizes gender as performance—as something people do in interaction—attributes gender differences to sex role stereotypes, normative expectations, differential social opportunities, and access to power. It also holds that individual change will not be sufficient to overcome existing patterns of behavior. As many feminists have argued, gender inequalities will not be reduced without restructuring the social environment, social opportunities, and the sex role prescriptions for behavior. Until women and men are recognized as status equals, social roles, norms, and expectations for men and women will not change, and gender differences in interaction will continue to be reproduced.

Overview of the Book

In the chapters that follow, I examine various dimensions of conversational interaction to explore the question of sameness and difference in the communication styles of men and women. I provide a narrative review of the literature intended to raise questions about polarized conceptions of men and women in interaction. The research studies are drawn from a variety of different disciplines—psychology, sociology, linguistics, communication studies, women's studies, and organizational behavior. Researchers are not always aware of the work of colleagues in different disciplines, and in writing this book I hope to bring research from a variety of disciplines to the attention of all. Each chapter includes an assessment of the research findings and of existing theoretical explanations for the data. All results reported are those that have reached statistical significance.

In chapters 2 and 3 I examine gender differences in the roles

men and women play in groups. In chapter 2 I focus on gender differences with an emphasis on behavior, directed both to helping
groups achieve their tasks and to providing emotional support and
resolving tensions between group members. Men have been held to
be more task oriented, and women to be more concerned with the
social and emotional aspects of group interaction. I examine the
magnitude of the differences between men and women in their
emphasis on task and expressive behavior. I also look at the conditions under which differences between men and women in task and
expressive behavior are maximized and minimized—that is, how
these behaviors are affected by the nature of the task assigned to
groups, the length of the interaction, how well participants know
each other, the sex composition of the group, and the specific role
demands placed on participants.

In chapter 3 I discuss gender differences in dominance, leadership, and hierarchy. Men are held to speak more and to assume leadership in mixed-sex task groups. The chapter begins by examining
studies of initially leaderless groups to determine whether men
speak more and are more likely to emerge as leaders than women.
The magnitude of the gender differences found in those studies is
reviewed, as are the situational factors that influence the magnitude
of those differences. I devote the remainder of the chapter to the
question of whether men and women behave differently when leadership roles or other male stereotypic roles are assigned to them. In
other words, if leadership behavior is legitimized for women, and
women are seen to possess equal competency at the task and given
equal power and authority, do they interact differently as leaders?

The next two chapters focus on gender differences in language
and speech. In chapter 4 I review the literature on interruptions.
Many people have taken interruptions to be an indicator of power
and dominance in interaction. Men are held to interrupt more than
women and to interrupt women more than other men. In this chapter I examine the meaning of interruptions and the functions they
may serve in interaction. While interruptions may be used to assert
dominance, they may also be used to express support and agreement. I examine studies to determine whether there are gender differences in the use of interruptions as mechanisms of power and
dominance.

Other gender differences in language are the focus of chapter 5.
A variety of speech features have been held to characterize the
speech of women: tag questions, qualifiers and hedges, questions,
minimal responses (e.g., *um-hum, yeah*), and intensifiers. Many have

taken these speech features to be expressions of hesitancy and uncertainty. I discuss the meaning of these speech features in chapter 5 and examine studies to determine whether there are reliable gender differences in speech and the extent to which the use of "women's" speech features varies with the socioeconomic status and social role of the speaker, the content of the conversation, and the conversational setting.

Gender differences may be reflected not only in the interaction process, but in the content of conversations. Gender differences in self-disclosure, in conversation content among adolescent and adult friends and acquaintances, and in conversation content among strangers in laboratory encounters are examined in chapter 6. I raise questions about the extent to which the finding that women are more self-disclosing than men is affected by variables such as the research methodology employed, the social role of the speakers, or the gender of the conversational partner.

In chapter 7 I focus on gender stereotypes and the consequence of these stereotypes for the perception, evaluation, and treatment of speakers. I address a variety of questions. To what extent are our perceptions of gender differences greater than actual behavioral differences? Are men and women perceived differently even if they exhibit the same behavior? To what extent do our gender stereotypes affect our evaluation of speakers? Are speakers of either sex who use speech features associated with women seen more negatively than speakers who do not use these speech features? Do differential perceptions of men and women become self-fulfilling prophecies for behavior in conversations?

The final chapter draws together what we now know about gender differences in interaction. The various theoretical explanations for gender differences in interaction put forth to account for the data in each chapter are compared and assessed in terms of their utility in accounting for the data. Elements from each of the disparate perspectives are woven together to provide an understanding of gender and communication. I raise questions about the politics of a search for gender differences or similarities, and the consequences of locating the source of gender differences in the individual or in the larger social context. Given what we know, I discuss directions for future research on gender and communication.

2

Task and Expressive Roles in Groups

Groups of individuals that interact over time tend to develop different roles or expectations about how participants will behave and the qualities they will exhibit. Forty years ago, Talcott Parsons argued that all small groups develop two fundamental types of roles—an instrumental role that is directed to helping the group achieve its task and an expressive role that is directed toward providing emotional support to group members.[1]

The traditional nuclear family, according to Parsons, provided an example of role differentiation along instrumental and expressive lines: the father is concerned with adaptive-instrumental activity (holding a job and providing financial support), whereas the mother is concerned with integrative-expressive activity (being involved with the emotional support and care of children). Parsons argued that even where women hold jobs, the traditional jobs they hold as teachers, social workers, nurses, and secretaries have primary expressive components and are thus analogous to the role of wife and mother in the family.

From our contemporary perspective it is clear that at best Parsons's description of the family in the 1950s represents a selective vision of families. The model never characterized many families, leaving out, for example, families in which both husband and wife worked outside the home out of economic necessity. Nor did it recognize the unpaid labor women do inside the home as "work" that requires instrumental skills. The role of the mother in the traditional nuclear family entails a great deal of instrumental activity, and much of the behavior directed to the care of children is instrumental behavior that may or may not be accompanied by emotionally supportive behavior. However, the question of whether men and women enact different roles in interaction along instrumental and expressive lines has continued to be a topic of interest to the present day.

Overall Assessment of Gender Differences

Interaction Process Analysis

In order to study instrumental and expressive behavior in groups, we need a method to assess the ongoing interaction process. In 1950 Robert Freed Bales provided such a methodology when he developed Interaction Process Analysis (IPA), a 12-category system for analyzing conversational interaction.[2] Bales's original scoring system was revised in 1970[3] and has served as the basis for a large body of research on small group interaction over the years.

The 12 categories of IPA were grouped into four subsets, two indicative of instrumental or task activity, and two indicative of expressive or social-emotional activity. Task activity includes three types of "questions" (asks for opinion, asks for suggestion, and asks for information) and three types of "attempted answers" (gives opinion, gives suggestion, and gives information). Expressive behavior includes three categories for "positive reactions" (seems friendly, dramatizes, i.e., jokes, tells stories, shares fantasies, and agrees), and three categories for "negative reactions" (disagrees, shows tension, and seems unfriendly). As any group struggles to resolve a problem or complete a task, the interaction moves between instrumental and expressive acts, between a focus on the task itself and a focus on resolving tensions and re-establishing solidarity between group members.[4] IPA was to be scored by unobtrusive observers who break interaction down into "acts" (equivalent to single simple sentences) and place each act into 1 of the 12 categories.

The research reviewed in this chapter is based primarily on studies of interaction using IPA or revisions of it. There are both strengths and weaknesses to the use of this methodology. IPA relies on the act-by-act assessment of interaction by objective observers rather than global questionnaire assessments of interaction done in retrospect by either participants or observers. Questionnaire results are not always comparable to the results from act-by-act scoring of interaction. For example, recall that William Kenkel had 25 married couples discuss how they might spend $300.[5] Interaction was scored using IPA, and subjects also reported after each session on who did the most talking and other aspects of task and expressive behavior. Less than half of the 50 participants accurately judged who did more of the talking. Subjects were poor judges of task and social-emotional behavior and worse judges of social-emotional than of task interaction as measured by IPA. For expressive activity, 7 judged accurately; for who gave the most ideas and suggestions, 17 were accurate. Our perceptions of our interactions reflect our subjective biases and may not be in agreement with objective counts on how many times particular behaviors occurred. The strength of IPA is that it provides an objective perspective on the interaction process.

There are limitations to the use of IPA. Behavior is recast through the lens of a system that in subtle ways introduces biases into what we think we have objectively recorded. According to the scoring conventions Bales set up, each act must be categorized as either task or expressive and cannot be both simultaneously, although in his later work Bales conceptualized task and expressive behavior as independent dimensions.[6] Thus, the higher a person scores on expressive behavior, the lower that person will score on task behavior, and vice versa.

The majority of social-emotional acts that occur in group interaction fall into the categories "agrees" and "disagrees." But a recent critique of IPA by Cecilia Ridgeway and Cathryn Johnson points out that agreeing and disagreeing with another person's task suggestions could equally well be considered to be task acts, a necessary part of the evaluation and resolution of task solutions.[7] Agreements and disagreements have a task-oriented component.[8] Because women exceed men in positive reactions[9] and their task component is not recognized, the scoring system tends to overestimate the social-emotional emphasis of women and to underestimate their task emphasis. In addition, in Bales's scoring system, an opinion or a suggestion will be scored as social-emotional behavior—either as "seems friendly" or "seems unfriendly"—"if an element of interpersonal feeling is present."[10] Thus, if women use or are heard to use more of an emotional tone, their task contributions will be counted as social-emotional behavior.

Research Evidence for Sex Role Differentiation

With these cautions in mind, let us turn to the research evidence. Initial evidence for sex role differentiation along instrumental and expressive lines in small groups other than the nuclear family came from a study of 12 mixed-sex jury deliberations carried out in the

1950s by Fred Strodtbeck and Richard Mann.[11] Subjects were drawn from the regular jury pools of courts in Chicago and St. Louis and engaged in mock jury deliberations. Thus, jurors differed not only in gender but in age and social class. Each jury was composed of 12 jurors and contained from 1 to 6 women. Jurors listened to recorded trials and had to deliberate the case and return a verdict.

Strodtbeck and Mann found that women exceeded men in positive reactions, whereas men exceeded women in attempted answers. There were no gender differences on the combined social-emotional category negative reactions. They noted, "The data suggests that men *pro-act*, that is, they initiate relatively long burst of acts directed at the solution of the task problem, and women tend more to *react* to the contributions of others."[12]

Many studies using IPA or a variant of the 12 categories have supported the original findings by Strodtbeck and Mann that in groups men show more task behavior and women more social-emotional behavior.[13] While the case has been made that men are instrumental and women expressive, a closer examination of these studies suggests that this stereotyped description of men and women is an exaggeration of the data, that the differences are small to moderate in magnitude, and that role differentiation along instrumental-expressive lines by males and females does not appear consistently in all group situations.

The Magnitude of the Difference

Let us begin by examining the magnitude of the gender differences that have been found. In an early review of four studies of mixed-sex groups using IPA, Lynn Anderson and P. Nick Blanchard assessed the magnitude of the differences that had been found in studies of gender and role differentiation. They found that women were significantly higher than men by only 8% on the combined positive social-emotional categories and that men were higher than women by 8% on the combined active task categories.[14] There were no differences on the negative social-emotional or passive task categories (questions). Thus, gender differences were found on two of the four subsets of IPA, and they represented only an 8% difference between men and women.

The review by Anderson and Blanchard of two studies of single-sex groups showed that women exhibited 5% more positive social-emotional behavior in single-sex groups than men, and men showed 9% more active task behavior than women in single-sex groups.

Anderson and Blanchard point out that the majority of interaction in all groups by males and females is task behavior, that on average across studies, 75% of male interaction is task behavior, and 67% of female behavior is task behavior. The review, although based on a small sample of studies, suggests that gender differences exist but that they are small in magnitude and far from absolute. Both men and women devote themselves primarily to the task, and both men and women engage in social-emotional activity. An 8% difference between men and women has been misrepresented as a polarized difference.

Anderson and Blanchard reanalyzed Strodtbeck and Mann's data, showing that 79% of men's interaction was in the task categories, whereas 63% of women's interaction was. Strodtbeck and Mann in fact report, "By and large, the jurors' interaction profiles are quite similar. In the face of this similarity the direction of attention to the differences associated with sex roles should not be permitted to obscure the determinative influences of the problem situation."[15] Their general conclusion that women were more reactive and men more proactive is generally quoted, rather than their recognition of the considerable similarity between the profiles of men and women.

To say that men proact and women react must not be taken to mean that women do not direct the majority of their interaction to task behavior, or that men do not engage in social-emotional behavior. Anderson and Blanchard cautioned that we must be careful how we choose to cite research findings, noting the tendency for cultural stereotypes and prejudices to determine what we choose to cite. This tendency to cite differences between men and women even when the data show considerable similarity has continued over the years.[16]

Meta-analytic Findings

There are no published meta-analyses of the literature on gender and role differentiation, but an unpublished meta-analytic review of this literature was carried out by Linda Carli, who examined 15 studies of social-emotional behavior and 17 studies of task behavior.[17] Carli found women's behavior to be more social-emotional in orientation (mean effect size d ranges from $-.59$ to $-.36$) and men's behavior to be more task oriented (d ranges from .59 to .35).[18] An effect of $d = .2$ is considered to be small in magnitude with an 85% overlap in the distributions of men and women, whereas an effect of .5 is considered to be moderate with a 67% overlap in the distributions.[19] Thus, Carli found a moderate effect for task and expressive behavior. In correlational terms, Carli found that knowledge of the sex of group members accounted for less than 10% of the variance in task and social behaviors.

The Interaction Context

Although gender differences in role differentiation along instrumental and expressive lines have been found in many studies, the appearance of gender differences is inconsistent from one study to another. In the most recent narrative review of this literature, Susan Wheelan and Anthony Verdi note that out of 28 studies of task behavior, 19 find men to be more task oriented while 9 show no gender differences.[20] Out of 20 studies of social-emotional behavior, 16 report women contribute more, while 4 find no differences. Thus, gender differences do not appear in a third of the studies of task-oriented behavior and in 20% of the studies of social-emotional behavior.

In order to account for the variability in results from one study to another, we must consider the situational context of the interaction in each study. An analysis of contextual variables such as the intimacy of the relationship between the participants, the status and role of the participants, the length of the interaction, the demands of the task, and the sex composition of the group will provide an understanding of the conditions that determine the magnitude of the gender differences that emerge along instrumental and expressive lines. It is important to keep in mind that these contextual variables do not operate independently but interact with each other. Although I discuss them separately, each contextual variable influences the other.

The Impact of the Social Context of Interaction on Gender Differences

Intimacy of Participants and Length of the Interaction

Two studies suggest that gender differences in task and social behavior are greater in groups of strangers than in groups of individuals who know each other well. Robert Leik studied 9 families consisting of a mother, father, and college-age daughter.[21] Each family member interacted in three types of groups: "homogeneous" groups composed of all mothers, all fathers, or all daughters; "structured" groups composed of a mother, father, and daughter all from different families; and the original family groups. Groups had to reach consensus on issues having some relevance to family values or goals. Traditional task and social roles appeared in interaction with strangers, but not in the original family groups. Males when interacting with strangers were more instrumental and less emotional than were females (both daughters and mothers). Mothers played a dual role in family groups, sharing the task sphere with their husbands and the emotional sphere with their daughters.

Gerold Heiss studied undergraduate unmarried couples whose relationships varied in their degree of intimacy: 24 couples who were casually dating, 10 who were serious daters, and 20 who were engaged.[22] Couples were given 20 minutes to discuss topics about family life on which they disagreed. Overall, men dominated in the task areas (were higher on both questions and attempted answers). However, the difference was significant among casual daters but not among the committed dyads. In casually dating couples women gave more positive reactions than men, but there were no gender differences in the other two groups of couples whose relationships were more intimate. Thus, we must be careful not to generalize findings based on college students who are strangers in a laboratory study to couples or families who are involved in actual ongoing intimate relationships.

In a study of married couples, George Levinger found that both partners are task specialists and neither are social-emotional specialists. Levinger studied 60 middle-class couples whose marriages ranged from 4 to 24 years long.[23] Levinger had each marital partner answer questions about task performance (e.g., how frequently they pay the bills, go grocery shopping) and social-emotional performance (e.g., how often they praise their partner, make an effort to see their partner's point of view in an argument). Levinger found that both men and women were task oriented, although they differed in the type of tasks they generally performed. Men and women showed equal levels of social-emotional activity on five out of six items assessing social-emotional behavior. Levinger argues that "doubt is cast on the stereotype that the wife is principally interested in social-emotional relations while the husband forages merely for the material things in life. If the husband is indeed emotionally absent, the wife's ability to sustain social-emotional relations in the marriage is clearly limited."[24]

Gender differences may be greater in groups meeting for short periods of time than in groups meeting for longer time periods. The original work by Bales and his colleagues on small group interaction was carried out in the laboratory with groups that met for several sessions.[25] The trend in research since that time has been for groups to meet for a single session, and often for sessions as short as 5 or 10 minutes.

Wheelan and Verdi in their 1992 review of the literature found few studies of task and social-emotional behavior in which subjects met for an extended period.[26] Their own research was based on a 4-day group relations conference whose purpose was to help members study group and organizational dynamics by becoming participants in that interaction. The conference was attended by 27 individuals ages 24 to 58, including administrators and professionals from a variety of occupations. Members met in single-sex and mixed-sex group sessions that ran for 4½ to 7½ hours.

The interaction process was not scored with IPA, but the scoring system did include two categories comparable to task and social-emotional behavior and involved act-by-act scoring of interaction. Wheelan and Verdi scored pairing statements, defined as "expressions of warmth, friendship, support and intimacy with others. These statements show solidarity, suggest agreement, assistance, or reward."[27] They also scored work statements, which "represent purposeful, goal-directed activity and task-directed efforts."[28] During the first of nine 30-minute intervals, men had more work statements, women more pairing statements. After this time period, there were no gender differences in task or social-emotional behavior.

These data suggest that gender differences are likely to be greatest in magnitude in initial interactions among strangers and may be mitigated when people get to know and interact with each other more extensively. Because the majority of the research on interaction has been carried out on strangers in brief encounters, we may tend to find more evidence for gender differences than we would if we had more studies based on people who know each other well and interact over time. Strangers have knowledge of gender but no personal information about each other; they are thus more reliant on stereotypes in the absence of other information.[29] It is interesting that when interacting in the traditional nuclear family group, women did not confine themselves to expressive behavior but simultaneously engaged in both task and social-emotional behavior, and that the performance of social-emotional behavior was mutual for men and women in marriage. Because we have little process data from ongoing intimate relationships, we know less about the extent to which men and women in these relationships differ in their emphasis on task and social behavior than we do about gender differences in short encounters among strangers.

Demands of the Task

The nature of the interaction that occurs in a group depends in part on the particular task demands that a group faces, and the distribution of acts into the 12 IPA categories by group members will vary with the demands of the task.[30] Research suggests that when the task given to a group draws on male roles and expertise assumed to be more typically acquired by men, men will be more task oriented than women. When the task draws on female roles and expertise assumed to be more typically acquired by females, females will be more task oriented than males.

Elaine Yamada and her colleagues studied 28 all-male, 28 all-female, and 32 mixed-sex dyads that had to interact in four role-play situations.[31] Half of the situations were female linked and required subjects to take the roles of registered nurses and kindergarten teachers, and half were male-linked situations that required subjects to take the roles of mathematicians and airplane pilots. Participants had higher rates of task behavior in roles linked to their own sex than in roles linked to the opposite sex. In other words, females showed more task behavior in the role of nurse or kindergarten teacher than they did in the role of mathematician or airplane pilot, whereas males showed more task behavior as pilots or mathematicians than they did as nurses or kindergarten teachers. Participants had higher rates of social-emotional behavior in situations linked to the opposite sex. Males performed more social-emotional behavior in female-linked situations than male-linked, and females performed more social-emotional behaviors in male-linked situations than female-linked.

The study suggests that when people are secure about their knowledge base, they will show a higher task orientation than when they feel less secure about their knowledge and expertise. When people feel less secure in their knowledge, they contribute less task behavior and do more work to maintain solidarity between group members. If tasks used in research studies draw on roles or expertise that is more commonly associated with being male, we would expect men to show a greater task emphasis and women to show a greater social-emotional emphasis, but these findings may be accounted for by the nature of the task itself. For example, the original study of jury deliberations by Strodtbeck and Mann required subjects to discuss negligence and damages, areas that men may have felt more competent to discuss than women.[32]

The level of task behavior shown by men and women in interaction depends on the particular role demands they face. When women are authorized to play a role that demands a high level of task behavior, they show the same task emphasis that men do. Linda Carli studied 64 single-sex and 64 mixed-sex dyads.[33] Each subject was paired with a partner who disagreed with him or her on the topics for each of two discussions. Recognizing that knowledge of the topic might influence behavior, Carli chose topics for discussion on which men and women rated themselves to be equally knowledgeable. For the first discussion, subjects had 10 minutes to agree on ideas that were most important in forming an opinion on the topic for that discussion. Before discussing the second topic, one person was randomly selected to try to persuade the other. Persuaders had to convince their partners that their own ideas were the most important.

In single-sex dyads, persuaders engaged in more task behavior than nonpersuaders and asked fewer questions. Both male and female persuaders increased their task contributions from the first discussion (where they did not have the role of persuader) to the second (where they did have the role of persuader). There were no gender differences in mixed-sex groups in the second discussion. While traditional patterns of role differentiation appeared in the first encounter, they were mitigated by the assignment of men and women to a role that required an emphasis on task behavior and the legitimation of that role for women.

When women gain experience at a task, they have been found to show an increase in task orientation in mixed-sex groups. Marlaine Lockheed and Katherine Hall carried out a study of 4-person groups of high school students whose task was to play a board game moving a token through a maze.[34] When 8 mixed-sex groups played the game, males initiated 56% of the task-related acts. In a second condition, subjects played the game in all-female or all-male groups. There were no gender differences in the amount of task activity in single-sex groups. Subjects from these single-sex groups were then reassigned to mixed-sex groups and played the game again, having been provided with the opportunity to develop expectations for their own competence at the game. For females who participated first in an all-female group and then in a mixed-sex group, the number of task-oriented acts increased. Thus, as females felt more competent at a task, they showed more task activity.

These studies suggest that higher levels of task activity by males in groups will occur when the tasks draw on roles, interests, or expertise more commonly acquired by men. The data reveal that when women have greater expertise at a task, when they are authorized to play roles that demand high levels of task behavior, or when they are given the opportunity to acquire higher expectations for their own competence, gender differences disappear or are reversed.

Sex Composition of the Group

Another factor that affects the relative expression of task and social-emotional behavior by men and women in interaction is the sex composition of the group. Two aspects of the sex composition of groups have been considered—the relative proportion of men and women in the group and whether groups are single sex or mixed sex.

Do men and women behave differently when groups are equally balanced by sex than when one sex is in the minority? Distinctiveness theory suggests that in a group setting, the persons with the more distinct characteristics will be more apt to notice and focus on their own distinctive traits and to be noticed by other members.[35] When one is in the minority in a mixed-sex group, gender is more salient, and gender differences may be exaggerated.

Rosabeth Kanter studied the sales force of a large industrial corporation in which women were in the minority. She found that these women had higher visibility than other group members and that there was a tendency for them to be trapped in stereotypic roles.[36] The saleswomen were mistakenly taken to be wives and secretaries; that is, their characteristics were distorted to fit existing stereotypes of women. In addition, they were afraid to be too successful for fear their success would make their male counterparts look bad, or that they would be seen as too aggressive.

Women in the minority may be more likely to act in stereotypic roles to gain social acceptance. Dafna Izraeli tested Kanter's theory of proportions in a study of trade union committees in small- and medium-sized Israeli factories.[37] Izraeli found empirical support for Kanter's propositions. Role entrapment was greater when women were in the minority in groups than when groups were balanced by sex. Women in the minority were more likely to be viewed as having been elected primarily to look after the special needs of women. Rather than being seen as individuals in their own right, they were assigned to attend to the social-emotional role of looking after women.

Several studies provide evidence to suggest that gender differences in task activity are greatest when women are in the minority in a mixed-sex group. Richard Johnson and Gary Schulman studied five types of 4-person groups: 15 all-male groups; 16 all-female groups; 20 balanced groups with 2 males and 2 females; 15 groups with 3 males and 1 female; and 19 groups with 3 females and 1 male.[38] Groups were given 30 minutes to discuss the case of a successful businessman who was brought before a Congressional Committee and asked to provide information about people he knew in his 20s who were members at the time of the Communist Party Cell. The businessman was threatened with a contempt charge if he was unwilling to give information. The groups had to decide what he should do.

After the discussion, each member had to rate each other member on 11 items measuring task-oriented and social-emotional activity. When factor analyzed, the 11 items produced a task factor including 7 items and a social-emotional factor including 4 items. In the balanced groups the men scoring highest on task activity had higher levels of task activity than the top-scoring women. For women who were the highest scorers on task activity, their level of task activity went down with each reduction of the proportion of women in the group. Thus, men exceeded women in task activity in balanced mixed groups; and as groups increasingly favored men in number, the task contribution of the top-level female task contributor decreased. The most task-oriented women showed a suppression of task behavior in accordance with sex role norms when they were in the minority in groups. In conjunction with the discussion of task biases considered earlier, we need to question whether the particular task chosen by Johnson and Schulman favored greater task contributions by men. Subjects were asked to take the point of view of a businessman testifying before a predominantly male body of Congress.

Charlan Nemeth and her associates carried out two studies of jury deliberations, finding traditional gender differences in the first but not the second study.[39] One difference between the two studies was the sex composition of the groups, suggesting that more traditional sex role differentiation occurs when mixed-sex groups are not balanced but have more male than female members. In the first study, Nemeth and her colleagues created 28 six-person mixed-sex groups composed of college students. Men were in the majority in half the groups (14 groups had 4 males and 2 females), 12 were equally balanced by sex, and 2 had female majorities (4 females and 2 males). Subjects read testimony of a case of a husband accused of murdering his wife. They were given 2 hours to discuss the case and come to a decision. Males scored higher on task behavior; they gave more suggestions, opinions, and information than females overall and as a percentage of their total acts. Although traditional gender differences emerged, they were modest in magnitude: 77.7% of men's activity was in the task categories versus 63% of women's activity.[40]

Nemeth and her colleagues then ran a second study of 6-person mixed-sex jury deliberations in a law school trial court. There were fewer groups in this study, and their sex composition differed from the first study. Two groups had 4 females and 2 males, three groups were evenly balanced, and a single group had 4 males and 2 females. In this study they found no gender differences on any of Bales's categories: 65% of men's activity was in the six task categories versus 63% of women's activity.[41]

In accounting for the lack of gender differences in the second study, the authors suggest the main difference involved the way in which the evidence was presented to the jurors. (In the first study subjects were given written information; in the second study groups witnessed the trial and had to rely on their memories.) The authors did not note the difference in the sex composition of the groups. In the first study women were in the minority in half the groups (14 of 28), whereas in the second study women were in the minority in only one of six groups. The widely cited study by Strodtbeck and Mann of 12-person jury deliberations involved predominantly male groups, containing from 1 to 6 women.[42] Thus, it appears that role differentiation along gender lines may more likely occur in mixed-sex groups when women are in the minority.

Rates of task and social-emotional behavior by men and women in single-sex groups have been compared to rates in mixed-sex groups to see if the presence of members of the opposite sex influences the relative task and emotional emphasis of men and women. Some researchers have found the overall rates in the two kinds of groups to be comparable.[43] Other researchers have found greater role differentiation in single-sex than in mixed-sex groups: men place a greater emphasis on task behavior in interaction with other men than in mixed groups, while women place a greater emphasis on social-emotional behavior in interaction with other women than in mixed groups.[44] The inconsistency in results from one study to another can be accounted for by differences in the particular measures used of task and social-emotional behavior, the particular nature of the interaction context, and the magnitude of the differences that serve as evidence for gender differences.

It is useful to look closely at two studies that are often cited to show that gender differences are greater in single-sex than in mixed-sex groups. These studies illustrate the problem of how small differences may become exaggerated when cited in later reviews.

Jane Piliavin and Rachel Martin studied 15 all-female, 16 all-male, and 46 mixed-sex groups of 4 members each.[45] Groups held a 10-minute discussion about the case of a girl who discovered her roommate was using heroin.[46] In comparing the behavior of men and women in single-sex groups to their behavior in mixed-sex groups, Piliavin and Martin found women dramatized more in all-female groups than in mixed groups, whereas men disagreed more, asked less for suggestions, and gave fewer suggestions in all-male groups than in mixed groups. Thus, the behavior of women in single-sex and mixed-sex groups differed on only 1 of 12 IPA categories. The finding that men showed different behavior in single-sex and mixed-sex groups was based on 3 of 12 IPA categories, but together, the 3 categories accounted for less than 2% of the total acts scored in the 12 IPA categories. Although the study has often been cited as evidence that in mixed-sex groups gender differences are moderated—that men are less combative and more willing to listen in interaction with women than with men—these conclusions have been drawn from extremely small differences.

Research by Linda Carli, cited previously, also found greater gender differences in single-sex than in mixed-sex dyads.[47] Carli used a modification of the IPA categories.[48] She studied 32 female, 32 male, and 64 mixed-sex dyads. Subjects were paired with a partner who disagreed with them about the two topics for discussion. For the first discussion, pairs were given 10 minutes to come up with a joint list of three ideas they felt were most important to forming an opinion on the topic.

Carli found no gender differences in mixed-sex dyads, but she did find larger stereotyped differences in single-sex than in mixed-sex dyads. Males used more positive social behavior and less task behavior when paired with a female than a male partner. Females showed a higher rate of task behavior, more disagreement, and a lower rate of positive social behavior when paired with a male than with a female. Although Carli reports that "men and women show a variety of less sex-stereotyped behaviors when interacting with those of the opposite gender,"[49] the magnitude of these differences should also be noted. In mixed-sex groups, women devoted 58% of their interaction to task behavior, in single-sex groups, 52%. The difference is 6%, statistically significant but small. In mixed-sex groups, 1.37% of women's interaction was disagreement, whereas in single-sex groups, .10% of their interaction was disagreement, again a difference that is quite small in magnitude.

In the second discussion, one partner was randomly chosen to try to persuade the other that his or her ideas were the most important. Although Carli found women showed more task behavior in the first discussion when paired with a man than with a woman, she found in the second discussion that when women played the role of persuader, their partner's sex had no effect on their use of task behavior. Thus, Carli found only partial support for the contention that role behavior is more gender stereotypic in single-sex than in mixed-sex groups. The effect is quite small in magnitude and is mitigated by the demands of the task.

It appears, then, that the task emphasis by females in a mixed-sex group decreases as the proportion of men in the group increases. Being in the minority in a group draws attention to a person's distinctiveness and increases visibility. There are pressures on minority members to gain acceptance that may lead to the enactment of more sex role stereotypic behavior. The effect of the group's sex composition on the relative task and social-emotional emphasis of males and females remains uncertain, as research findings are inconsistent from study to study. Where differences have been found, they are quite small in magnitude and depend on the particular task demands placed on the participants.

Assessment and Explanation of the Findings

When we consider studies of role differentiation in groups as a whole, we find a greater emphasis by men on instrumental/task behavior and by women on expressive/social-emotional behavior. Thus, men have been portrayed to be task oriented and women to be expressive, but the data do not support such polarized descriptions of the behavior of men and women. Women, like men, direct the majority of their interaction to task behavior. Men, like women, engage in expressive behavior, but to a lesser degree. If we search the literature for statistically significant gender differences on task and expressive behavior, we find them in many studies.

There are other equally valid ways, however, to read the same research findings. The magnitude of the differences is not large. Gender accounts for less than 10% of the variance in task and expressive behavior according to Carli's meta-analysis. Moreover, the research is based primarily on white, middle-class samples. We know little about how these gender differences interact with race and class.

The Personality Approach

Strodtbeck and Mann attributed gender differences along instrumental and expressive lines to the socialization of men and women.[50] They believed that the tendency for men to select a task emphasis and women to select a social-emotional emphasis becomes internalized in the personalities of males and females. This explanation does not adequately account for the individual and situational variability in the data. Some women exceed men in their rates of task activity. Rates of task and social-emotional behavior for males and females vary depending on the intimacy of the participants, the length of the interaction, the nature of the task, and the sex composition of the group. Gender differences along instrumental and expressive lines are mitigated when group members get to know one another as individuals, when they interact over time, and when the roles participants must enact require instrumental behavior. Women, in fact, have been found to be more task oriented than men when the task draws on female roles and expertise. Men show a greater level of task activity when working on tasks that draw on roles or expertise more commonly acquired by men, and they show more social-emotional behavior when the situation involves taking on female roles. If men and women simply developed different interaction styles, we would find greater behavioral consistency from one setting to the next. We need explanations that take the situational context into account.

Status Characteristics and Expectation States

A widely accepted explanation that has been put forth to account for the data is the theory of status characteristics and expectation states.[51] Success at a task is assumed to require competency or task ability. Group members try to gauge the task abilities of other members in order to maximize their hopes for success. When direct information is lacking about the relative competency of group members, they will rely on external status to form expectations. Members will develop expectations about the potential value of other members' contributions by generalizing from the value placed on the external status characteristics of each individual.

A diffuse status characteristic is defined as having two or more states that are differentially valued (e.g., sex has the states male and female). People hold different expectations for performance competency for each state, and stereotypes exist about specific qualities and skills possessed with each state. In a society where men have greater status than women and are seen as possessing greater dominance and prestige, higher expectations will be formed for men, and these expectations will become self-fulfilling prophecies. If sex operates as a diffuse status characteristic, the theory predicts that men will be more influential in mixed groups because of their presumed task-related competence. Group members will expect men as high-status persons to have greater performance ability, men will be given more opportunities to participate, and men will be more likely to have performance evaluated positively. Group members will assume the status characteristic is relevant to performance unless prior belief establishes it as not relevant. Gender differences according to this theory should disappear if women can be shown to have greater task-related competence.

The theory applies to ad hoc mixed-sex task groups in which members meet as strangers in a societal context where greater status accrues to men. In this context, men would be expected to be more competent at the task and would be granted more opportunity to demonstrate task-related behavior. According to the theory, women would be expected to show more task activity than men in groups when the task draws on roles or expertise more commonly acquired by women. In this context, group members share expectations for female task competency. The theory also predicts that when individuals know each other well and can draw on knowledge about each other rather than stereotypes, gender will play a less important role in determining who shows more task orientation.[52]

The theory accounts for the higher level of task activity by men and was extended by B. F. Meeker and P. A. Weitzel-O'Neill to account for the higher level of social-emotional activity by women.[53] Meeker and Weitzel-O'Neill suggested that task contributions by a group member who has low status will be assumed to be motivated by that person's desire to enhance his or her status. They argue that although it is acceptable for group members who possess high status (that is, men) to enhance their status, it is not legitimate for women who do not "deserve" higher status. Thus, before the task contributions from women will be accepted in a group, there must be evidence that a woman is cooperatively motivated. High rates of social-emotional activity by women are a way to demonstrate that their task contributions are motivated by concern for the group rather than by concern for status.

Research by Cecilia Ridgeway supports this hypothesis.[54] Ridgeway ran 40 groups composed of 3 same-sex subjects and an opposite-sex confederate (i.e., a person who posed as another subject but was working for the experimenter and had specific instructions about how to behave). In the *group-oriented* condition the confederate acted friendly and cooperative, accompanying task statements with comments about the importance of cooperation. In the *self-oriented* condition the confederate was less friendly and cooperative and more distant. Motivation had a dramatic effect on female confederates in otherwise all-male groups. Female confederates in male groups achieved high influence when group oriented but low influence when self-oriented. Motivation had no impact on how influential male confederates were in female groups.

Ridgeway's data suggest that as low-status individuals, women need to be cooperative and friendly in order to be heard. Research by Sara Snodgrass suggests that other aspects of women's social-emotional orientation may have more to do with their subordinate role than with their gender.[55] Snodgrass studied 9 all-male, 9 all-female, and 18 mixed-sex dyads of undergraduates who interacted for one hour.[56] One member of the dyad was randomly assigned to be leader, the other to be the student. Interpersonal sensitivity was defined as the correlation between items in which person A rated how he or she thought person B felt with B's ratings of his or her own feelings. Subordinates showed more sensitivity to leaders' feelings than leaders did to subordinates' feelings, but there were no gender differences. Snodgrass argued that subordinates may have a greater need to be aware of feelings and reactions of superiors in order to respond to their needs and acquire favor.

In a follow-up study Snodgrass observed 96 pairs of subjects.[57] Twelve male and 12 female principal subjects interacted with 4 other subjects: a male boss, a female boss, a male employee, and a female employee. Thus, each principal subject served twice in the role of leader and twice in the role of subordinate. All other subjects interacted with only one partner. Dyads interacted for an hour on three tasks—an interview, an assembly task, and a decision-making task. Interpersonal sensitivity was assessed as previously defined. Again, there were no gender differences in interpersonal sensitivity (i.e., women leaders showed no more sensitivity to their partners than male leaders), but subordinates were more sensitive to how they were being seen and the impression they were making than leaders were.

What then motivates task and social-emotional behavior? From the perspective of expectation states theory, task behavior results from being knowledgeable and having task competency, or from being perceived to be knowledgeable and competent at the task. Social-emotional behavior is a form of ingratiating behavior that less powerful group members use to have their ideas heard and accepted, to acquire favor, and to get their needs met. People focus on social-emotional behavior when they lack or are perceived to lack knowledge and competency at the task.

It is problematic, however, to assume that social-emotional behavior has a single meaning. Social-emotional behavior is used by high-status as well as low-status members of groups; it must not be regarded solely as the behavior of the powerless. Forms of social-emotional behavior like interceding or mediating or moderating a difficulty are used by more dominant members of groups. The same social-emotional behavior takes on a different meaning when used by a high-status individual in a group than when used by a low-status member. For example, praise from a low-status member could be considered to be ingratiating behavior, whereas praise from a high-status member would not be.

Social Role Theory

It can also be argued that gender differences in task and social-emotional behavior derive from differences in the social roles played by men and women in society. Alice Eagly argues that because men are assigned to different roles in work and family life than women— roles that carry more power and status and require instrumental competence—men will be believed to be agentic and task oriented.[58] Women will be believed to be more communal and emotionally expressive because they play domestic roles and fill occupations that require these traits.

The performance of very different roles in society by men and women leads to differential behavior, which in turn creates different stereotypic expectations for men and women. In the process of enacting different roles, men and women also acquire sex-typed skills and beliefs that further contribute to gender-stereotypic behavior. According to social role theory, people are expected to behave in a manner consistent with their gender roles; such behavior is considered to be socially desirable, and people tend to comply with social norms for behavior. Thus, the greater task orientation of men and expressive emphasis of women is consistent with gender roles and fulfills stereotypic expectations.

From this perspective, social-emotional behavior is not ingratiating behavior; it is an expression of the norms for feminine behavior. Women are expected to be communal, to be expressive and concerned with the interpersonal relations between participants, and they may pay a price if they do not display expected gender-related behaviors.

Future Directions

We know more about task behavior than we do about social-emotional behavior—a form of behavior that is extremely important to the successful functioning of any group. Clearly, social-emotional behavior may be motivated by a variety of concerns. We need to focus attention more specifically on the type of behavior that falls into the IPA category "seems friendly." This category includes a wide variety of behaviors: acts of support, approval, reassurance, sympathy, nurturance, moving the group forward on the task by mediating or moderating a conflict, yielding, or conceding a point.[59] In research studies, this category of acts has extremely low rates, representing less than 5% of the interaction,[60] but even though infrequent, it has important cumulative effects over time on a social system.

Women are believed to be the ones who hold relationships, families, and groups together by doing the necessary social-emotional work. Literature on urban kinship shows family networks to be held together by women.[61] Much of the work women do to maintain social systems like families and extended families, however, is primarily instrumental work. Women exchange resources, babysitting, or meals out of social need. This behavior serves an instrumental purpose. We need to think carefully about how to determine whether a behavior is task or social-emotional in orientation, or whether it is both simultaneously. We lack process data over time in long-term intimate relationships or groups to better determine the kind of social-emotional behavior that women and men exhibit to help maintain social systems, what motivates this behavior when it is performed, and how it is related to power and status.

Groups that interact over time develop roles other than the two fundamental task and expressive roles described by Talcott Parsons. Although considerable attention has been given over the years to determining whether men are more instrumental and women are more expressive, other types of gender-related roles develop in groups that are deserving of future attention. Some roles are produced not by the differing styles of men and women but by the differential treatment of men and women.

For example, Rosabeth Kanter, in her work on organizations,

suggests that women may be trapped in a variety of roles based on their gender, and that these roles limit their ability to express themselves or to demonstrate their task competence.[62] She describes the role of mother, an emotional specialist who listens in a noncritical fashion, sympathizes, and accepts; the role of seductress or sexual object, who introduces competition and jealousy; the role of pet, who amuses and serves as a cheerleader; and the role of iron maiden, who is tough, forthright, and demands treatment as an equal. Women in these roles are not valued for their task-related competence. Even the iron maiden is viewed with suspicion because she is seen as threatening and dangerous. Men may likewise be trapped in the role of protector, provider, seductor, or aggressor based on their gender.

Gender differences in roles may be produced by differential perceptions and responses to individuals based on gender. We need to go further in examining the impact of gender stereotypes on the entrapment of men and women in different types of roles in groups.

3

Dominance and Leadership in Groups

Dominance and leadership are characteristics associated with men and masculinity.[1] Consistent with this notion, research on mixed-sex discussion groups shows men to take the lead and dominate by talking more than women[2] and to emerge more often as leaders in groups that are initially leaderless.[3] We could conclude from this evidence that the widely held stereotype of male dominance and leadership is actually an accurate depiction of reality, but before doing so we need to consider alternative perspectives on these data.

This chapter is divided into two sections. In the first section I consider the features of the participants and the situational context that make men more likely than women to emerge as leaders and to display dominance in initially leaderless groups, and those contexts that mitigate this effect. In the second half of the chapter I look at the behavior of women and men in actual leadership positions. If we legitimize leadership for women by assigning them to leadership roles or to other male stereotypic roles, to what extent do men and women show similar displays of dominance and leadership in these positions?

Emergent Leadership

The Measurement of Leadership

Who is more likely to emerge as the leader in a group that is initially leaderless, a man or a woman? To answer this question, we need to define and measure leadership behavior. Several different definitions of leadership have been widely used.

Verbal Participation in Groups One of the most popular measures used to determine who dominates or emerges as the leader in an initially leaderless group is amount of verbal participation. Speaking in a group takes up time and it draws attention toward the speaker and away from other members. Those who speak the most are those who receive the most interaction, whereas those who speak infrequently are rarely addressed.[4] There are a variety of ways to assess amount of verbal participation: speaking time, number of words spoken, number of acts initiated.[5]

Task, Social-Emotional, and General Leadership Who emerges as the leader of a group has also been assessed by measures of task-leadership, social-emotional leadership, and general leadership. The task leader is the person identified as contributing the most to helping the group achieve its goals. The social-emotional leader is the person identified as doing the most to reduce tensions and establish and maintain satisfying relations between group members. A leader can be identified more generally by asking group members who the leader of the group was. To assess who is the task or social-emotional leader, some researchers use act-by-act scoring of interaction to determine who contributed the most task or expressive acts. Other researchers rely on general ratings of task, social-emotional, or general leadership done by either group members or objective judges.

Relationship Between the Measures Whether leadership is measured by time talking, task leadership, or general measures of leadership, the results are similar. Because task activity as scored by Interaction Process Analysis usually accounts for over two thirds of the interaction in a group, total task activity and total verbal participation are highly correlated.[6] It also turns out that when group members or objective judges are asked to name leaders, they point to those who talked most and did the most to help the group achieve its goals. A review of the literature on leadership status and verbal participation rates by R. Timothy Stein and Tamar Heller shows very high correlations (over .70) between verbal participation and task and general leadership.[7] Similarly, a meta-analysis of participation rate and leadership emergence in small groups by Brian Mullen and his colleagues shows participation rate to be a very clear predictor of leadership emergence.[8]

While verbal participation, task leadership, and general leadership assess similar aspects of leadership behavior, these measures are not related to social-emotional leadership. Stein and Heller's review found almost no relationship (mean correlation of $r = .16$) between verbal participation and social-emotional behavior (i.e., behavior directed toward establishing solidarity between group members and reducing tensions). Task and social-emotional leadership are independent forms of leadership that may or may not be integrated within the same person.[9]

Researchers have focused attention primarily on task or general leadership rather than on social-emotional leadership, and in so doing they may not have captured a form of leadership that may be more permissible or prevalent for women. It is possible that women provide leadership of a different form than men, but the research does not provide as much information about social-emotional leadership.

Overall Findings on Gender and Leadership

The majority of research on leadership in mixed-sex groups shows males to emerge as leaders more frequently than females. In an analysis of 64 data sets discussed in 29 studies of gender differences in power and prestige in mixed-sex task groups, Marlaine Lockheed found 70% of the data sets revealed more male activity, influence, or leadership, 17% revealed no gender difference, and 12.5% favored females.[10] In a recent review of 56 studies of gender differences in amount of talk, Deborah James and Janice Drakich found men talked more in 42.9% of the studies; there were no gender differences in 28.6% of the studies; in 25% of the studies the results were equivocal; and in only 3.6% of the studies did women talk more than men.[11] Clearly, women are unlikely to assume leadership more than men, but there are many studies that find no gender differences. Nor do these literature reviews give us information about the magnitude of the effect of gender on leadership.

The Magnitude of the Difference Information about the magnitude of the effect of gender on leadership is provided by Alice Eagly and Steven Karau's 1991 meta-analysis of the data on leadership emergence.[12] Their meta-analysis supports the conclusion that men are more likely to emerge as leaders in mixed-sex groups than women, but it shows the effect to be modest in magnitude. The meta-analysis was based on 58 studies of leadership emergence in mixed-sex, initially leaderless task-oriented groups, most of which were laboratory studies using college students as research subjects.

Men were found to emerge as leaders more frequently than women when task leadership was assessed (mean weighted effect size d = .41) and when general or unspecified leadership was assessed (mean weighted d = .32 and .29, respectively). Less than 20% of the studies in the meta-analysis included measures of social leadership (behavior directed to maintaining satisfying interpersonal relations), but women were found to emerge as leaders when social leadership was assessed (mean weighted d = -.18).

Recall that an effect size d of .2 represents a small effect with an 85% overlap in the distributions of males and females, whereas an effect size of .5 represents a moderate effect with a 67% overlap in the distributions of men and women.[13] Thus, the effect size for task or general leadership is small to moderate, and for social-emotional leadership it is small. The meta-analytic findings reveal that while men are more likely to assume leadership in groups than women, in many situations women emerge as leaders in initially leaderless groups.

We need to go beyond the overall meta-analytic findings, then, to determine the aspects of the interaction context that account for the variability in the findings. Leadership is a process that takes place in interaction between individuals and the particular characteristics of the situation.[14] The question we need to ask is what the characteristics of participants and the interaction situation are that account for the fact that men do not always assume leadership in groups but that make men more or less likely to emerge as leaders in groups.

Status

High-status individuals are more likely to talk longer and to emerge as leaders in interaction than individuals who are low status. Feminists have long noted that status differences have been confused with differences due to sex.[15] Because greater status and power are conferred to men in this society than to women, status differences may account for gender differences in some studies. Research by Barbara and R. Gene Eakins demonstrates how gender may be confounded with status in studies of leadership.[16] Seven faculty meetings attended by 6 males and 4 females were recorded in a university department. Eakins and Eakins found that while men took more turns than women and spoke longer per turn than women, the number of turns taken followed a hierarchy of status based on rank and length of time in the department. Thus, status within the group served as the basis for rates of participation, just as gender did.

Work by Fred Strodtbeck shows how status differences between individuals based on roles and positions in society are brought into small group discussions and serve as the basis for differences in speaking time within a group.[17] Ten couples were studied from each of three cultures in the Southwestern United States; cultures that varied in terms of the relative position of men and women: Navaho Indians, Mormons, and Texan farmers. The Navaho society is matriarchal; Mormons are patriarchal; and Texan farmers are more egalitarian. Spouses filled out identical questionnaires and were asked to arrive at common answers where responses differed. There was a significant relationship between the spouse who talked the most and the spouse who won the most decisions. For Navahos, the wives won more decisions, for Mormons, husbands won more decisions, and there were no significant differences between husbands and wives for the Texans. The study suggests that interaction is shaped by power elements of the larger social and cultural context in which the interaction takes place. Members of groups that hold more power in society are more dominant in small group interactions.

Consistent with this perspective, Strodtbeck and Mann found that the status an individual possesses in the larger society is brought into a small group interaction and influences participation rates.[18] In their study of 12-person jury deliberations they drew on participants from regular jury pools in Chicago and St. Louis. Men were found to originate more acts than women, but high-status persons were found to initiate more interaction than low-status persons.

Because we rely so heavily on college students as subjects for our experiments, we study males and females who enter an interaction as equals in terms of their status as students. We do not have many studies of groups whose members vary widely in status—the kind of studies that would be necessary to determine the relative influence of gender or status. The few we have suggest that talking time is greater for those with higher status. However, even when college students interact, differences in the status of men and women in society may be carried into small group interactions in terms of stereotypes and expectations for task competency. Males may be expected to be better able to help the group to achieve its goals, and they may be afforded more opportunities to take the lead. The impact of status differences between men and women in the larger culture in shaping expectations for leadership is discussed later.

Personality

One of the better predictors of who will take the lead in leaderless discussion groups is personality. Between 48% and 82% of the variance in leadership has been found to be accounted for by personality traits.[19] Some individuals tend to assume a larger share of speaking time than others regardless of their conversational partners.[20] Individuals who are high in performance self-esteem, dominance, activity, and ascendancy—personality traits associated with masculinity—may be more likely to emerge as leaders. However, the situation is complex for women who possess these personality traits because sex role prescriptions for behavior in many settings dictate that men should be in charge and take the lead. Despite the power of personality in shaping behavior, when sex role prescriptions for behavior conflict with personality dispositions for women, sex role prescriptions serve to inhibit the direct expression of personality. Personality dispositions turn out to be better predictors of leadership behavior for men than for women because they are sex role congruent, and they are better predictors of leadership in single-sex groups than in mixed-sex groups.[21]

Performance Self-esteem Individuals who believe that they are capable of performing competently at a task and have high expectations for their own performance are more likely to emerge as leaders than those who have low expectations. When men and women hold equivalent expectations about their task competency, research has shown there to be no gender differences in task leadership.[22]

Research by Patricia Andrews provides a nice demonstration of this effect.[23] Andrews assigned 64 subjects to 4-person groups based on scores on the Performance Self-Esteem Scale (PSE).[24] Each group had a high- and a low-performance self-esteem male and a high- and a low-performance self-esteem female. Groups were given 15 minutes to discuss what could be done to improve the quality of teaching at the university. In postsession ratings, members and observers were asked to indicate who they felt to be the leader of the group. People with high-performance-related self-esteem were named to be leaders 73% of the time, were seen as giving more problem-relevant information, and were believed to offer more sound opinions. People with low-performance self-esteem were named to be leaders only 23% of the time. When PSE is high, either sex is likely to be chosen as leader.

If women are as likely as men to assume leadership when they feel capable of performing a task competently, but men are more likely to be found to be leaders in research studies, we need to look carefully at the tasks that have been assigned to groups. We need to see if studies of leadership are based on tasks that favor male skills and expertise—tasks that men approach with higher expectations for their own task competency. The influence of the task on the emergence of leadership is discussed in a later section.

Masculinity and Femininity Individuals possessing sex-stereotypic masculine characteristics are more likely to assume leadership initially than persons possessing a sex-stereotypic feminine orientation, as shown in research by Bonnie Spillman and her colleagues.[25] Because the masculine sex role is associated with an instrumental orientation, individuals possessing masculine traits would be expected to initiate more task behaviors in groups. Spillman and her colleagues tested subjects on the Bem Sex Role Inventory, a measure of the degree to which subjects perceive themselves to possess sex-stereotypic masculine and sex-stereotypic feminine characteristics, and they assigned 66 students to mixed-sex groups of 5 to 8 members. Groups met for four 1-hour meetings to discuss and provide solutions to a variety of problems. At the end of each session, members filled out social and task leadership ratings.

Masculine and androgynous individuals (those possessing both masculine and feminine characteristics) had higher total task leadership scores than feminine persons after the first meeting, although the difference was not significant at later meetings. Thus, the assumption of traditionally valued feminine characteristics was not conducive to task leadership in an initial encounter, but it was not an impediment to the assumption of leadership as group members became better acquainted over time.

Spillman's work raises an important question about another potential bias to research studies. If we study groups that last but a single session, we may be more likely to find men have an initial advantage in being named as leader, but the effect may be diminished over time. The length of the interaction on leadership emergence is considered in a later section.

Dominance Dominance has been the most widely studied personality predictor of leadership emergence in groups. Research on single-sex groups shows dominance to be a good predictor of leadership. For example, research by William Rogers and Stanley Jones on single-sex groups shows that more dominant individuals take up a larger proportion of speaking time in a group.[26] In their study of 18 same-sex dyads composed of one high-dominance and one low-dom-

inance individual engaging in 15 minutes of interaction, high-dominance individuals held the floor twice as long as low-dominance
individuals. Dominance, however, has less ability to predict behavior in mixed-sex groups. In a study that has now become a classic,
Edwin Megargee demonstrated that dominance is a good predictor
of leadership emergence in single-sex groups, but that sex role
norms have more influence than personality variables on the manifestation of dominance by women in mixed-sex groups.[27] His findings have been replicated by many other researchers.

Megargee tested students on the Dominance Scale of the California Psychological Inventory. Eighty students were formed into either
single-sex or opposite-sex pairs including one person high in dominance and one person low in dominance. Pairs were shown an
upright box and told to remove certain nuts from a set of bolts on the
box as quickly as possible. To do the job, they had to pick a leader to
stay outside the box to remove nuts with a wrench and a follower to
enter the box with a screwdriver to hold the bolt in place.

In single-sex groups, the high-dominance partner assumed leadership: for male pairs, 75% became leaders; for female pairs, 70%
became leaders. In mixed-sex pairs, however, the male assumed
leadership regardless of the dominance of the individuals. When personality was consistent with sex role expectations and a high-dominance man was paired with a low-dominance woman, men assumed
leadership in 90% of the cases. The most striking results were produced in the condition where a woman high in dominance was
paired with a man low in dominance, and personality ran counter to
sex role norms for interaction. High-dominance women assumed
leadership over low-dominance men only 20% of the time.

Megargee tape-recorded the discussions between pairs preceding
the choice of leader. The tapes revealed that when high-dominance
females were paired with low-dominance males, 91% of the time
they appointed the low-dominance partner to be leader. It was not
the case that low-dominance men were more assertive, but rather
that high-dominance women were reluctant to assume leadership
and expressed their dominance indirectly by appointing their partners to be leaders. Megargee's study illustrates the conflicts faced by
dominant women in interaction with men in some settings — conflicts between personality dispositions and sex role requirements —
and the study points to the power of sex role norms in influencing
overt leadership behavior.

Megargee's work attracted the attention of the research community, and four replications and extensions of his original study were

carried out in the 1980s.[28] In two of these studies, even though the tasks varied,[29] the results were quite similar to those of Megargee. High-dominance women were found to assume leadership over low-dominance men 30%[30] and 35%[31] of the time. In a third study, high-dominance women gained equality with low-dominance men and assumed leadership 50% of the time.[32] These three studies suggest that despite the vast changes in consciousness about sex roles, and sex role change in society between the original study in 1969 and the follow-ups over 15 years later, the conflict between personality dispositions and sex role stereotypic prescriptions for behavior persists. This conflict causes high-dominance women to suppress their expression of leadership and pressures men to assume leadership. Only one replication and extension of Megargee's study, discussed following, found contrasting results, with high-dominance women assuming leadership over low-dominance men 71% of the time.[33]

The follow-up studies provide further information to help explain the behavior of high-dominance women with low-dominance men. The work of Linda Nyquist and Janet Spence demonstrated that although high-dominance women appointed their partners to be leaders, they expressed their dominance behaviorally in the interaction.[34] Dominant women may be reluctant to assume overt leadership over men, but they may exert leadership behavior within the follower role. The study by Robin Fleischer and Jerome Chertkoff demonstrated that high-dominance subjects were more likely to want to be leader than low-dominance subjects, but high-dominance women had less desire to be leaders than high-dominance men.[35] High-dominance women may show less preference for the leadership position because women are not expected to be leaders.

The most recent extension and replication of Megargee's study has produced findings that contrast with that of Megargee's original study, and it provides further clues to the factors that inhibit the expression of dominance in high-dominance women.[36] Beverly Davis and Lucia Gilbert ran 61 mixed-sex dyads that extended the conditions studied by Megargee. They studied high- and low-dominance pairs, as well as pairs with both partners high or both partners low on dominance. Subjects participated first in a 7-minute discussion. They were given a list of 12 specialist teachers, 7 of whom would have to be dismissed by a school board due to budget cuts. After making their individual decisions, group members came together to make a team decision. Following this discussion, subjects performed the same task that was carried out by Megargee's subjects (i.e., removing nuts from a set of bolts using a wrench).

In the initial group discussions, high-dominance individuals spoke more, had more successful influence attempts, and were rated as more forceful than low-dominance subjects. Thus, in the initial discussions, personality was a good predictor of behavior. Subjects then engaged in the task used by Megargee. When sex role prescriptions for behavior were consistent with personality dispositions, personality was a good predictor of behavior. The most striking finding, however, was that when a high-dominance woman was paired with a low-dominance man, 71% of the high-dominance women became leaders. This result contrasts sharply with the 20% found by Megargee and the 35% to 50% found in later studies for this condition.

The distinguishing factor in the study by Davis and Gilbert is the insertion of the interaction prior to the selection of leader. Davis and Gilbert gave group members the opportunity for the personal characteristics of each partner to become known. Subjects engaged in a discussion on an issue where neither males nor females were likely to have greater expertise. Despite the fact that pairs interacted for only 7 minutes, the fact that subjects were not complete strangers but had some knowledge of each other had an impact on their behavior.

The research by Davis and Gilbert also suggested that women alter their dominance expression in response to the dominance level of their partner. Davis and Gilbert were able to compare high-/low-dominance pairs with pairs who had similar levels of dominance. High-dominance women assumed leadership over high-dominance men only 31% of the time, but they assumed leadership with low-dominance men 71% of the time. With a male high in dominance, 67% of high-dominance women picked their partner to lead. With a low-dominance man, 57% of high-dominance women picked themselves to lead. Thus, women were quite sensitive to the dominance levels of their male partners; they held back in the presence of highly dominant men but not in the presence of low-dominance men. The same pattern held for low-dominance women. When both partners were low on dominance, equal numbers of men and women became leaders, but 100% of low-dominance women with a high-dominance man picked their male partner to be leader. Low-dominance women held back entirely in the presence of high-dominance men but not in the presence of low-dominance men.

This series of studies reveals first that dominance is an important predictor of leadership behavior in single-sex groups and in mixed groups where personality dispositions and sex role prescriptions for behavior are consistent. When sex role norms for interaction are incompatible with personality dispositions, as is the case when a high-dominance woman is paired with a low-dominance man, personality expresses itself in more subtle ways and is no longer the clear predictor of overt leadership behavior. High-dominance women show less preference for being named leaders than high-dominance men; they express their dominance by assigning male partners to be leaders, particularly when their partners are dominant, and by displaying dominance behaviors during the task. However, the research of Davis and Gilbert suggests that when individuals interact with each other even for a brief time and are not simply strangers in an initial encounter, personality (as opposed to gender role stereotypes) will play a larger role in predicting interaction in mixed-sex groups. In this situation, high-dominance women assumed leadership over low-dominance men, but the women remained cautious in assuming leadership over highly dominant men.

Summary Personality dispositions such as dominance are better predictors of leadership in single-sex groups than in mixed-sex encounters,[37] although performance self-esteem has been found to be predictive of dominance and leadership for women in mixed groups. Women are more likely to express dominance and to assume leadership when they know they can perform competently at the task. Men are more likely to emerge as overt leaders in brief mixed-sex encounters among strangers, even if the women present are more dominant in personality. Leadership is associated with masculinity, and the behavior of men and women follows the dictates of sex role norms in initial encounters rather than personality dispositions. The data suggest that the greater emergence of males as leaders than females may be attributed not to their more dominant personalities, but to the avoidance of overt leadership by females. When participants have some knowledge of their partners, women are more likely to avoid leadership positions when they are interacting with high-dominance men than with low-dominance men.

Sex Composition of the Group

The studies reviewed here demonstrate that men and women behave differently depending on the sex of their partners in interaction. When meeting others as strangers, women are more inhibited in expressing dominance in the presence of men than in the presence of other women. Women have been found to talk less in mixed-sex task groups than they do in all-female groups.[38]

Comparison of Behavior in All-Male and All-Female Groups When comparisons are made of all-male and all-female groups, males have been found to establish a clearer hierarchy of leadership than females. Mary Fennell and her colleagues had 10 all-male and 10 all-female 4-person groups come to a unanimous decision about how to rank order 15 items salvaged from a plane wreck for their survival value.[39] In 6 of 10 male groups, the most active group member held that position through the entire discussion and was the most active on questions, directions, and statements. This pattern was characteristic of only 3 of 10 female groups.

Consistent with this pattern, in a study conducted for my dissertation research I found that all-male groups established a more stable dominance hierarchy of speaking than all-female groups.[40] I ran two all-male, two all-female, and two mixed-sex groups of 5 to 7 members each that met in five 1½-hour sessions with the task of getting to know each other. The same males were the most active speakers in every session and never missed sessions. In all-female groups, there was greater flexibility in the rank order of speaking across sessions. Women had a preferred place in the rank order of speaking, but they showed more flexibility in the rank they assumed from session to session. If females missed sessions, they were able to assume higher ranks in later sessions. I also found that in all-male groups, males addressed over 30% of their interaction to the group as a whole rather than to individuals, a style that has been considered to be an exercise of power or influence in a group.[41] In all-female groups, females addressed less than 10% of their interaction to the group as a whole.

Comparison of Behavior in Single-Sex and Mixed-Sex Groups Our perspective on these findings shifts when we contrast the behavior of males and females in single-sex groups with their behavior in mixed-sex groups. In mixed-sex groups, unlike all-male groups, my research revealed flexibility in the rank order of speaking. Males addressed less than 9% (rather than 30%) of their interaction to the group as a whole. In other words, the behavior of men resembled that of women in mixed-sex groups; there was a sharp contrast between expressions of dominance and hierarchy by males in all-male and in mixed-sex groups.

Male-Male, Female-Female, and Male-Female Dominance Exchanges Some very interesting research using assessments of dominance as it is expressed in the ongoing interaction process similarly demonstrates that men display a greater emphasis on displays of dominance in interaction with men than women do with women or than men do with women. The male emphasis on dominance is particularly striking when comparisons are made of interaction of men and women in single-sex groups; it is mitigated when men interact with women.

Judi Miller studied 48 undergraduates in single-sex dyads with the task of imagining themselves in a situation where they wanted to go to a concert but all the tickets had been sold but one.[42] They were given 5 minutes to role-play who would get the single remaining ticket. Each interaction was coded as one-up, one-down, or one-across in conjunction with the previous one. A one-up move is nonsupportive and assertive, a one-down move is supportive and nonassertive, and a one-across move extends the previous response in a neutral, noncommittal way. Men used more one-up moves than women, women more one-down moves than men. Women showed more submissiveness than men and more often responded to one-down moves by moving down.

Similar findings for all-female groups have been reported by Donald Ellis, who analyzed contiguous acts in two consciousness-raising groups that met periodically over a 3-month period.[43] Groups tried to create a supportive atmosphere where members would feel safe to share feelings, and they discouraged the establishment of leaders or of any hierarchy. Each act was coded for relational control as dominant, submissive, or neither. The most frequent relational mode was equivalent symmetry, or acts that were neither dominant nor submissive, followed by the same. Very little competitive symmetry occurred; that is, dominance followed by dominance, or dominance followed by submissiveness. It is important to note that Ellis studied only women in all-female interactions; he provides no comparison with women in a mixed-sex context. In addition, by studying a women's consciousness-raising group, he has selected a context for all-female interaction in which a feminist ideology prevails and norms call for nonhierarchical, supportive interactions.[44]

Not only do men in all-male groups show a greater emphasis on dominance than they do in mixed-groups, they show a greater emphasis on dominance in their interactions with men in mixed-sex groups than they do with women in those groups. In a study of a married couples group therapy by Anne McCarrick and her colleagues, males were found to show greater competition with other males than they did with females, or than females did with each other.[45] The group was composed of 5 male ministers and their wives, who ranged in age from 27 to 53. They met for an initial 15 sessions—3 sessions lasting 8 hours, all others lasting 2 hours. The group met 2 years later for another 15 sessions.

Males were more likely to respond to other males with a one-up response (e.g., giving orders, interrupting, asking questions demanding answers, giving nonsupport responses) than females were to other females or than males were to females. Females were more likely to respond to one-down messages with one-down responses (e.g., giving support responses, using noncomplete phrases that invite others to take control), and females were unlikely to give one-up responses to one-down messages. By contrast, men attempted dominance when not challenged. The greatest likelihood of a one-up response was seen by males addressing males, but males showed less competition with females.

It is interesting to link the greater emphasis on competition in male-male interactions to findings by Wendy Wood and Nancy Rhodes on social-emotional behavior in male-male encounters.[46] Wood and Rhodes carried out a sequential analysis looking at the patterning of contiguous sets of acts as scored by a modified version of Interaction Process Analysis. College students participated in 3-person mixed-sex discussion groups with a male or female majority. Discussions lasted 75 minutes. Women were more likely to respond to a positive act with another positive act than with a task act, and this tendency was particularly strong for women to other women. Men were more likely to respond to a negative act with another negative act than women were, but this was particularly true for men to other men. Women were less likely to respond to negative acts at all, and this tendency was most pronounced with other women. In other words, males were more likely to escalate conflict with other males, females to avoid it with other females.

These data suggest then that if we compare men and women based only on behavior in single-sex groups, men appear to be much more concerned with dominance and hierarchy than women. Not only are these concerns about dominance and hierarchy heightened in interactions between males, but research by Donald Ellis and Linda McCallister shows this to be particularly true for masculine sex-typed men.[47]

Ellis and McCallister tested subjects on the Bem Sex Role Inventory. From a pool of 200 subjects, they formed groups that had subjects who were either all sex-typed masculine (including 14 men and 1 woman), all sex-typed feminine (including 13 women and 2 men), or all androgynous (including 6 men and 6 women). Subjects had to decide on three books and three symbolic items that they considered to be representative of our country. Interaction was coded for control bids (i.e., attempts to dominate or structure the relationship), deference (i.e., submissiveness to another), or equivalence (i.e., bids for mutual identification). Groups composed of sex-typed masculine individuals generated significantly more relational control bids than the other groups. They were more concerned with control—with directing and structuring the interaction. In the sex-typed masculine groups, control bids were responded to with control, and deference was more likely to be followed by control. Sex-typed feminine groups were characterized by relational equivalence—by equivalence followed by equivalence. Thus, it is not sex alone that predicts the male emphasis on dominance and leadership, but identification with the masculine gender role.

These data should not be taken to suggest that women will not exert dominance against women in all-female groups. If we consider dominance as attempts at controlling another's behavior, then we have research by Cecilia Ridgeway and David Diekema that shows that women are quite capable of exerting dominance against other women just as men are against other men.[48] Ridgeway and Diekema studied 21 all-male and 21 all-female 4-person groups, each composed of two confederates and two naive subjects. The group was asked to make a decision about an insurance settlement in a jury case and had 12 minutes to decide upon an award level from $0 to $25,000. The main confederate argued for an award of $0, the second confederate for an award of $15,000. In half the groups the main confederate was aggressive, hostile, and challenging toward the second confederate, who reacted in a neutral fashion. The main confederate never attacked the naive subjects. Ridgeway and Diekema found that in both all-male and all-female groups, the naive subjects intervened with dominance acts or controlling behaviors (e.g., dismissing arguments, interrupting, showing hostility and negative affect, giving counterarguments). When we consider the total number of acts initiated by men and women, there was no difference in the proportion of acts that were attacks.

Proportion of Men and Women in the Group The degree to which men and women display dominance may depend not only on whether interaction takes place in a single-sex or mixed group, but also on the relative proportion of men and women in the group. Research evidence shows no clear patterning to dominance and leadership emergence by men or women as the proportion of women in a group decreases. According to the meta-analysis by Alice Eagly and Steven Karau, effect sizes were quite variable when women were in the minority, but strangely enough, men were less likely to emerge as leaders when they were in the majority ($d = .24$) than when groups were evenly balanced by sex ($d = .49$). There is some evidence to suggest that being a solo woman in a group is detrimental to task performance and hence leadership potential,[49] and that being a solo female in a group is more disadvantageous to emergent leadership than being a solo male.[50]

Summary When we consider the sex composition of the group, we find that the male emphasis on dominance and hierarchy is heightened for men who possess more sex-typed masculine characteristics and mitigated when men interact with women. The data suggest that the establishment of dominance and hierarchy are of greater concern between men than between women, or between men and women. Does this mean that females pay less attention to issues of dominance and hierarchy? In my own research I found there were women who dominated sessions in all-female groups, but these women expressed concern about being too dominant and promised to be quiet in later sessions.[51] Women who are dominant and competitive fear they will pay a price in social rejection. In the second half of this chapter I examine the behavior of men and women in roles that sanction dominance behavior for women to see if their behavior is similar to that of men.

Task

If the task given to a group requires skills, abilities, or interests that are more typically acquired by men than by women, men are more likely to emerge as leaders; if tasks favor abilities that are more often acquired by women, women tend to emerge as leaders.[52] Eagly and Karau in their meta-analysis found that men were more likely to emerge as leaders on masculine tasks ($d = .79$) than on gender neutral tasks ($d = .58$) or on feminine tasks ($d = .26$).[53] Thus, there is a large effect when tasks are masculine, a moderate effect when tasks are neutral, and a small effect when tasks are feminine. When the tasks given to groups required greater social complexity (e.g., interpersonal problem solving, negotiation, extensive sharing of ideas, purely social interactions), men were less likely to emerge as leaders ($d = .23$). Eagly and Karau noted that unfortunately the nature of the task became confounded with the length of time the group met, which is a factor I discuss later. Because groups that meet for longer periods of time often work on tasks of greater social complexity, the length of time that the groups meet is a potentially confounding variable.

Masculine and Feminine Tasks Several studies provide illustrative examples of how task requirements influence the emergence of leadership for males and females. Joyce Carbonell noted the masculine bias to the task used in Megargee's experiment, which involved fixing a machine by unscrewing bolts.[54] She created a comparable "feminine" task involving garment workers. Subjects had to use a needle and thread to sew on buttons in contrast to Megargee's task in which subjects had to use a screwdriver and wrench to remove nuts from bolts. In single-sex groups, as in the original study, high-dominance partners assumed leadership over low-dominance partners (for males 75%, for females 69%). When high-dominance males were paired with low-dominance females, 75% of the men assumed leadership. When high-dominance females were paired with low-dominance males, 56% of the women assumed leadership, whereas only 20% of the women assumed leadership in this condition in Megargee's study, and 30% in Carbonell's replication of the original experiment. Thus, high-dominance women were more likely to assume leadership when faced with a feminine task than a masculine one. It is interesting to note, however, that while the task favored female skills or interests, women were only slightly more likely than men to take the lead.

Similarly, John Dovidio and his colleagues found that whether males or females talk longer depends on how familiar the topic is to their sex.[55] They assigned 48 students to mixed-sex dyads that had 3 minutes to discuss each of three topics—one masculine topic (automotive oil changing), one feminine (pattern sewing), and one neutral (vegetable gardening). Females held the floor longer on the feminine topic, males on the male topic, and males also spoke longer and initiated speech more often on the neutral topic.

Finally, Diane Wentworth and Lynn Anderson compared groups working on masculine, feminine, and neutral tasks.[56] Ten mixed-sex, 4-person groups were assigned to each task condition. In the masculine task condition, groups had to decide how to invest a $10,000 inheritance a young cousin had received. In the feminine task condition, groups had to advise a young female friend how to spend a $10,000 inheritance for her wedding. In the neutral task condition, groups had to advise a young married couple how to spend a $10,000 inheritance designated solely for entertainment. Groups held 20-minute discussions, and members filled out postsession ratings on leadership.

Men were more likely to be perceived as leaders on the masculine task than women (89% of emergent leaders were male). Women were not significantly more likely than men to emerge as leaders on the feminine task (60% of emergent leaders were female), but they were significantly more likely to assume leadership on the feminine task than the masculine one. Subjects also rated their own expertise on the task. There was a significant interaction between gender typing of task and sex: males were more likely to see themselves as knowledgeable about the masculine task, women the feminine task.

Biases Toward the Use of Masculine Tasks Men are more likely to be designated leaders or to speak more in studies that use tasks such as presentation of arguments to prove one's point[57] or getting the best deal for one's side in a confrontation.[58] Competitive debate and confrontation are forms of interaction sanctioned for males, but they require a style that violates norms for the display of femininity. The tasks given to groups in many laboratory studies draw on such styles or skills. If such tasks are used in an experiment and men assume leadership, the findings are rarely attributed to the tasks but are attributed to the sex of the participants.

Studies of informal discussion do not yield a clear pattern in regard to sex and leadership or total amount of verbal participation, but the variability in results suggest that males emerge less consistently as leaders when the task is less structured, when group members are free to talk about whatever they like, or where the task requires the discussion of more personal feelings and values of group members. Some studies find no sex-related differences in rates of participation when discussion is informal and non-task oriented,[59] some find women to speak more than men and be more likely to assume leadership,[60] and some find men to speak more than women.[61]

Summary When tasks draw on knowledge, styles, or skills stereotypically associated with men, men are more likely than women to emerge as leaders, and the effect size is large ($d = .79$).[62] When tasks are less structured, talk is informal, or when tasks draw on the skills and expertise of women, women are more likely to emerge as leaders than when tasks draw on male styles or skills ($d = .23$). It is important to note, however, that the data do not show women to be significantly more likely than men to emerge as leaders under conditions that favor female leadership; the gender differences are mitigated but not always reversed.

Length and Intimacy of the Relationship

As members get to know each other's attributes and task-relevant competencies, sex becomes less salient in predicting leadership in mixed groups. Men are often found to have higher verbal participation rates in mixed-sex laboratory task groups that last less than 20 minutes.[63] Eagly and Karau in their meta-analysis found that men are more likely to emerge as leaders in groups lasting less than 20 minutes ($d = .58$).[64] The effect size decreases as the length of the group's meeting time increases: for single session meetings lasting more than 20 minutes, the effect size is .38, and for studies of interaction that last more than a single session, the effect size is reduced to .09. Thus, the overall finding that men are more likely to emerge as leaders than women is highly dependent on the fact that we have studied interaction in very brief or onetime encounters.

Groups Meeting More Than One Session Bonnie Spillman and her colleagues studied groups that met for four sessions and found surprisingly that women emerged as leaders initially, but that gender influenced only initial leadership emergence.[65] In this study it was the females who had higher task and social leadership scores after the first two sessions, but there were no gender differences in leadership after either of the last two sessions. The authors had hypothesized that males would initially be rated higher on task leadership. To account for the findings, they examined the personality tests taken by the participants and discovered that the majority of the women did not fit stereotypical sex role expectations. Only 36% of the women were sex-typed feminine, and the women were more autocratic than the men.

Craig Schneier and Kathryn Bartol studied 52 groups of 4 to 7 members that met in conjunction with a course in personnel administration over 15 weeks on assigned projects.[66] At the end of the semester members were asked to name a leader. There were no differences in the proportion of females and males being designated as emergent leaders. Thus, in groups meeting over longer periods of time, gender is not always predictive of leadership designation.

Intimacy of the Relationship Between Group Members The majority of research studies of gender and leadership are based on the interaction of strangers. When studies are done of individuals in more intimate relationships, gender is less predictive of leadership behavior. Gender differences in rates of verbal participation are greatest when participants do not know each other well.[67] William Kenkel found no gender differences in speaking time in his study of discussions among married couples about how to spend a gift of $300.[68] In this study, husbands and wives filled out personality tests including assessments of dominance prior to the discussions. Seventy-five percent of the dominant wives talked as much or more than their husbands, and half the submissive wives talked as much or more. What makes this interesting is that research on strangers discussed earlier shows high-dominance women are inhibited from expressing leadership; but in married couples, high-dominance women may be less inhibited in the expression of verbal dominance.

We find examples in research on married couples of wives dominating discussions with their husbands. Sibilla Hershey and Emmy Werner studied 28 couples ages 23 to 35.[69] In 14 couples the wives were associated with a Women's Center, whereas in the other 14 couples the wives had no association with any organization. Each member of the couple responded individually to how they would deal with 10 hypothetical situations, and couples were then asked to discuss the situations together and to come to a mutual decision.

Hershey and Werner found that in couples where the wives were active in the women's liberation movement, wives spoke longer in interactions with their husbands, whereas husbands spoke longer in relationships where wives were not active in the movement. Although the study does not address the issue of whether more dominant women were attracted to the women's movement, or whether the women's movement gave women an ideology that made them more outspoken, it is clear that in intimate relationships many women express dominance.

While amount of verbal participation in a group may be a good measure of dominance and leadership in a group of strangers meeting for a short period of time, we need to consider whether who talks the most is always an appropriate measure of dominance and leadership in more intimate relationships. Power differences that have been established in ongoing intimate relationships are often but not always reflected in who speaks more in interaction.

Peter Kollock and his colleagues studied 35 homosexual (including both male homosexual couples and lesbian couples) and heterosexual couples.[70] Couples were categorized based on questionnaire data as power balanced or power imbalanced in terms of decision making. Subjects were given five short stories to read and were asked to resolve the conflicts faced by characters in the stories. In homosexual couples, the more powerful person spoke more. In heterosexual couples balanced in power, there were no gender differences in speaking time. Thus, in intimate heterosexual relationships when men and women have equal power, men are not more likely to speak more.

When heterosexual couples had a more powerful male, that male was found to talk more; in fact, those males spoke more than any other group of males in the study. These data all suggest that knowledge of who has the most power in an intimate relationship is predictive of who will dominate discussions verbally. However, the most perplexing finding was that when heterosexual couples had a more powerful female, she was found to talk more than females in traditional or balanced couples but less than her male partner. Despite the actual power difference that existed in the intimate relationships of these heterosexual couples, when a woman was more powerful than her male partner, he seemed to increase his loquaciousness. The authors speculate that these men may feel the need to draw attention to themselves in the dialogue out of discomfort with the role reversal in power in the relationship.

Summary The finding that men are more likely to emerge as leaders is in part an artifact of the situation in which leadership has been studied. Much of the literature on small groups is based on brief interactions between strangers, often as short as 5 to 10 minutes and usually lasting a single session. While gender differences in leadership emergence occur in short encounters, these gender differences are mitigated in interactions that continue over many sessions. We have too few studies that score ongoing interaction of longer duration. In interaction between people who are in ongoing intimate relationships, whether or not a man dominates depends more on power differentials, personalities, and attitudes of the individuals involved and less on gender than it does in interaction among strangers.

The study by Peter Kollock and his associates suggests that we might need more subtle measures of leadership if we are to focus our attention on dominance and leadership in long-term groups or more intimate relationships. Time talking might be a good measure of leadership in an initial encounter but not in a long-term relationship.

Recapitulation of Gender and Leadership Emergence In the first part of this chapter I looked at who emerges as the leader in a group, men or women. The research literature reveals that men tend to emerge more often as leaders in initially leaderless groups, but that the effect is small to moderate in magnitude. The magnitude of gender differences depends on a variety of features of the participants and the interaction situation. Men do not always dominate mixed-sex conversations; many studies report no gender differences in rates of verbal participation.[71] Men do not consistently stress dominance and hierarchy in their interactions; their style depends on the gender of their partners in interaction. Men are more likely to dominate and emerge as leaders in short, onetime encounters, when group members are strangers, or when the task draws on skills or interests that are associated with men or more typically acquired by men. When participants have some knowledge of each other, are in an intimate relationship, are engaged in less structured tasks or tasks that draw on the skills and expertise more commonly acquired by females, and interact over time, gender differences are mitigated and sometimes reversed.

It is interesting to note that even when women have more power in a relationship, are more dominant in personality, or when task skills draw on feminine skills or interests, women may not be more likely to emerge as leaders than men. It appears that women are inhibited in the expression of dominance and leadership because these behaviors and roles are not legitimate for them. The question that I address in the second half of this chapter is what happens when we legitimize leadership for women—when we study women who hold positions of rightful authority or who are in roles that require male stereotypic dominant behavior. Do women under these conditions behave similarly to men, or do they exhibit a different communication style?

Comparison of Male and Female Leadership Behavior

Leadership Styles

In the remaining portion of this chapter I examine the behavior displayed by men and women who hold positions of leadership or who are assigned to stereotypically masculine roles. Alice Eagly and Blair Johnson carried out a meta-analysis covering 162 studies of gender differences in the leadership styles of men and women.[72] The review covered studies of task and social-emotional styles, as well as democratic and autocratic styles. Before turning to the results of their meta-analysis, we should note that most of the research studies they covered used individuals' ratings of their own leadership styles or subordinates' ratings of leaders rather than actual interaction data. Only 36 of 370 sex comparisons that were examined in the meta-analysis were based on actual observation of a leader's behavior.

The danger with using ratings of leadership style is that it is impossible to determine the degree to which sex role stereotypes have influenced these evaluations. There are studies in which employees in organizations are asked to rate managers on communication behavior, and some of these studies find gender differences. John Baird and Patricia Bradley, for example, studied 150 employees from three organizations and found that the employees saw female managers as more concerned and attentive than male managers, and male managers as more dominant and directive than female managers.[73] It is not possible to determine the extent to which these perceptions are accurate representations of differential behavior on the part of male and female managers. Research has shown that men and women who behave identically as leaders are evaluated differently.[74] Studies of actual interaction are less prone to this type of bias. In chapter 7 I discuss the ways in which knowledge of a person's gender influences our perceptions and evaluations of his or her behavior.

Other biases affect questionnaire assessments as well. Subordinates' perceptions of managers do not agree with self-reports by managers, nor do subordinates within a work group agree strongly with each other in their perceptions of managerial style.[75] In addition, women may be less likely to report dominant and competitive behavior than men. Sara Snodgrass and Robert Rosenthal found that when women were assigned the role of leader they rated themselves as less dominant than male leaders did, but these differences were not perceived by objective observers.[76] Thus, females imagined their behavior to be more in line with traditional sex roles than it was.

Returning to the meta-analysis by Eagly and Johnson, we see that they found male leaders were not more task oriented than female leaders ($d = .00$), meaning that there was a 100% overlap in the distributions for men and women. There was a very small tendency for women to show more of an interpersonal orientation (mean weighted $d = .04$). The strongest evidence for gender differences in leadership behavior was that women showed a more democratic style than men (mean weighted $d = .22$), but again, it was a small effect. In the meta-analysis, gender differences were found in the laboratory studies but not in field studies conducted in organizations.[77] Eagly and Johnson concluded that organizations use criteria for selecting managers and have mechanisms for socializing managers into their roles that minimize any tendencies men and women might bring to their positions to lead or manage differently with distinct male or female styles.

Florence Denmark similarly concludes that many of the assumptions that women managers are basically different from men are not supported by the empirical data; these assumptions simply reflect sex role stereotypes. Numerous studies of actual leadership behavior in organizational settings have found no gender differences.[78]

Social Roles

One way we can understand why men and women behave similarly as leaders is that behavior is determined to a large extent by the situations and social roles in which we find ourselves. People behave differently in the role of group leader and the role of group member. Anderson and Blanchard compared the rates of task and social-emotional behavior of group members to group leaders in mixed-sex groups.[79] Men showed a 27% increase and women a 29% increase in task behavior when they were in leadership roles as compared to member roles. Both sexes intensified their task emphasis when in leadership roles. But men and women differed little as task or social-emotional leaders. Anderson and Blanchard found gender differences in task and social-emotional leadership to be quite small, with male leaders initiating 4% to 5% more task activity than female leaders, and female leaders exhibiting 4% to 5% more social-emotional activity than male leaders.

The extent to which we express dominance and submissiveness may have more to do with the roles we play than with our gender. D. S. Moskowitz and colleagues had 181 adults who worked at least 30 hours a week monitor their social interactions for 20 days, filling out a form for every interaction that lasted at least 5 minutes.[80] The degree to which people displayed dominance at work could not be predicted by their gender, but it could be predicted by their social role. People showed more dominance and less submissiveness toward people they supervised than toward bosses or co-workers. Supervisory roles called out more dominance behavior, subordinate roles called out more submissive behavior.

Many believe that female leaders are more concerned than male leaders about establishing positive relationships—that they are more caring and less hierarchical than their male counterparts. Nancy Wyatt has argued that the leadership style we attribute to women may be better explained by the situations in which they find themselves.[81] She studied leadership in a group of 40 women who made up the Weaver's Guild, a group of women ranging in age from their 20s to their 70s, who had an interest in handspinning and hand-weaving. Most of these women were married, few were employed. The women in the Weaver's Guild were competent women who did not have opportunities to pursue their own careers. Women left the Guild when they found full-time employment. Wyatt found that the women who were identified as leaders emphasized caring and con-nection, were not comfortable talking about power, refused to claim power, and resisted hierarchy. Power and hierarchy were not rele-vant concepts for understanding the dynamics of the group or its leadership.

We could conclude from this data that women are different from men, that they prefer a style of caring and mutual sharing of respon-sibility and avoidance of hierarchy. Wyatt, however, argued that the behavior of the women leaders was constrained by their powerless-ness. She found the most compelling explanation of her findings in Kanter's work on women in organizations.[82] Kanter noted that pow-erless groups of co-workers who were outside the career advance-ment ladder in an organization focused on peer relationships and establishing a supportive group culture. The Weaver's Guild offered peer support to a powerless group of women. Wyatt concluded:

> Women in the Weavers Guild behave as they do, valuing responsibility and connection, because it serves their interests best to do so in the sit-uations in which they find themselves. The issue of why and how these women find themselves in such situations seems to me another question altogether.[83]

Assignment to Stereotypically Masculine Roles

Research shows that men and women behave similarly when they are assigned to roles that require stereotypically masculine behav-ior such as assertiveness, dominance, or autocratic leadership. Linda Carli compared interaction patterns of all-male, all-female, and mixed-sex dyads who held two discussions under two different sets of instructions.[84] Subjects were paired with someone who dis-agreed with them on the topics for both discussions. For the first discussion, subjects had 10 minutes to agree on the three most important ideas in forming an opinion on the topic. For the second discussion, one subject was instructed to be as convincing as possi-ble about the importance of his or her ideas. Based on Interaction

Process Analysis, subjects assigned the role of persuaders showed an increase in their task behavior from the first to the second discussion and showed increased disagreements and decreased agreements in the role of persuader. Male and female subjects responded similarly to the instructions to convince their partners; that is, both sexes showed an increase in stereotypical masculine behavior under these instructions.

Helen Klein and Lee Willerman studied the interactions of 112 women. They assigned each woman to a 3-person group with either 2 female or 2 male confederates.[85] In the first 10-minute discussion, typical levels of dominance were assessed. In the second interaction, they told subjects to try to be the leader, to be as assertive and dominant as possible so that maximal levels of dominance could be assessed. They scored the content of subjects' verbalizations for dominance (i.e., forceful, assertive statements). There was a significant difference in the amount and content of verbal participation under typical and maximal conditions. Under maximal instructions, women showed greater dominance behavior. Although females were significantly less dominant with male than with female confederates in the typical situation, they were equally dominant with male and female confederates in the maximal condition. The data show clearly that women have the capacity to exhibit more dominance and do so when the behavior is legitimized.

A final study illustrates females' capacity to enact more stereotypically masculine behavior when the role demands it. Christopher Stitt and his colleagues studied 678 students in 6-person groups.[86] Each group had a leader and 5 subordinates. Leaders were given instructions about how to lead their group to produce as many paper airplanes as possible. Autocratic leaders were told to make decisions without considering the opinions of the other group members, to be aggressive and to give orders. They were to decide how many airplanes were to be produced and who was to do what job. Democratic leaders were told that all decisions must be made by everyone in the group. Groups were given 10 minutes to plan on how many airplanes to make and how to divide up production of the planes. Groups were then given a 5-minute production period. Although there were significant differences for democratic and autocratic leaders on 13 of 14 variables measuring leadership behavior, male and female leaders displayed comparable leadership behaviors in each condition. Thus, females exhibited autocratic types of behavior when the role demanded it.

Group members arrive with preexisting stereotypes about appropriate behavior for their sex. When sex-typed masculine behavior is legitimized for women, their behavior shifts to a style that is comparable to that of men. Research shows that the presence of female role models exhibiting stereotypically masculine behavior can enhance the expression of those behaviors in women as well.[87]

Changing Performance Expectations for Women

When women are assigned to leadership roles or to stereotypically masculine roles that require dominance and assertiveness, and dominance and leadership are legitimized for women, men and women are found to behave similarly. There is also evidence to suggest that men may display more dominance and assertiveness because they are assumed to be more competent in performing group tasks, and that if these expectations are changed, women perform similarly to men.[88]

Assigning Women Higher Status Than Men A number of studies have looked at the impact of assigning women higher status positions, greater expertise, or greater competency at a task to determine whether the behavior of women under these conditions will be similar to that of men. Wendy Wood and Stephen Karten assigned 144 students to 4-person mixed-sex groups with 2 males and 2 females.[89] Subjects were first given a series of aptitude tests. One male and one female were randomly chosen to receive high-status scores of 350, and the other 2 members were given low-status scores of 234 and 226. In the comparison condition no scores were given out. Subjects then had 15 minutes to reach a unanimous decision about a case of a female college student suspected of using heroin. Five minutes of interaction were scored using Interaction Process Analysis, and members rated each other on competence.

When subjects were aware of their scores, high-status individuals were perceived to be more competent than low-status individuals, and they showed higher rates of verbal participation and task orientation than low-status persons. However, there were no gender differences in task behavior, and men were not seen as more competent than women. In the comparison condition when no scores were given out, gender differences mirrored status differences: men spoke more, engaged in more active task behavior, and were perceived as more competent. Thus, when women were believed to have task competency, stereotypic gender differences were reduced, and behavior was based on perceptions of competency rather than gender.

Assigning women to higher status roles may reduce sex differences but may not completely eliminate them. Helena Leet-Pellegrini found that even when women were given greater expertise at a task than their male partners, they did not reach the level of leadership behavior that males did.[90] Leet-Pellegrini studied 70 pairs, all male, all female, and mixed sex, who had 10 minutes to discuss the negative effects of television violence on children. In equally informed pairs, partners discussed the topic as nonexperts. In unequally informed pairs, one partner was made the expert and given topically relevant information to read before the conversation. Participants and objective judges rated subjects on dominance and control. Experts talked more than nonexperts, whereas there was no imbalance in talking time for equally informed pairs. Although experts dominated, male experts took up more talking space relative to their partners than female experts did, were perceived as more dominant by subjects, and were rated by objective judges as more controlling of the conversation than female experts. Actual mean scores are not reported by the author, and it is possible that the size of these effects may have been small.

Assigning Women Greater Task Competency Than Men Two studies provide compelling evidence that gender differences are reduced when women are believed to possess greater task competency. Meredith Pugh and Ralph Wahrman gave 44 subjects 40 trials in which they had to decide whether a large green rectangle containing black and white geometric shapes had more white or black.[91] Each subject was assigned a fictitious opposite-sex partner. On 25 trials subjects were informed that their partner disagreed with their choice. They were also told that making the correct choice was of prime importance, and that it was both legitimate and necessary to use their partner's judgment. Subjects then made a final choice. Women deferred to men more than the reverse, suggesting that subjects assumed men had greater competency at the task than women.

The experiment was repeated, but this time subjects were told that previous studies had shown women to be just as likely as men to do well at the task. The results remained unchanged. The experiment was again repeated with 40 subjects who were told women are better than men on a skill relevant to spatial judgment ability. Before they were given the 40 trials, subjects were given a picture with hidden figures embedded within it and asked to identify as many hidden pictures as possible. Women were given a picture whose hidden figures were easy to identify, and men were given a picture whose hidden figures were quite difficult to identify. Consequently, women got 9 or 10 correct, men only 2 or 3 correct. Women became more influential than they were in the original study, and men less influential, but women did not gain the advantage over men—they came out equal. Subjects were asked to come back the next day and were told they had a new partner of the opposite sex. No significant difference between the scores of men and women was found.

The study reveals the power of expectations in shaping behavior. Men were assumed to be superior at the task, even if subjects were told that men and women had equal abilities. It was necessary to demonstrate female superiority—to actually show that females have greater task competency—in order for females to gain equality. Even when females were shown to have superior task ability, they didn't gain the advantage over men. More evidence of ability is required for a woman than for a man to overcome initial performance expectations. There is a double standard for performance expectations, with a stricter standard for ability imposed on women than on men.[92]

David Wagner and his colleagues found that when women *believe* that they are more competent than men at a task, they will exert more influence than when they believe they are less competent than men.[93] Sixty female subjects were given a pretest supposedly to measure their task ability. They were then assigned to one of three conditions. In one condition they were given no feedback on their ability, in one they were told they had low ability and their male partner had high ability, and in the final condition they were told they had high ability and their male partner had low ability. Subjects were also told that the past research on the test they took had shown that males showed superior ability to females.

Subjects had to perform a task ostensibly involving the same ability measured by the pretest. They had to decide whether the top or bottom of two figures had more black or white. As in the studies by Pugh and Wahrman, subjects made an initial choice, and the experimenter communicated to them their partner's choice. Subjects then had the opportunity to make a final decision. Subjects were told that their partner disagreed with their initial choice on 20 out of 25 trials. The proportion of time females stayed with their initial choice was .735 when they believed they had more ability than their partners, .51 in the condition where they were given no feedback, and .372 when they believed they had less ability than their partners. Thus, the more confidence women had in their own task ability and in the superiority of their ability in relation to their partner, the more likely they were to be influential in mixed-sex groups.

Wagner and his colleagues then replicated this study using 63 male subjects. The mean percentage of time subjects stayed with their initial choices was .72 for males in the no-feedback condition— dramatically higher than .51 for women. When males believed they had more ability than their partners, the proportion of males who stayed with their initial choice was .779. When they believed they had less ability than their partners, it was .479, significantly lower than the no-feedback condition.

The results of this study show that gender inequalities can be reduced in situations where the task is explicitly associated with gender if women can be shown to be more capable of performing the group task than men. Telling a woman she is capable increases her behavior almost to a level that results from telling a man he is capable (.735 versus .779). But telling a man he is not capable does not reduce his expectations as much as telling a woman she is not capable (.479 versus .375).

Increasing Women's Beliefs in Their Task Competency The data suggest that if women have greater confidence in their own task-related ability they will be more likely to assume leadership. Jayne Stake found that women with low performance self-esteem, when given information about their task-related competency 2 to 5 days before a group discussion and assigned to lead the discussion based on that competency, show greater leadership behavior in dyadic interaction than their male partners.[94] Stake found that females who believed in their task competency scored higher than males on "gives task-related orientation, information," and "draws attention, repeats, clarifies." Leadership behavior was promoted in women in mixed-sex groups when those women were given time to assimilate information about their task-related ability, but it was not promoted when they were simply given information at the start of the interaction.

Norman Maier demonstrated that, as leaders, women need to be committed to and confident about a course of action in order to perform similarly to men.[95] Maier studied 96 mixed-sex groups engaged in a role play in which a foreman attempted to get his workers to change their work methods. All foremen were given the facts of the situation, and an obvious management solution was suggested to half of them. When given a solution, male and female leaders did not differ in their ability to have their solutions adopted, but women leaders were less effective when not supplied with a solution. It is important to note the masculine biases inherent in this experiment. All participants played the roles of males whose work was to assemble fuel pumps. Women may have been more effective without the management solution if the task they were involved in had not had such a strong masculine bias.

Taken together, these studies demonstrate that there is often an implicit assumption that males possess more task ability than females. When females are led to believe they possess greater task competency than their male partners, they show more verbal participation, active task behavior, and influence. Gender differences are reduced and the behavior of men and women becomes equivalent, yet women do not gain the advantage over men. There appears to be a double standard for women. It is not enough for women to be seen as equally competent; they are held to a stricter standard for ability and must be more competent than men to come out equal.

When experimenters try to manipulate performance expectations immediately before a group begins (by giving false feedback about the relative competency of group members), this information may not be sufficient to overcome long-standing beliefs and expectations about the self and others. When personality assessments are done of performance self-esteeem (as in research discussed earlier in this chapter), we find leadership to be determined by high levels of performance self-esteem rather than by gender. Women with high levels of performance self-esteem truly believe themselves to be more competent at the task. When women had 2 to 5 days to assimilate information about their greater task competency, they were more likely to show leadership behavior than when they were given feedback immediately prior to the interaction. We may need to achieve more profound social change in beliefs about women's task competency to enable women to exceed men in displays of dominance and leadership.

Explanations and Conclusions

Although research shows that men are more likely than women to emerge as leaders in initially leaderless groups, it also shows that gender is not a good predictor of dominance and leadership when groups meet for extended periods of time, when participants know each other well, and when tasks draw on skills and expertise more commonly acquired by women. Gender differences in leadership are diminished when leadership is legitimized for women and role demands call for stereotypically masculine behavior (e.g., persuasiveness, assertiveness, or autocratic leadership). If women are seen to be more competent at the task than men, are confident in their own task ability and course of action, and are exposed to female role models exhibiting masculine role behavior, gender inequalities are reduced and women display more leadership behavior.

Two theories have been put forth to account for these findings. Both place great weight on the importance of gender-related expectations in determining leadership behavior. Both theories address the ways in which society's gender inequalities in status become important in shaping interaction processes as they set expectations about who should lead in groups. Expectation states theory addresses expectations about the greater task competency of men, whereas social role theory accounts for expectations that extend beyond task-related competency to more general expectations about the performance of sex-typed masculine and feminine behavior. There is considerable overlap between the two theories and in the predictions they make about leadership behavior.

Expectation States Theory According to expectation states theory, as discussed in chapter 2, gender differences in group behavior are produced by differential expectations for the behavior of men and women. These expectations derive from gender differences in power and status in society. Male dominance is built into the familial, economic, political, and legal structures of society. In a society where men have greater status than women and are seen to possess greater dominance and prestige, men will be assumed to possess greater task-related competency. As a consequence, they will offer more task behavior in groups, will be given more opportunities to participate, and their contributions will be more highly valued. Expectation states theory attributes male leadership in mixed-sex task groups to men's higher status and the consequent expectations for their task competency. It predicts that gender differences will be mitigated when women are given greater task competency, when members have prior knowledge about each other's task competency, or when groups are assigned tasks that draw on female skills and expertise. In other words, gender differences in behavior will be mitigated when expectations are changed about the relative competency of men and women.

Expectation states theory originally addressed itself specifically to expectations about how competent each group member might be at the task. It did not address gender role expectations that extend beyond expectations for task-related competency. We bring to our interactions expectations about other types of gender-appropriate behavior, for example, expectations that women will be communal and concerned with relationships. If high-dominance women choose not to be leaders, as in the research by Megargee, it may have less to do with subjects' expectations about their task-related competency than with the violation of expectations that men should lead. Expectation states theory has been extended, however, to address expectations for social-emotional behavior as well as task competency in shaping the behavior of group members.[96]

Social Role Theory A second explanation for gender differences in dominance and leadership is social role theory, developed by Alice Eagly (also discussed in chapter 2).[97] Eagly argues that the differing social positions of men and women in society account for gender differences in social behavior. The roles assigned to men in our society carry more power and status than those assigned to women, and the difference in the roles assigned to men and women in the family and in society lead to the creation of different stereotypic expectations for behavior. We see men as leaders; leadership positions in our societal institutions are filled primarily by men. Men will be believed to be more dominant because they fill these high-status roles that require leadership behavior. Thus, we come to expect this behavior from men; men are expected to display dominance. We see women in domestic roles and occupations that require more emotionally expressive behavior. Because we do not see women in high-status roles that require the display of dominance and leadership behavior, we are less likely to expect this behavior from women. We expect instead expressive behavior based on the roles we see them fill in society. Social role theory postulates that people will behave consistently with their gender roles. The emergence of men rather than women as general or task leaders is consistent with their differential occupational roles in society.

Social role theory contends that gender roles will be salient only to the extent that other social roles are not more salient, and it predicts that gender differences in short laboratory encounters will be greater in magnitude than those in organizational settings where other roles are more salient. In organizational settings when men and women hold similar jobs, or in situations where leadership is legitimized for women, the constraints of the leadership role will be more important determinants of behavior than gender. The theory also accounts for the fact that when women are believed to be more competent at a task, they will be expected to be more competent at performing the task and will be more likely to take the lead.

Both expectation states theory and social role theory suggest that as long as gender inequalities exist in status and social roles in society, people will come to small group interactions with differential expectations for the behavior of men and women that become self-fulfilling prophecies. People expect men to be leaders, and there are normative pressures for men and women to fulfill these expectations.

In a recent study, Janet Swim tested the accuracy of people's beliefs about gender and leadership against behavioral data from Eagly and Karau's meta-analysis on gender and leadership emergence.[98] Swim asked students to indicate the percentage of men and of women they believed to fall at each point on a 6-point scale from very unlikely to become a leader to very likely to become a leader. She turned these ratings into a measure of perceived effect size for leadership emergence by males and found it to be quite large ($d = 1.04$). The actual effect size reported by Eagly and Karau was .41 for task leadership and only .32 and .29 for general or unspecified leadership. Thus, subjects tended to be quite inaccurate in their expectations about leadership, assuming gender differences in leadership to be quite large and much greater than they actually are. As long as men are expected to lead and to be more competent and capable of leading, they will take the lead.

The data on emergent leadership and leadership behavior demonstrate that men and women are capable of a range of behavior, and that when traditional expectations for the behavior of men and women are overcome—when leadership is legitimized for women and women are seen as highly competent—gender differences in leadership are diminished. There may be many styles of leadership; some leaders are more democratic, others more autocratic, some are more task oriented, others more attuned to relations between group members. It is problematic to associate these styles with leaders of a particular gender; they are more a matter of individual differences.[99] Both men and women are capable of showing all of these styles.

The data show that when women are put into positions now held by men, gender differences in behavior are mitigated. The behavior we attribute to men may be better attributed to their roles than to their gender. Research has focused primarily on task or general leadership, but the research that has addressed social-emotional leadership shows that men and women in leadership positions basically do not differ in social-emotional orientation.[100] Good leaders need to focus both on the task and on establishing and maintaining satisfying relations between group members, and these behaviors are performed by good leaders regardless of their gender.

4

The Function and Patterning of Interruptions in Conversation

Men and women convey information about who they are, their intentions, and their relative positions through the way they speak. Gender differences in the use of language have drawn the attention of many researchers in linguistics, sociolinguistics, communication studies, and psychology. Interruptions, a speech form commonly viewed as a mechanism of power and dominance in conversation, have been of particular interest to the research community. Many researchers believe that interruptions provide a behavioral measure of dominance in everyday social experience because they involve a violation of the current speaker's right to speak, are used to usurp that person's turn, and are used to control the topic of conversation. Interruptions thus provide a measure that we can use to determine whether the greater power and dominance of men in society is reflected in ordinary face-to-face interaction between men and women.

The Research Findings

Interest in gender differences in interruptions was sparked by research by Don Zimmerman and Candace West, a study that has now been widely cited.[1] Zimmerman and West recorded 31 segments of conversation in public places such as coffee shops and drugstores. Twenty of those conversations took place between same-sex pairs—10 male pairs and 10 female pairs—and the remaining 11 conversations took place between mixed-sex pairs. All conversants were between the ages of 20 and 35. Interruptions were defined as simultaneous speech that penetrated into the structure of the speaker's utterance, more than two syllables away from the terminal boundaries of a possibly complete utterance.

Zimmerman and West found that in conversations among people of the same sex, the interruptions were equally divided between the two speakers. In conversations between men and women, on the other hand, men did almost all of the interrupting. Of the 48 interruptions recorded in mixed-sex conversations, 96% were by men. Based on the assumption that interruptions violate the current speaker's right to a complete turn by usurping that speaker's turn space, Zimmerman and West viewed men in cross-sex conversations as asserting asymmetrical rights to the control of topics. Repeated interruptions were followed by topic changes. Thus, it appeared that speakers who were continually interrupted took this as a signal of a lack of support for the continued development of a topic.

The initial study by Zimmerman and West was followed up by Candace West in an examination of 5 male and 5 female college students conversing in mixed-sex dyads in a laboratory.[2] Although the original study involved acquaintances in natural settings, the follow-up study involved strangers in a controlled laboratory setting. Subjects were told to relax and get to know one another prior to a discussion of bicycle safety on campus. Twelve minutes of speech was tape-recorded and transcribed. Researchers observed 28 instances of deep interruptions. In 75% of those instances females were interrupted by males. Males interrupted females 12.1 syllables from the beginning of their turns, whereas females interrupted males 25.4 syllables into their turns. The patterning of interruptions provided evidence for the power difference between men and women and the way that men "do" power in face-to-face conversation.

Evidence accumulated that men do more of the interrupting in conversation than women do[3] and that men interrupt women more than women interrupt men.[4] A critical reevaluation of the literature on interruptions, however, suggests that there may be more studies that report no gender differences in interruptions than there are studies that find such differences,[5] and that interruptions may be used for many functions in conversation other than to convey dominance.

Let us look again at the 1975 study by Zimmerman and West. First, it is important to note that there were only 7 instances of interruptions present in the 20 same-sex conversations that were recorded, and that these 7 interruptions occurred in only 3 of the conversations. These interruptions were evenly distributed between the two speakers—3 by one speaker, 4 by the other. Given the small sample of interruptions, this is an extremely unreliable database on which to accept the conclusion that interruptions are equally divided between the speakers in same-sex conversations but unequally distributed in cross-sex conversations. In the 11 mixed-sex conversations, one quarter of the interruptions came from a single subject—a male student who repeatedly interrupted a female teaching assistant in her attempt to explain a concept. A single subject can skew a data set when the sample size is so small, and researchers can base conclusions on that subject's sex that may well be erroneous. The results can with equal likelihood be attributed to that subject's personality or to the context of the interaction.

Zimmerman and West give the reader an exact account of their data. A problem occurs when the findings are reported out of their original context by later researchers who rely on the general conclusions. The limitations of the original findings are rarely presented to later readers; instead, generalizations are presented as if the data could be interpreted in a single fashion. This study has become a classic. It is cited in all literature reviews on gender and interruptions, and though the overall finding of gender difference is widely known, few know what the data actually look like.

The Interpretation of Interruptions

The Theory of Turn Taking in Conversation

The appropriateness of studying interruptions as a vehicle of dominance derived from a theory of turn taking in conversations developed by Harvey Sacks and his associates—a model that has served to guide much of the research on interruptions.[6] Sacks and his colleagues studied the organization of turn taking in conversations by tape-recording natural conversations. They noted that conversations are remarkably orderly, that only one person talks at a time, and that the transitions between speakers are finely coordinated. Sacks and his colleagues developed a model of the techniques used to allocate turns in conversations that they believed to be universal—to apply to all conversations regardless of the topic, the setting, the number of speakers involved, or the identity of those speakers.

Sacks and his colleagues break conversation down into small units that range in size from single words to sentences. Speakers are entitled to one such unit. When the first unit is completed, a change of speaker can meaningfully occur, and another speaker can take the floor from the first speaker. Three rules govern the patterning of speaker change. According to rule one, the current speaker may select the next speaker; for example, by name, by directing a question to another person, or by nonverbal cues like eye contact. The designated speaker then has the right to the next turn and is the only party to have that right. If the current speaker does not select the next speaker, rule two follows. The second rule is that self-selection will govern the right to speak, that the next speaker will be the one who selects himself or herself first. If self-selection does not occur, rule three is put into operation: the current speaker has the right to take up the floor again. If the current speaker does not take up the floor again, rule two—self-selection—follows. If any rule is carried out, the rule set begins again with rule one. The turn-taking system assigns a speaker the exclusive right to speak to the first possible completion of a unit, and it works to minimize the occurrence of gaps between speakers or overlaps in speech.

According to the model proposed by Sacks and his colleagues, interruptions are violations of the turn-taking rules for conversation. Zimmerman and West's interpretation of their data on cross-sex interruptions follows from this model of turn taking. According to the model, male interruptions are violations of the rules of turn talking; they are attempts to usurp the exclusive right of women to talk to the possible completion of their utterances.

The greater frequency of use of interruptions by males than females provided evidence for the greater power and dominance of men in everyday social experience, and the study of gender differences in interruptions had widespread popular appeal. A large literature developed based on the assumption that interruptions were indicators of power and dominance. Studies that found men to interrupt more than women in mixed-sex conversation were taken as evidence for male dominance, whereas findings of no gender differences or of greater use of interruptions by women were overlooked.

A Reexamination of the Model of Turn Taking

We need to raise questions about the model of turn taking, for it serves as the basis for much of the research on interruptions. Not all conversations fit the model of turn taking proposed by Sacks and his colleagues. In an examination of transcripts of conversations of more than two people, we find a great deal of simultaneous speech, often making it difficult to tell exactly whose turn it is. Rather than one speaker talking at a time, conversation is often characterized by overlaps in speech, even in more formal settings like staff meetings.[7]

Deborah Tannen[8] and Jennifer Coates[9] have found simultaneous talk to be quite common in the conversation of friends. Tannen, for example, recorded 2 1/2 hours of conversation at a Thanksgiving dinner attended by 4 males and 2 females. There were numerous instances where overlaps abounded, yet the conversation proceeded in an animate and smooth manner. The overlaps were cooperative; speakers built on one another's sentences by chiming in to complete sentences along with the speaker. While the model proposed by Sacks and his colleagues defines these interruptions as violations of the speaker's rights to the floor, Tannen interprets these overlaps as indicative of cooperation. Simultaneous talk is accepted and expected in informal friendly conversation and may be unrelated to dominance and power. Interruptions in this context signal interest and give conversation animation.

Tannen's interpretation of her data is consistent with Starkey Duncan's findings on simultaneous speech.[10] When a person is speaking in face-to-face conversations, the listeners are not mute. In his analysis of 19 minutes of two dyadic conversations, Duncan noted many instances of simultaneous speech, which he labeled back-channel signals. These included a group of minimal responses (e.g., *m-hm*, *yeah*, *right*), sentence completions, requests for clarification, and brief restatements. These are not claims to a turn; listeners use them to provide the speaker with useful information.

Identifying Interruptions

It is clear then that the definition of an interruption is complex. Which instances of simultaneous speech should be considered interruptions? In fact, researchers have used many different criteria to identify interruptions. Many (beginning with Zimmerman and West) have noted that minimal responses like *yeah*, *uh-huh*, and *umm*, which are used as signals of support, interest, or attention, are functionally different from the type of interruption that violates the turn space of another. They have followed Duncan in excluding minimal responses from definitions of interruptions. Not all researchers, though, make explicit whether they have included or excluded minimal responses.

While Duncan considered sentence completions, requests for clarification, and brief restatements to be equivalent to minimal responses and believed these did not constitute a turn, most researchers have considered these behaviors to be forms of interruptions. These behaviors, like minimal responses, are functionally different from interruptions that violate the turn space of another.

Some researchers have suggested that an interruption must be "successful" to be indicative of dominance—that is, the speaker must yield the floor to the interrupter[11]—but not all studies have made this distinction. It is difficult to interpret the results of a study on interruptions, or to compare the results from two different studies, when there are no clear criteria for what constitutes an interruption.

In order to identify an interruption, we must decide whether the speaker has reached a possible completion point. There are no absolute criteria that are used either by speakers involved in a conversation or by those analyzing a conversation for determining where those possible completion points lie.[12] Whether a particular instance of simultaneous speech is actually an interruption may depend on a subjective judgment as to whether a speaker has finished his or her first point or has been monopolizing the floor. How severe a violation has occurred thus depends on the context—on what occurs before as well as after the interruption. The occurrence of simultaneous speech alone does not reveal whether the speaker has had a sufficient chance to express his or her thought.

The Multiple Function of Interruptions

As the research by Duncan and Tannen demonstrates, interruptions may serve more than one function. Thirty years ago, people raised questions about the assumption that interruptions were solely mechanisms of dominance. Marvin Shaw and Orin Sadler suggested that interruptions could be supportive in nature and used to express agreement and to reinforce the current speaker.[13] In a study of 10-minute discussions by heterosexual couples about interpersonal relations problems, Shaw and Sadler noted that women in this context interrupted their partners more than men did. The finding appeared contradictory to the expectation that men would dominate women, and the data not only raised questions about the assumption that interruptions are expressions of dominance but also pointed to the desirability of breaking down interruptions into functional subcategories. As Michael Natale and his colleagues noted, "It could be that vocal interruptions are either positive (emotional) or negative (competitive) according to situational determinants."[14]

A number of researchers have subdivided interruptions with

interesting results. Marianne LaFrance and Barbara Carmen studied 72 students in same-sex dyads who engaged in 7-minute conversations.[15] When LaFrance and Carmen did not find men to use significantly more interruptions than women, they broke interruptions into two types—interruptive questions and interruptive statements—and found there to be no correlation between the two (for males, the correlation was $r = -.09$, for women $r = .00$). The frequency of use of interruptive statements bore no relationship to the frequency of use of interruptive questions. Females used more interruptive questions than males did, and interruptive questions are less likely to be dominance related than interruptive statements. Thus, the subdivision of interruptions yields information about the use of interruptions by men and women that is masked when we simply add all instances of interruptions together.

Carol Kennedy and Carl Camden went a step further and broke interruptions into five types:[16] (1) clarification—interruptions that ask for clarification of the speaker's meaning; (2) agreement—interruptions that demonstrate support, understanding, or agreement; (3) disagreement—interruptions that challenge, reject, or contradict the speaker; (4) tangentialization—interruptions that show awareness of the speaker's statement but make light of the message; and (5) subject change—interruptions that reflect no awareness of the speaker's statement and have no common theme. Kennedy and Camden grouped the first two types of interruptions (clarification and agreement) together as confirmation interruptions. They considered disagreements to represent rejection interruptions, and they grouped tangentialization and subject change together as disconfirmation.

Kennedy and Camden studied 35 graduate students ages 23 to 46 in six naturally occurring mixed-sex seminars of 4 to 9 members. Each seminar was taped for 1 hour. They found women to interrupt more than men in this setting, and they noted that almost half the interruptions were confirmation interruptions (38% indicated agreement and 11% clarification). Only 19% were disagreements, and 32% were disconfirmation. Thus, there were significantly fewer disconfirmation and rejection interruptions than confirmation interruptions.

Kathryn Dindia used a similar classification of interruptions in a study of 10 female, 10 male, and 10 mixed-sex dyads of unacquainted students who were given 30 minutes for unstructured conversation without a specific topic assigned for discussion.[17] Dindia found that 55% of male-female and 61% of female-male interruptions expressed agreement. Frank Willis and Sharon Williams found that a third of the interruptions in their sample could be classified as agreement.[18] It is clear from this research that interruptions cannot be assumed to be dominance related and that gender differences in interruptions have been interpreted as evidence of power differences when the majority of interruptions in many conversations do not serve this function.

Julia Goldberg has conceptualized interruptions as falling on a continuum between two poles—power-oriented interruptions and rapport-oriented interruptions—with neutral interruptions in the center of the continuum.[19] The difference between power- and rapport-oriented interruptions is a matter of degree. Neutral interruptions do not arise from any listener wants but are used to repeat, repair, or clarify an utterance. The interrupted speaker continues to speak after the neutral interruption is completed. Both power and rapport interruptions satisfy listener wants. If a listener wants to be listened to and cuts off the other speaker in order to be heard—often with a topic change—the interruption is power oriented. Rapport-oriented interruptions express solidarity, interest, and concern and are acts of collaboration and cooperation. They encourage the development of the speaker's talk.

Clearly, interruptions may be used to serve a variety of functions, but we are only beginning to understand their full complexity. An agreement interruption may or may not be used to usurp the turn space of another, just as a disagreement interruption may or may not be disruptive to the speaker. We must analyze postinterruption behavior to determine the reaction of the current speaker to being interrupted, whether the current speaker yielded or not, and whether that interrupted speaker relinquished and then regained the floor by reinterrupting.[20] A review of the research on gender differences in interruptions reveals that interruptions have too often been studied without an appreciation of the complexity of their identification or interpretation.

The Situational Context

To understand interruptions more fully as they function in conversation, we must take a variety of other contextual variables into account—for example, the topic of conversation, the setting, the relationship between the participants, the sex composition of the group, and the personalities of the participants. These situational variables will influence patterning of interruptions in conversation. The real question we need to ask is whether men and women use interruptions to serve different functions and, if so, are those differences influenced by the situational context of the interaction?

Length of Interaction and Speaking Time of the Participants

Frequency of Occurrence of Interruptions In many conversations interruptions occur infrequently. Zimmerman and West found only 7 interruptions in their 20 same-sex conversations.[21] Lynn Smith-Lovin and Charles Brody found 17.4 interruptions to occur per quarter-hour,[22] and Peter Kollock and his colleagues similarly found 18.6 per quarter-hour.[23] To study interruptions, we need to take samples of conversation that extend for a long enough time period to establish stable rates of interruptions. How can we interpret the results of studies that find no gender differences in interruptions when the interactions studied lasted only 5 or 10 minutes? It is striking to note how many of the studies of interruptions are based on very brief conversations, often 10 minutes or less in duration.[24] Interaction over such short time periods yields a very low rate of interruptions, and a single individual can easily skew the results.

Speaking Time of the Participants Michael Natale and his colleagues found that the single best predictor of interruptions in dyads is the speaking time of the conversational partner.[25] The longer a person speaks, the more likely he or she will be interrupted. Natale and his colleagues studied 12 male, 12 female, and 12 cross-sex dyads of unacquainted students who were instructed to speak freely for 30 minutes. Using a multiple regression analysis, Natale and his colleagues found that speaking time of the conversational partner explained 63% of the variance in interruptions and that the gender of the speaker accounted for only 7% of the variance. This means that knowledge of whether speakers are male or female provides little ability to predict how much they will interrupt, but a good prediction can be made from knowledge of how long their partner speaks. Although men interrupted more than women, there were no gender differences in the percentage of successful interruptions that resulted in the interrupter gaining the floor. Gender then contributes little to predicting the frequency of interruptions when compared to the predictive power of the speaking time of the conversational partner.

In order to interpret interruptions, we need to know the length of the speaking time of all participants in a conversation. Some researchers have counted the total number of interruptions that occurred in conversation and examined the percentage of those interruptions that were initiated by males versus females. For example, Stephen Murray and Lucille Covelli coded 45 minutes of single-sex or mixed-sex interaction from each of six settings, identified 400 interruptions, and found that women interrupted twice as often as men.[26] The sample size is considerable, but if women both spoke more and interrupted more than men, they may not have interrupted more than men in proportion to how much they spoke.

We need to examine the proportion of total utterances by men and by women that are interruptions. If women are interrupted more than men, the results must be interpreted differently if women spoke less than men than if there was equality in the speaking time of men and women. In the original study by Zimmerman and West, for example, the authors count only the frequency of interruptions by males and females; they do not put that finding in the context of the total amount of speech by males and females.

One limitation, then, to our understanding of interruptions is the fact that we have not paid careful enough attention to the length of the interaction and the length of speaking time of the participants. Interruptions occur infrequently, so we need to study conversations of some length. Interruptions can only be interpreted in the context of how long each person speaks. We are more likely to interrupt a conversational partner who goes on at length and to interrupt more if we speak more.

Setting and Task Demands

We cannot properly understand gender differences in interruptions apart from the setting in which a conversation takes place and the task demands placed on the participants. The frequency and type of interruption that occur differ if strangers are working on a competitive task in a laboratory than if friends are engaged in informal social conversation.

Informal and Personal Conversations A high rate of simultaneous talk occurs when conversation is informal and personal, and these interruptions tend to be rapport rather than power oriented, as shown in research by Kathryn Dindia. Dindia studied 10 male, 10 female, and 10 mixed-sex dyads of strangers.[27] Each dyad had 30 minutes for unstructured conversation, with no specific task or topic for discussion. In these informal conversations Dindia found that 55% of male-female and 61% of female-male interruptions were agreement interruptions—that is, confirming responses.[28]

Several studies suggest that interruptions during informal personal talk are frequent in all-female groups where norms call for being sensitive and supportive of each other's points of view, and they may be more frequent in all-female than all-male groups. Jennifer Coates studied a women's group over a 9-month period.[29] The women knew each other well and held 3-hour sessions at people's homes every 2 weeks. These conversations did not operate by the norm of one person talking at a time. There were numerous instances of simultaneous speech that Coates considered to be instances of participants jumping in too soon out of enthusiasm to participate. When a woman ended an utterance by petering out or tailing off, others would complete her turn, resulting in simultaneous speech. At times, two women talked simultaneously on the same theme with no sense of competition or vying for turns. There were interruptive questions and interruptive comments. The more frequent use of this pattern of simultaneous speech among women than men has been reported in several studies of informal conversation.[30]

These studies show that in personal informal settings there are frequent interruptions that complete phrases and show confirmation and agreement, and these interruptions occur without a sense of competition for turns. In addition, this pattern of interruption is more characteristic of groups of women than groups of men. Studies that find higher interruption rates among women than men tend to be those that have looked at contexts that are more informal and conversations where talk is personal.

Two Types of "Floor"　Carole Edelsky noted that even within the same ongoing conversation in a meeting there are times when interaction is more formal and times when it is less structured and more informal.[31] Edelsky studied five informal meetings of a committee that dealt with issues of program and scheduling. The committee was composed of 7 women and 4 men, some of whom were familiar colleagues, others of whom were close friends. The meetings lasted from 1 1/2 to 2 hours. Edelsky found one type of "floor" in which a single speaker would hold forth, report, and solicit responses and in which conversation was marked by orderly, one-at-a-time speaking. A second type of "floor" was marked by simultaneous speech, deep overlaps, and two or more people jointly building on one idea in more informal collaborative talk. Men held forth and took longer turns in the first type of floor, and they spoke less in the second type of floor.

The data suggest that there is a style of conversation that may be more typical of women's groups—the second type of floor—in which interruptions abound and are collaborative, and that even within a mixed-group task context there may be periods when there is a shift to this collaborative type of interaction. Deborah Tannen's study of mixed-sex conversation over Thanksgiving dinner suggests that a collaborative type of floor may occur in mixed-sex groups when the participants know each other well and are engaged in informal conversation.[32]

Interaction in Formal Laboratory Settings The setting of the interaction can have an impact on the rate of interruptions. The rate and nature of interruptions in conversations in formal laboratory settings may not be comparable to interruption rates in more relaxed informal settings. Michiko Nohara ran two experiments under different conditions.[33] In the first experiment 4 male, 4 female, and 4 mixed-sex pairs had 10 minutes to discuss a case about an individual accused of murder. They had to come to a unanimous disposition decision about the defendant. The conversations were held in a casual living room and taped by a hidden recorder. In the second experiment dyads were brought into the laboratory with a one-way mirror and conspicuous microphones.

The rate of interruptions was higher in the formal laboratory than in the casual living room setting, and there was a greater tendency for one partner to do more of the interrupting in the laboratory setting. Partners interrupted more equally in the casual setting. While females tended to interrupt more than males in the casual living room, males tended to interrupt more in the laboratory setting. The time period of 10 minutes is quite short for establishing stable rates of interruptions, and interruptions were not subdivided by function. Still, the data suggest that when conversations are task oriented, the laboratory setting may call out more dominance-related behavior, particularly by males for whom it is sex role appropriate. This would explain the higher frequency of interruptions overall in the laboratory setting compared to the casual setting, the higher frequency of interruptions by males, and the greater asymmetry in interruptions between partners. An analysis of interruptions by type would be necessary to permit further understanding of this effect.

Task-Oriented Groups Many of the studies which find that men interrupt more than women are laboratory studies of goal- or task-oriented groups of 30-minutes duration or less.[34] In laboratory studies of task-oriented groups of more than 2 members, males are found not only to interrupt more, but also to interrupt females more than males.[35] The most informative study of task-oriented groups was carried out by Lynn Smith-Lovin and Charles Brody, who coded interruptions as supportive (expressed agreement, made positive requests for information), negative (expressed disagreement, raised objections, introduced a topic change), and neutral and looked at the success of each interruption.[36] Smith-Lovin and Brody studied 31 six-person groups, varying in sex composition from all male to groups including from 1 to 6 females. Groups were offered $30 for the best solution to a task. The odds of a male interrupting a male were half the odds of a male interrupting a female. Males did not interrupt more than females did, but they interrupted females more.

Smith-Lovin and Brody found negative interruptions to be very rare, but the odds of a woman yielding the floor to a man after a negative interruption were three times as great as the odds of a man yielding the floor. The authors attempted to address the question of how the type of interruption was affected by the sex of the interrupter, the sex of the person interrupted, and the sex composition of the group, but they found a complex interaction between all of these variables. The majority of interruptions fell into the neutral category. When men were speaking, women were less successful than men in gaining the floor by interrupting them with a neutral elaborating comment. When women were speaking, both sexes were equally successful in gaining the floor by interrupting them. The findings reveal not that men interrupt more than women do, but that males interrupt females more than males and that males are more difficult to interrupt successfully than females are.

In a later study, Lynn Smith-Lovin and Dawn Robinson also found no gender differences in rates of interruptions, but they did find that females were at higher risk of being interrupted than males.[37] The studies by Smith-Lovin and her associates point the way for future studies in their attempt to look at interruptions in context along with a variety of situational variables.

Tutorials There are situations that explicitly call for interruptive behavior, as shown by Geoffrey Beattie in a study of tutorial groups at the University of Sheffield.[38] In this setting women interrupted as much as men. Beattie studied 10 tutorial groups, 5 with a male tutor, 5 with a female tutor. Seven of the tutorial groups were mixed sex, while 3 female tutors had all-female groups. Each group had 3 to 6 students. Beattie analyzed 491 minutes of conversation. There were no overall gender differences in interruption in this setting, and males did not interrupt females more than males. The English university system provides a context in which students must show what they know, and interruptions are the way to gain the floor. When females are in a role that demands competition and assertion, they are as likely to use interruptions as males.

Summary An analysis of the effect of setting and task on interruptive behavior suggests that in informal personal conversations interruptions occur frequently, are often supportive and noncompetitive, and are more frequently found among groups of women than among groups of men. These findings contradict the stereotype that men interrupt more than women in conversation. Second, the belief that men interrupt more than women and that women are interrupted more than men is based on short task-oriented or competitive conversations among strangers in laboratory settings. In the context of a task group in a laboratory, expectations for males to be more competent at the task may call out more dominance from males and may lead females to yield the floor more readily than males when interrupted. Finally, when interruptive behavior is necessary to show what you know in a tutorial, both men and women interrupt others with equal frequency and success.

Status and Power

People have argued that the greater use of interruptions by males is a display of dominance and a reflection of the more powerful position of males in this society. If men have greater power and status than women, the independent influence of gender and status is difficult to determine. An examination of the literature reveals that across a range of settings and relationships, high-status and more powerful individuals are more likely to interrupt than low-status and less powerful individuals. Also, power and status may be confounded with gender in some studies. For example, in studies of interaction between parents and children, it is parents who interrupt more than children.[39] Don Zimmerman and Candace West draw the analogy between females and children, both of whom may have restricted rights to speak and may be ignored and interrupted.[40] Because not all interruptions are dominance related, however, there are instances when low-status individuals interrupt more than high-status individuals.

In work settings, it is the individuals with higher rank or status who interrupt more and the low-status individuals who are interrupted more. A study by Barbara and Gene Eakins is often cited to support the proposition that males interrupt more than females and that women are interrupted more than males, but a careful look at their data reveals that gender is confounded with status.[41] Eakins and Eakins tape-recorded seven faculty meetings attended by 6 males and 4 females in a university department. Eakins and Eakins found than men interrupted more than women, but men also spoke more. When the data were analyzed for proportion of interruptions to total number of turns taken, the highest quotients were "generally" male, but a woman had the highest proportion of interruptions to turns taken. The authors also found that a greater proportion of women's than men's turns were interrupted. They do not report the relative rank of each male and female faculty member, but they do report that for the two lowest ranking women, over half their turns were interrupted, that the woman who was interrupted most frequently held no Ph.D., and that the woman who was interrupted least frequently had the greatest seniority. The male who received the least interruptions had the highest rank, and the male who was interrupted the most had the lowest rank. These data suggest that status as well as gender accounts for the differences between individuals in rates of interruption in this setting.

In another study of colleagues at work, Nicola Woods recorded nine conversations with a hidden tape recorder.[42] Each conversation took place between 3 colleagues who differed in occupational status. Woods randomly selected 2 minutes of conversation from each group for analysis, yielding a small number of interruptions, so the data are at best suggestive. Both females and males talked through more possible transition places when they were in the high-status role than when they were in the role of subordinate, and subordinates were more successfully interrupted than speakers in higher status positions. The same women were successfully interrupted more frequently when they were in the subordinate position than when they were in the high-status position. Thus, the rate of interruptions varied with the status of the participants in the conversation, and being successfully interrupted was inversely related to status.

In a study discussed earlier of homosexual and heterosexual couples in intimate relationships, the power of the partner in the relationship rather than the sex of the partner was found to predict interruptions, with more powerful persons successfully interrupting more than their less powerful partners.[43]

A Consideration of Function and Context   Before concluding that higher status individuals always interrupt more, we need to consider the type of interruption and the situational context. In a laboratory simulation of an organization with two employees and a manager, Cathryn Johnson analyzed interruptions in 40 groups using Smith-Lovin and Brody's coding scheme.[44] She found no gender differences in the overall use of interruptions, but subordinates had higher rates than managers of positive interruptions (interruptions that express agreement, request elaboration, or complete the speaker's thought) and equal amounts of neutral interruptions. She found few negative interruptions that expressed disagreement, voiced objection, or changed the topic.

The study points to the necessity of subdividing interruptions. On the surface, the results appear to contradict the notion that high-status individuals interrupt more, but when the type of interruption is considered, we see that the interruptions used by low-status individuals expressed agreement and were not dominance related.

In his study of English university tutorials, Geoffrey Beattie found that students interrupted tutors more than tutors interrupted students.[45] In this context, students tend to address their remarks to the tutor rather than to the other students present. To make a good impression and show what they know, students must take the floor from the tutor before it goes back to another student. The role of the tutor is to encourage the students to speak, and thus tutors are less likely to interrupt the speech of students. The study points to the importance of keeping the role demands of a situation in mind when trying to interpret conversational behavior.

Likewise, in a study of doctor-patient interactions, there were no significant differences in the number of successful interruptions by patients and physicians. Julie Irish and Judith Hall videotaped 25 female and 25 male physicians interacting with a male and a female patient.[46] Despite their higher status, physicians did not do more interrupting than patients. Moreover, interruptions by physicians were not indicative of dominance but were requests for elaboration. Doctors successfully interrupted with questions more than statements, whereas patients successfully interrupted with statements more than questions. Physicians' interruptions are attempts to seek information; patients' interruptions may be attempts to get their story heard. There were few gender differences. The study, like that by Beattie, reveals the importance of subdividing interruptions by function and taking the situational context into consideration.

The findings on status suggest that the greater frequency of male interruptions and of male interruption of females may not always be a function of gender. It may well be a function of status within a given situation. High-status and more powerful individuals tend to interrupt more than low-status and less powerful individuals, and low-status individuals are interrupted more than high-status individuals in many settings.

The relationship between status and interruptions is imperfect. There are interruptions that are not dominance related and settings where role demands require being heard. Thus, there are conversations in which there is no relationship between status and interruptions and conversations in which low-status individuals do more interrupting than high-status individuals.

Sex Composition of the Group

Interrupting Members of the Same or the Opposite Sex Research provides no clear answer to the question of whether men and women interrupt members of their own and the opposite sex at equal rates. Some studies find that men interrupt women at a higher rate than they interrupt other men,[47] whereas others report that interruptions by men and women are not affected by the gender of their partners.[48] Smith-Lovin and Brody found that although men interrupt women more than men, women interrupt men and women to an equal extent.[49] Julie McMillan and her colleagues report that women interrupt women more than men,[50] but Dindia reports that women interrupt men more than women.[51] It is worth noting that none of these studies find men interrupt men more than women.

We need a classification of interruption by type to understand whether the kind of interruptions used by men and women is different with members of the same sex and members of the opposite sex. It would also help to determine the extent to which interruptions of women by men are dominance related. The inconsistency of findings from one study to another results as well from differences in the length of interaction studied, the interaction setting, and the task demands of the interaction—variables that have been demonstrated to have an impact on gender differences in interruptions. Because studies were conducted over a period of 25 years, during which extensive gender role change has occurred, inconsistencies may also be due to temporal factors.[52]

Interruptions in Single-Sex and Mixed-Sex Groups Several studies compare interruption rates in single-sex and mixed-sex dyads, but again the findings are inconsistent. While some researchers have found there to be more interruptions in mixed-sex dyads than in same-sex dyads,[53] others have found higher rates of interruptions in single-sex dyads (either all male or all female) than mixed-sex dyads.[54] Studies have yielded different findings in regard to the issue of how equally interruptions are distributed between participants in single-sex and mixed-sex conversation. Zimmerman and West found interruptions to be used equally by partners in single-sex conversation but unequally in mixed-sex conversation. The sample of interruptions for single-sex groups, however, was only 7, and thus the results are not highly reliable.[55] Some researchers have found interruptions to be unequally distributed between partners in all groups regardless of whether they were all male, all female, or mixed sex,[56] suggesting that personality variables as well as gender play a role in accounting for rates of interruption. Nohara found the most pronounced differences in the frequency of interruptions between two speakers to occur in all-male dyads.[57]

Personality

Because researchers have taken interruptions to be indicative of power and dominance, they have carried out studies to determine whether individuals who score higher on the personality trait of dominance are more likely to interrupt others in interaction than individuals who score low on dominance. The evidence is contradictory, and results are difficult to compare across studies due to differences in the particular measures of dominance and interruptions used, as well as differences in other situational variables such as the sex of the subjects, the degree to which they are acquainted, and the task assigned. Although there is evidence from some studies that dominance predicts interruptions, the finding must be qualified by these mediating variables.

Competitive Interactions Studies by Derek Roger and his colleagues reveal that highly dominant individuals, particularly when interacting with other highly dominant individuals, are more likely to interrupt. Derek Roger and Andrea Schumacher gave a large pool of subjects the dominance subscale of Edwards Personal Preference Schedule, and they selected the 72 highest and lowest scoring males and females to serve as subjects.[58] Subjects were assigned to single-sex pairs of three types: 2 high-dominance individuals, 2 low-dominance individuals, and 1 high- and 1 low-dominance individual. Subjects had 10 minutes to discuss a topical issue on which they disagreed with the task of convincing their partner of their point of view. Individuals high in dominance were found to interrupt successfully (that is, gain the floor from the speaker) more than those low in dominance, and the rate for successful interruption was greater in high-high dominance dyads than in low-low or high-low dominance pairs.

Derek Roger and Willfried Nesshoever followed up this experiment with a study of mixed-sex dyads.[59] High and low scorers on the Edwards Personal Preference Schedule were assigned to 7 mixed-sex dyads in one of four dominance conditions: a male and a female subject both high on dominance, a male and a female subject both low on dominance, a high-dominance male with a low-dominance female, and a high-dominance female with a low-dominance male. Again, the task assigned to subjects was to convince partners of their own point of view during a 10-minute discussion. When a dominant male and a dominant female were paired, there were no gender differences in interruptions, and both partners showed a higher rate of successful interruptions than subjects in the other three conditions (who showed comparable rates of interruptions to each other). Thus, dominance rather than gender was predictive of rate of interruption.

Using a different approach to the assessment of personality, Kriss Drass assessed subjects' sex role identity by having subjects rate themselves on 24 characteristics.[60] Students were assigned to 13 female and 13 male dyads with the task of deciding which member of the dyad was most deserving of a fictional "outstanding undergraduate" award. Conversations lasted on the average only 5 to 7 minutes. The more malelike the subject in his or her sex role identity (aggressive, assertive, dominant), the more likely the subject was to interrupt.

It appears from these studies that when highly dominant individuals are paired, regardless of sex, and given a competitive task, the rate of interruption increases. Unfortunately, all of these studies are based on interactions lasting 10 minutes or less, which is a short time period to establish stable rates of interruptions. It is important to note that the results in the studies by Roger and his colleagues (that interruptions occur more frequently when highly dominant people are paired than when low-dominance individuals are paired) held for successful interruptions but not for unsuccessful interruptions, and that all of these studies involved competitive interactions. What if the task is not competitive?

Noncompetitive Encounters Nicola Ferguson studied 1 female who interacted for half an hour with each of 15 different female friends about whatever they wished.[61] All 16 subjects filled out self-ratings of dominance and were also rated by the main female subject on dominance. Dominance was not significantly related to the rate of interruptions. There is unfortunately no parallel data for male subjects, so it is impossible to tell whether the same lack of relationship would hold true for males in informal conversation. It is possible that the competitive and conflictual nature of the task used by Roger and his colleagues produced more dominance-related interruptions, whereas the interruptions in the study by Ferguson in informal, more personal conversation may not have been dominance related.

There are inconsistent findings in regards to the relationship between dominance and interruptions in studies of noncompetitive and nonconflictual task-oriented groups. William Rogers and Stanley Jones used Cattel's measure of dominance as well as Gough's adjective checklist to categorize people as high or low on dominance.[62] Subjects were assigned to same-sex dyads including one high- and one low-dominance individual. Eight male and 10 female dyads were given 15 minutes to determine a solution to a campus problem. High-dominance males interrupted partners more frequently than low-dominance males, but this was not true for females. Thus, on a more cooperative task, dominance predicted interruptions for males but not for females in single-sex groups.

In a study I carried out with my colleagues, we found dominance to predict interruptions for both males and females in single-sex groups but for neither sex in mixed-sex groups.[63] We tested subjects on the dominance scale of the California Psychological Inventory and assigned them to single-sex or mixed-sex groups of 5 to 6 members. Each group met for 40 minutes to discuss an ethical dilemma. We found no correlation between dominance and successful interruptions for either males or females in mixed-sex groups, but we did find correlations of $r = .37$ for males and $r = .53$ for females between dominance and successful interruptions in single-sex groups.

In sum, research has not consistently found high-dominance individuals to interrupt more than low-dominance individuals. Highly dominant individuals are found to interrupt successfully more when engaged in competitive encounters; successful interruptions are more likely dominance related in this context. However, the results are contradictory from study to study when individuals high and low in dominance are working on more cooperative, noncompetitive tasks. The fact that dominance does not consistently predict interruptions when interaction is noncompetitive and nonconflictual, and that dominance appears to be unrelated to interruptions in informal conversation, suggests that many interruptions are not power related in these contexts.

Assessment and Explanation of the Findings

Years ago, interruptions were seen to be a useful indicator of dominance in everyday interaction, and they drew the attention of many researchers. As our understanding of interruptions has become more sophisticated, it is clear now that interruptions may be used to serve a variety of functions in conversation. Interruptions may be used to express support, interest, concern, and agreement, as well as to usurp the turn space of another and to assert dominance. Researchers need to consider the intention of speakers when they assign meaning to an interruption, rather than assigning the same meaning to all interruptions. If a listener cuts off a speaker to change the topic, the interruption is power oriented; if a listener interrupts a speaker to express agreement and solidarity, the interruption is collaborative and cooperative. The reaction of the speaker to being interrupted is also important to our understanding of the phenomenon—not only whether the speaker yields the floor or regains it by reinterrupting, but also how a person experiences the interruption.

Even though a considerable research literature has developed on interruptions, we know less than we thought because of the limitations inherent in much of this research. Interruptions are infrequent in occurrence, and yet it is striking to note that we have based our understanding of interruptions on very brief conversations, often 10 minutes or less in duration. We have often counted interruptions by men and women without regard to their relative speaking time. Those who speak more would be expected to interrupt more. Until recently, researchers failed to break down interruptions by type, and yet we can only meaningfully understand them when they are subdivided by function.

My assessment of this research is consistent with a 1993 review by Deborah James and Sandra Clarke that concluded that the majority of the research has found no significant gender differences in interruptions.[64] The stereotype that men interrupt more than women is a misrepresentation of the data. The majority of studies have reported no gender differences in interruptions. In studies of informal personal conversation, it is women who are often found to do more interrupting than men, and conversation tends not to follow the norm of one-at-a-time speech but is filled with simultaneous speech that does not involve a vying for turns. When women have to show what they know, as in a British tutorial, or be heard in a visit to the physician, they interrupt as much as men. The finding that males interrupt more than females do and that males interrupt females more comes primarily from task groups of strangers in the laboratory, a setting in which gender is salient and sex role pressures are operative.

The primary explanation that has been put forth to account for gender differences in interruptions is that gender differences result from and reflect inequalities in power and status in society. Men as high-status individuals have the right to exert dominance over women, to usurp their turn space, and to limit their right to speak. According to the theory of status characteristics and expectation states discussed in chapter 2, members of task groups will expect men to have greater task competency than women. Thus, men will feel freer to cut into the turn space of women, and women will be prone to yield the floor to them more readily. The expectations associated with men's greater status in society, as well as actual status differences between group members, may contribute to the higher rate of interruption by males in competitive task settings. This explanation accounts for the fact that men have been found to interrupt women more in short, task-oriented interactions among strangers in the laboratory. It seems likely that men may use more dominance-related interruptions in this context.

What the power/status approach does not account for are interruptions that are not dominance related— interruptions that instead express agreement and rapport. From the power/status approach, powerless individuals would be expected to use more rapport-oriented interruptions as a form of ingratiating behavior. This explanation does not capture the nature of interruptions in informal, more personal talk. Those interruptions are rapport oriented and are used to express solidarity, interest, and concern. Nor does this explanation account for the lack of gender differences in interruptions in so much of the research.

Interruptions are governed by more than the power and status of the participants. The use of interruptions varies between contexts. Speakers show a shift in style not only as they move from one situational context to another, but also depending upon their interaction goals. The use of interruptions cannot be accounted for without attention to the situational context and the goals of the speakers.

Interruptions are more complex but no less interesting than they were seen to be in the past. We must move beyond the narrow question of whether men interrupt more than women to questions of whether there are gender differences in the use of a particular type of interruption in a specific situational context. We must move on as well to questions of the subjective experience of being interrupted. It would be important to know whether disagreement interruptions that challenge or reject, or interruptions that change the topic have a differential impact on men and women. Are women more sensitive to being interrupted than men? If women are interrupted the same number of times as men, are they more likely to withdraw rather than to regain the floor? We need to link our categorization of interruptions to the perceptions and experiences of those who are interrupted.

5

Language Use and Conversation Management

Scholars have engaged in considerable debate over the past two decades about the extent to which gender differences exist in speech and about the meaning of those differences. It is important to note that in the English language no speech forms are used exclusively by members of one sex and not the other;[1] men and women both use the same linguistic forms. Some have argued that there are consistent gender differences in the frequency with which certain speech forms are used. Others contend that stereotypes about gender differences in language far outweigh actual gender differences in speech. Controversy exists as to the meaning of the gender differences in language use that have been identified. A review of the research literature reveals the complexity of these issues and the problematic nature of many of the conclusions that have been drawn. Given the breadth of the issues that have been considered in regard to gender differences in language use, I have chosen to focus this chapter on language and will not consider paralinguistic features (e.g., pronunciation, pitch, intonation, loudness, grammatical form, hesitations in speech, laughing, and crying).

Robin Lakoff's Claims

Interest in women's speech was sparked by the writings of the linguist Robin Lakoff.[2] Lakoff examined her own speech and that of friends and acquaintances, using introspection and her own intuition, and compiled a description of "women's language." According to Lakoff, women's speech is characterized by a variety of forms.

Women use specialized vocabularies having to do with domains that have been relegated to them, such as cooking, decorating, and fashion. For example, women use precise discriminations in naming colors (words like *mauve, ecru*). Women use more "meaningless particles"—terms like *oh dear* or *goodness*—whereas men will use much stronger expletives like *shit.* Women are not allowed as strong expression as men are. Women use "empty" adjectives like *adorable, charming*, and *sweet*, which express emotional rather than intellectual evaluation.

Lakoff claimed women use many speech forms that express uncertainty and hesitancy. Women are more likely than men to use tag questions, which are midway between an outright statement and a question—for example, "Richard is here, *isn't he?*" Lakoff postulated that tag questions lack the assertiveness of an outright statement and the confidence of an outright claim. They allow the speaker to avoid commitment and conflict with the addressee by giving the impression of not being certain and looking for confirmation. Women's language is characterized further by the use of question forms with declarative functions. For example, when asked what time dinner will be ready, a woman might say, "Oh . . . around 6 o'clock?" The sentence has the form of a declarative answer to a question, but it also has a rising inflection, thus expressing an unwillingness to state an opinion directly. Women use declarative statements in question form to express uncertainty and to ask for confirmation.

Lakoff argued that women use more polite forms than men. Their requests and orders are made polite. For example, rather than saying, "Set the table," a woman might add *"please"* to the statement, ("Won't you set the table, please?") or phrase it as a question ("Will you set the table?"). Politeness involves the avoidance of strong statements and the use of more euphemistic forms. Women use more hedges and modals, such as *well, y'know, kind of, I guess, I think, I wonder*—terms that convey uncertainty. Women use the intensive *so*, which, according to Lakoff, by its imprecision, allows women to hedge on strong feelings and to back away from strong emotions.

Lakoff concluded that women's choice of speech style reflects their self-image. They speak with uncertainty and imprecision, with deference and politeness so they will not be called on to account for their opinions. She argued that the discrepancy between the speech of women and men is derived from the discrepancy in the positions they hold in society.[4] Lakoff wrote more recently, "Women's language developed as a way of surviving and even flourishing without control over economic, physical, or social reality."[5] Women's language is a symbolic expression of their lack of power. Given their social position, women must agree, be indirect, and not confront in order to get their needs met and to survive. Lakoff believes that women are capable of forthright communication but have developed a different style out of necessity.

Methodological Considerations

The Function of Speech Forms

Before examining the empirical literature that has developed to test many of Lakoff's claims or to examine gender differences in language more broadly, we must look at a number of methodological problems that plague research studies. First, Lakoff made claims about the function of many speech forms. For example, she claimed that *I think* is an expression of uncertainty or hesitancy, as in, "The play is at 8 o'clock, *I think*," and that tag questions are an expression of tentativeness or uncertainty. Many researchers accepted these assertions without question, assuming that use of these speech forms conveys a single meaning. But a single language form can serve a variety of functions depending on its context. If a woman says to her child, "*I think* it's about time you cleaned up your room," in this context *I think* is an expression of certainty rather than uncertainty. Speech forms are multifunctional and may even serve many functions simultaneously.[6] For example, a tag question such as, "You missed the last meeting, *didn't you?*" may soften a more negatively toned statement and may also encourage the addressee to respond.

There has been considerable debate in recent years about the meaning of speech forms like tag questions and qualifications in speech, and we must exercise care in interpreting the results of the many studies that take speech samples, add together all occurrences of a speech form like tag questions, and assume them to have a single meaning. Equally problematic are studies that create indices of hesitancy by adding together a variety of forms like *I guess*, *sort of*, and *kind of*. To assume that such an index represents uncertainty is to misrepresent many of the speakers' intentions, for each of these forms may be used to serve a variety of functions.

Controlling for Amount of Speech

To examine gender differences in the frequency of usage of any speech features, we must be sure that the speech samples include equal amounts of speech by men and women. Pamela Fishman, for example, collected 52 hours of tape-recorded conversation from 3 heterosexual couples in their homes.[7] She does not report whether equal amounts of speech were produced by men and women as a baseline for her analyses. Thus, when she finds that women asked 2½ times as many questions as men, it is impossible to determine accurately what this means. The finding takes on a different meaning if women talked twice as much as men, the same amount as men did, or half as much as men. Regrettably, many studies analyze gender differences in frequency of usage of speech features without using the amount of speech produced by men and women as a baseline for these comparisons, rendering their results uninterpretable.

With these cautions in mind (i.e., the a priori assignment of meaning to speech forms and the failure to control for the amount of speech of men and women), we can begin to examine the research literature. Some studies have looked at gender differences in the use of individual speech features like tag questions, intensive adverbs, and personal pronouns, whereas others have looked more generally at "women's language"—that is, at the frequency of use of a combination of speech features thought to characterize women's speech. I begin with an examination of the studies based on individual speech features and then move to a consideration of studies based on combinations of speech features. As is the case in any research area, people have given considerable attention to some language features, and collected little data collected on others. Susan Philips has pointed out:

> We have a situation in which most of those with linguistic training do not do empirical work, and the nonlinguists know very little about linguistic processes and do not seem to have made much effort to become linguistically sophisticated. For this reason, the forms that have been studied empirically are the ones that require the least linguistic background to identify, characterize, and explain to others.[8]

Individual Speech Features

Politeness

Lakoff claimed that women use more polite forms than men. Our understanding of politeness has been furthered by Penelope Brown and Stephen Levinson's theory of politeness, which conceptualizes politeness in terms of "face."[9] All participants in an interaction have both positive and negative face needs; that is, they have needs to be respected and needs not to be imposed upon. Positive face is achieved if one feels liked, respected, and valued. Expressions of disapproval, criticism, contradictions, and challenges all threaten positive face needs. Positive politeness is oriented toward the positive face needs of the addressee. Negative face is achieved when one feels constrained, imposed upon, and restricted in one's actions. When a request is made, the request automatically places some constraint on another person and poses an imposition on that person. Requests thus challenge negative face, or the speaker's need not to be imposed upon. Negative politeness is oriented to reduce a constraint imposed on another person. Politeness within this conceptual framework, then, is a way to meet positive and negative face needs.

We must consider the use of politeness within a situational context; it will be affected by power and intimacy in a relationship as well as by the magnitude of the face threat posed by a request.[10] Brown and Levinson postulate that in close relationships there will be less obligation to redress face in a request. In relationships with unequal status partners, the less powerful person will use more politeness strategies than more powerful persons. If women are of lower social status than men, they would be expected to use more negative politeness strategies. Politeness will be greater with requests of greater magnitude.

Lakoff suggested that there are many forms in which politeness can be expressed, only one of which is the use of the word *please*. Requests can be made more polite by phrasing a command as a question, by using modal constructions (for example, *might*, *may*, *could*), or by using weaker forms. These are forms of negative politeness oriented toward reducing an imposition on another person.

In a questionnaire study of politeness, Leslie Baxter asked 155 subjects to indicate the likelihood that they would use 32 tactics in a series of eight hypothetical situations.[11] Baxter found that females report less frequently than males that they would use face-threatening actions (e.g., commands, threats) and more frequently that they would employ negative and positive face-redressive tactics (showing understanding, sympathy, liking). Janet Holmes found women to use apologies more than men.[12] She had students collect 20 consecutive instances of apologies, generating a corpus of 183 apologies. Women produced 75% of the apologies.

We must apply caution in concluding that differences in the use of politeness by men and women are attributable to gender. Paula Johnson has argued that women do not have access to the same forms of power that men do.[13] Women do not hold positions of status in the social structure—positions that give them superior knowlege or expertise—and if they do, they are discouraged from using their resources directly by being viewed as pushy and unfeminine. Thus, women must rely on indirect strategies and more personal resources such as liking, affection, and approval. Women's greater politeness is related to their lack of many forms of power.

In a study designed to disentangle the effects of gender and power on the use of persuasion strategies used by men and women, Lynda Sagrestano found the effect of power to be more profound than the effect of gender.[14] She had 146 undergraduates respond to three different scenarios in which they imagined an interaction where they tried to influence a nonintimate friend. In each scenario they were either an expert compared to their partner, a novice compared to their partner, or their relative power was not specified. Men and women used similar influence tactics, but more powerful people used more direct strategies, and less powerful people used more indirect strategies. Less direct strategies can be considered to be forms of politeness. Janice Steil and Jennifer Hillman similarly found that power rather than sex was more predictive of strategy use and concerns for politeness.[15]

Direct imperatives or directives—for example, "Close the door"—pose a threat to the negative face wants of the other party in a conversation. They constrain or restrict the other's actions. A few studies have examined gender differences in the use of direct imperatives or directives. Judy Lapadat and Maureen Seesahai tape-recorded conversation in all-male and all-female groups using a concealed tape recorder in informal contexts.[16] Although they found that males used direct imperatives more frequently than females, the results are difficult to interpret because the authors do not state whether there were equal amounts of speech produced by males and females in their sample.

Bent Preisler studied 24 four-person discussion groups.[17] Each subject participated in both a same-sex and a mixed-sex group discussion of 43 minutes in which groups had to come to consensus about an issue. Men were found to use more imperatives than women in utterances that gave opinions, suggestions, and information—for example, "If you want to take action, do it on the spot."[18] Fathers have been found to use more directives in their speech while playing with their children than mothers.[19]

We must understand the use of directives, like the use of direct influence tactics, in the context of power as well as gender. Kimberly

Jones found no gender differences in the use of directives in a 3-hour business meeting of a group of morris dancers, but she did find that directives were related to the leadership role and to status in the group.[20] The female volunteer leader for the meeting initiated and received the most directives, and those who had been members of the team for 3 years or more used more directives than individuals who had been in the group for 2 years or less.[21] These data suggest we must be careful in isolating the effect of gender from that of role and status in understanding the use of imperatives—a language form that is face threatening and thereby less polite.

The study of gender differences in the use of politeness strategies, when framed in terms of positive and negative face, encompasses a broad range of behavior. Examples of positive politeness include exaggerated interest, agreement with the speaker, repeating part of what a speaker has said, hedging opinions, and use of the inclusive form *we*. Examples of negative politeness include avoidance-based behaviors such as indirect statements, hedges, deference, and questions rather than assertions. The question of whether women are more polite than men touches on language features that are addressed throughout this chapter.

Tag Questions

There has been considerable debate about whether Lakoff was correct in her claim that tag questions are more frequently used by women than men. Tag questions lie midway between a statement and a question and have a short question added onto the end—for example, "She's coming this weekend, *isn't she?*" The results from empirical studies are contradictory. Some studies report that women use more tags than men,[22] some report that men use more tag questions than women,[23] some report no gender differences,[24] and some report that it depends on the particular function of the tag used and the situational context.[25] Debate also continues about the function of tag questions—whether Lakoff was correct in her claim that tags indicate uncertainty and hesitancy.

Explaining Contradictory Results The early researchers of tag questions tended to tape-record conversations and look at gender differences in the frequency of usage of tag questions. Betty Lou Dubois and Isabel Crouch, for example, tape-recorded a small professional meeting with 15 to 25 people present to study the conversational give-and-take following each formal presentation.[26] They found that 33 tags were spoken by men and none by women. Maryann Hartman, to take another example, interviewed 12 male and 16 female elderly Maine residents (ages 70 to 93) in their homes for 1 1/2 hours and found that men used very few tags, whereas women used them frequently.[27] How can we explain the discrepancy in the results between these two studies?

There are significant differences in the settings, the sex and status of the participants, and the content of speech between the two studies. Hartman is a woman interviewing elderly women in their homes about their life histories. What Hartman found was that a high frequency of tag questions occurred in all-female conversations about personal topics. Dubois and Crouch recorded a professional conference. The setting is mixed sex and the talk is impersonal. They do not report whether men spoke more frequently than women. However, it is likely that the men assumed higher rank professionally than the women, were represented in greater numbers, and did more of the talking. In this context, tags may have been used by men to solicit information, whereas they may have been used for other functions in the interview setting. Taken together, these studies suggest that there is no simple answer to the question of which sex uses tag questions more frequently. Research may be more meaningful if it were reframed away from a search for the presence or absence of gender differences in tag questions and framed instead from a larger perspective that considers gender differences in the function of tag questions in particular situational contexts.

Functional Analyses of Tag Questions It is useful, then, to focus our review on those studies that have attempted to look at the function of tag questions and the situational context in which they occurred. Janet Holmes made an important contribution to the direction that research has taken in her focus on the communicative strategies that tags may express—in other words, on the reasons or motivations behind the use of tag questions.[28] Holmes suggests that tags, because of their interrogative form, generally function as devices for eliciting a response from the addressee.

Holmes analyzed a 43,000-word corpus drawn from radio, television, primary school classroom discussions, and casual conversations between friends. The sample included equal amounts of speech by males and females. She identified 90 tag questions in the sample and classified them by meaning into three categories.

1. *Modal meaning: Uncertainty*. The tag expresses uncertainty or requests reassurance, confirmation, or agreement—for example, "She's coming around noon isn't she?"[29]

2. *Affective meaning: Solidarity*. The tag conveys solidarity, facilitates the addressee's contribution to the conversation, and encourages that person to join in—for example, "Still working hard at your office are you?"[30]

3. *Affective meaning: Politeness*. The tag conveys politeness or softens a directive or a negatively toned speech act—for example, "You'd better not do that again had you?[31]

Holmes found a small overall difference between men and women. Women initiated 56.6% of the tags, men 43.3%. The most frequent type of tag used by women (59%) were tags with affective meaning that express solidarity. Women used tags with affective meaning more often than men did (59% for women versus 26% for men). Men on the other hand used more tags to express uncertainty than women (62% versus 35%). Thus, women used tags to maintain and facilitate conversation, men to express uncertainty. Holmes's data contradict Lakoff's claim that tags are used to express uncertainty. Only a third of the tags used by women served this function.

Holmes also found that tags were used more by people in leadership/facilitator roles—for example, teachers, hosts in informal conversation in their homes, and interviewers on television and radio. These individuals are responsible for making certain that the conversation proceeds smoothly; it is their role to encourage the other people to participate. Thus, the role of the speaker and the aim of the interaction are important variables in accounting for the use of tag questions. When Holmes compared the use of tags in formal situations such as television and radio talk shows and classrooms to informal situations involving casual conversation between friends, she found that tag questions occur more frequently in personal, informal conversation.

Holmes provides further evidence that contradicts the stereotype that women use tags to express uncertainty.[32] She analyzed a corpus of 24,000 words consisting of equal amounts of speech by males and females in matched contexts. Women were found to produce 63% of the tags overall. Holmes again classified tags by their function, and she found that 62% of the tags used by women were facilitative and expressed solidarity, whereas 35% of the tags used by men served this function. On the other hand, 40% of the tags used by men expressed uncertainty, and 29% of the tags used by women expressed uncertainty.

Attempts to use Holmes's categorization of tags have revealed the complexity of assigning single meanings to speech acts. Although Holmes noted that tags may serve more than one function simultaneously, she did not highlight the difficulties in assigning them to functional categories. In an attempt to use Holmes's functional categories, Deborah Cameron and her colleagues had problems reliably distinguishing between tags that simultaneously seemed to be both modal and affective.[33] For example, *"You were missing last week, weren't you?"* has an element of a softener but calls for confirmation.[34] A single tag may be multifunctional. Cameron and her colleagues examined 9 texts of 5,000 words each from the Survey of English Usage, a collection of conversational speech. The texts consisted of 3 all-male, 3 all-female, and 3 mixed-sex conversations. The total sample included 45,000 words. Cameron and her colleagues identified 96 tags, 62.5% used by men and 37.5% by women. Thus, where Holmes found women to exceed men in the use of tag questions, Cameron and her associates found men in their sample used tags more frequently than women.

Cameron and her colleagues classified tags as either modal (expressing uncertainty) or affective (expressing solidarity or politeness). An analysis by function showed that 75% of the tags used by women were affective and were used to facilitate speech, whereas 60% of men's tags were affective. Forty percent of men's tags were modal versus 25% of the tags used by women. Cameron and her colleagues found men to use a higher rate of tags overall and a higher proportion of those tags to be facilitative than Holmes did. Cameron and her associates also point out that two men in the sample had abnormally high scores for facilitative tags, that they had been aware of being recorded for the Survey, and that they may have been trying to elicit as much talk as possible. They may have been playing a facilitator role, and as Holmes's data reveal, people in this role use tags more frequently. The difference between the two studies in the frequency of tag usage by men and women indicates that the frequency of usage of speech forms is contingent on the features of the conversational setting and the roles and relationships of the participants. The findings are consistent between the two studies that tag questions are used to express uncertainty less frequently than they are used to facilitate speech, and both studies show that men use tags to express uncertainty more than women do.

In a second study Cameron and her associates examined the use of tags in encounters that are asymmetrical—where one participant is institutionally responsible for the conduct of the conversation.

They examined 9 hours of talk recorded from three broadcast settings: a medical radio call-in show, a classroom interaction on educational television, and a televised discussion program with a presenter and an audience. There were equal numbers of men and women in the sample in the role of powerful and powerless speaker.

Cameron and her colleagues identified 116 tags in this sample. Men used modal tags, which express uncertainty, more frequently than women (47% of men's tags and 20% of women's tags), whereas women used affective tags, particularly facilitative tags, more frequently than men (80% of women's tags and 52% of men's). In other words, if tag questions are used to express uncertainty, it is men who use them for this function more than women. Women are more likely than men to use tag questions to maintain and facilitate conversations. Facilitative tags were never used by powerless persons of either sex; they were used by powerful speakers to get others to speak at length. Cameron and her colleagues suggest that if women use more facilitative tags in conversations, they are using a strategy to control conversations. Thus, the use of tag questions by women should not be taken to be a marker of their subordinate status.

In a study of all-female speech in a woman's group, Jennifer Coates found that tags were used to facilitate conversation and to invite others to speak.[35] Over 9 months Coates recorded a women's group that held 3-hour sessions at people's homes fortnightly. Her analysis was based on 135 minutes of text. The vast majority of tags were found to be addressee-oriented, or affective—that is, they were used to facilitate interaction. Very few tags were used to elicit information. Half of the tags occurred in the middle of an utterance, for example, "I think the most difficult thing is is that when you love someone you you half the time you forget their faults (yes) *don't you* and still maybe love them but I mean. . . ."[36] Tags thus were used frequently to monitor the progress of the conversation—to check the "taken-for-grantedness of what is being said."[37]

Summary It is clear that tags cannot be taken a priori to indicate uncertainty. They may serve a variety of functions, and a single tag may even be multifunctional. Tags are used less frequently to express uncertainty than they are to express solidarity and to facilitate speech. Gender differences in the frequency of usage of tag questions depends on the content of the conversation, the roles of the participants, and the situational context. The data reveal no clear difference between men and women in the overall use of tag questions, but they do show women to use tags more frequently to express solidarity and men to use tags more frequently to express uncertainty.

A high use of facilitative tags is found in all-female personal conversation. Tags in this context are used as a form of "positive politeness" to encourage the others to join in the conversation and to check in with other speakers for support. Facilitative tags are also used by powerful speakers of both sexes in roles that require them to facilitate conversation—for example, teacher, host, and interviewer. Holmes got to the heart of the issue in 1984 when she wrote:

> Detailed analysis of the functions of different linguistic forms is a necessary prerequisite for the quantification on which generalizations about female and male usage may be based. It is crucial that such analyses draw on as broad and diverse a range of contexts as possible if unnecessary distortion is to be avoided.[38]

Questions

Lakoff claimed not only that women use more tag questions than men, but also that women use more declarative statements in question form. Many studies have examined gender differences in the frequency with which men and women ask questions in conversation, although few of those studies have distinguished questions in general from declarative statements in question form. Studies of small groups using Interaction Process Analysis (IPA) reviewed in chapter 2 reveal no consistent gender differences on the subcategory "questions" (which includes "asks for opinions," "asks for suggestions," and "asks for information"), but in scoring, IPA declarative statements in question form are not distinguished from other types of questions. Some studies find women use more questions than men or make more statements in question form than men,[39] but other studies find no gender differences.[40]

The Function of Questions As was the case with tag questions, questions can serve many different functions. Janet Johnson provides a variety of examples of questions serving different functions.[41] Questions can be used to advise (e.g., "Don't you have a coat?"[42]). They can be used to complain (e.g., a coach shouts to an official, "How 'bout callin' some fouls?"[43]). A question like "May I help you?"[44] is not only a request for information, it is an offer to help and a request to know why the addressee is there. Coates also suggests that in personal conversation, questions during another speaker's turn may be a sign of active listenership.[45]

Johnson carried out a study based on four 1-hour tape recordings of monthly meetings of two departmental groups at a large industrial corporation.[46] One group provided technical support to the other. The technical group included the same 3 men on all tapes. The group of users varied from meeting to meeting, but it always included 2 females and 2 to 5 male engineers and designers. The leader of the group was the computer graphics manager. The sample included 203 questions that were organized into three categories:

1. *Information questions.* For example, "Can you put in z-values?"[47]
2. *Confirmation devices.* These could be requests for feedback or checks for understanding—for example, "They automatically number them?"[48]
3. *Facilitation strategies.* These are used to structure or regulate the interaction—for example, "Have you been using them, Kathy?"[49]

Johnson found no gender differences in the number of questions used by men and women, but she did find that leaders used questions to facilitate interaction, whereas engineers used questions more frequently to request information. Unfortunately, this study has neither equal numbers of men and women in the group, nor equal amounts of speech by men and women. The findings for gender are therefore not reliable, but it does demonstrate the necessity of a functional analysis of questions and the importance of the role of a participant in interaction (e.g., leader, support staff, group member) in understanding the use of questions. Alice Freed has developed a taxonomy of question functions, seeing questions to vary along an information continuum, but gender differences in the use of questions using this taxonomy have not been explored.[50]

Intimate Couples One of the most widely cited studies of questions was conducted by Pamela Fishman, who collected 52 hours of naturally occurring conversation from 3 heterosexual couples in their homes.[51] The couples had known each other for 3 months, 6 months, and 2 years, were white, professionals, and between the ages of 25 and 35. Fishman placed tape recorders in their homes for 4 to 14 days. She found that in 7 hours of tapes, men asked 59 questions, and women asked 150, or 2½ times as many questions as men. She noted that women had more trouble starting conversations and keeping their topics going, and she suggested that questions solve the problem of ensuring a response to their utterances. Questions demand answers. She noted that women used the question opening *d'ya know what* twice as often as men. This is a form that is used by children as a way to ensure their right to speak. The use of *d'ya know what* suggests that women, like children, have more restricted rights to speak.[52]

Task Groups Two studies address Lakoff's claim specifically. Jennifer Simkins-Bullock and Beth Wildman studied 13 all-male, 13 all-female, and 13 mixed-sex dyads who had 15 minutes to come up with a list of 10 mutually agreed upon suggestions to improve the university's orientation procedures.[53] Females made more suggestions in question form than males did in mixed-sex groups. Similarly, Julie McMillan and her colleagues studied 6 all-female, 2 all-male, and 10 mixed-sex groups of 5 to 7 members.[54] Groups had 30 minutes to solve a murder mystery. Women used more imperative constructions in question form than men did in mixed-sex groups, and they did so more in mixed-sex groups than in all-female groups. The differences are small in magnitude, and the results are based on very few occurrences. McMillan and her colleagues found men in mixed groups to average .56 and women to average 1.86 imperatives in question form. Simkins-Bullock and Wildman do not report the actual means for men and women.

Marjorie Swacker's study of the question-and-answer session at a professional meeting revealed gender differences in the way in which men and women asked questions.[55] For men, 72% of their questions were preceded by scholarly background information; for example, "Both Fries and Francis have stated that the normal one-word adjective position is before the noun. How does this compare with . . . ?"[56] For women, only 19% of their questions were preceded by this type of information. Thus, men used questions to establish their knowledge and credentials; questions for men were a way to use power. Expert power is based on having superior knowledge,[57] and Paula Johnson has hypothesized that it is used more frequently by males than females because they are the acknowledged experts in this society.[58]

Summary There is insufficient empirical evidence to test the hypothesis that women use declarative statements in question form more than men. The weight of the evidence from studies using Interaction Process Analysis suggests that women do not ask more questions than men. But IPA does not distinguish questions posed as statements with a rising intonation from other question forms, and it may still be the case that women ask questions in different forms or to serve different functions than men do. The existing literature suggests that such a functional analysis is imperative. Questions can be asked to request information, suggestions, or opinions, to show active listenership, to complain, to advise, to facilitate further interaction, and even to establish one's knowledgeability. Future studies need to examine questions by looking at the functions they serve and by exploring whether the use of certain types of questions varies not only with gender but also with the status and role of the speaker in an interaction and the nature of the interaction.

Qualifiers and Hedges

Lakoff claimed that women use more qualifiers or hedges—words that convey uncertainty such as *kinda, I guess*, and *I think*—than men. People use qualifiers or hedges to attenuate the force of a statement. There is no consistent list of words agreed to be hedges. Hedges include a variety of forms: verbs (e.g., *seem, I believe, I reckon, I suppose*), adverbials (e.g., *maybe, perhaps, probably*), epistemic modals (e.g., *could, might*), and discourse features (e.g., *kind of, sort of, I mean, you know*).[59] Each study that has attempted to test Lakoff's claims has included a different set of words as hedges, and many researchers do not even make explicit in reporting their findings the list of words they have included, making comparisons across studies difficult.

To further complicate the matter, Janet Holmes's research makes clear that a single form like *I think* can take on a variety of meanings.[60] It may have a different meaning depending on whether the stress is on *I* or on *think*, on whether *I think* is pronounced with a rising, falling, or fall-rise intonation, and on its position in a sentence. For example, "They're stones or brick *I think*" is more tentative, whereas "*I think* I'll have some cake" is more deliberative.[61] *I think* can be used by a speaker to express confidence in his or her proposition—not uncertainty—as in, "Well, *I think* when times are hard you've got to have something to look forward to."[62]

The frequency with which men and women use qualifiers and hedges has been found to depend on the age of the speakers that have been studied. Research by Frances Sayers and John Sherblom on adult males ages 60 to 80 shows older males use higher rates of qualified speech than college males do, meaning that gender differences found in college samples may not apply to older populations.[63]

If we look at the overall pattern of results across studies, we see that some empirical studies find women use more qualifiers or modal constructions than men,[64] but others find no gender differences or find that gender differences rely on the particular function of the qualifier and the context in which it appears.[65] This inconsistency between studies is brought about by the differences in the settings studied, the characteristics of and relationship between the participants, and the definitions of qualifiers or modal constructions used. Because qualifications and modal constructions may be used to serve a variety of functions, it is less informative to look at overall gender differences than to look at gender differences in the function of qualifiers in particular contexts.

A Functional Analysis of the Use of "I think" It is most useful to begin by examining the work of linguists like Holmes and Coates, who have looked at gender differences by carrying out functional analyses of linguistic forms like qualifiers and hedges. Holmes divided instances of *I think* into two broad functional categories.[66] The *deliberative* use of *I think* includes instances that express confidence and add authority and weight to a proposition. Here, *I think* is in the initial position. The *tentative* use of *I think* includes instances that express uncertainty, that soften the force of a proposition, or that attenuate the force of a speech act. The tentative use can occur because the speaker is uncertain, or because the speaker takes account of the addressee's feelings. For example, "*I think* you better go now"[67] expresses politeness or rapport and has an affective meaning. In its tentative use, *I think* can occur in any position in a sentence with any intonation. Holmes noted the difficulty in reliably distinguishing between the two categories of *I think*. Often a decision cannot be made about how to classify an instance of *I think* without looking at the context in which it occurs in the conversation.

Holmes studied a 25,000-word corpus containing equal amounts of male and female speech in carefully matched social contexts. She found a total of 70 instances of *I think* in this corpus. The deliberative function of *I think* represented 49% of the instances in the data set, calling into question the assumption that *I think* is an expression of uncertainty. Overall, women used *I think* in its deliberative form as frequently as men, but they exhibited fewer instances of the tentative use of *I think*. In formal contexts such as television and radio interviews and classrooms, women used *I think* more frequently in its deliberative function than men did, whereas in informal contexts men used the deliberative form of *I think* more than women did.

When the instances of *I think* were broken down by context, the numbers became too small to be reliable, but Holmes postulates that in public, formal contexts women may increase their use of *I think* to add weight and authority to their opinions, while in informal conversation women do not have to do this. According to the data on gender stereotypes, men are often assumed to have greater competency than women due to their higher status in society. Because of this, women may have to work harder than men in formal contexts to impress others that they are as competent as men.

Although *I think* has often been taken to be a hedge, Holmes's research suggests that half the time speakers use *I think* they use it to serve the opposite function—to express confidence in the speaker's proposition and to add authority to it. Whether men or women use *I think* more frequently to add weight to their opinions depends on the situational context; men use it more in informal contexts, women in formal contexts.

In her interview of elderly Maine residents about their life histories, Hartman noted that there were many more qualified statements made by women than by men.[68] She found "I don't think so; I don't know as they did; perhaps; I suppose; I don't know; I think so; course perhaps I'm not telling the whole truth as it should be told, but; I just feel; it seems to me"[69] to be present in the speech of women but not men. Women may have used these forms to serve the same function as *I think* in its affective meaning—to take the addressee's feelings into account, to soften their speech rather than express uncertainty about their propositions, and to avoid imposing their viewpoint on another person.

Epistemic Modals Coates examined gender differences in the use of epistemic modals, or utterances in which speakers explicitly qualify their commitment to the truth of a proposition they express.[70] Examples of epistemic modals include *perhaps, I think, sort of, kind of, probably,* and *I mean.* Coates makes clear that epistemic modals may take on different meanings, but they are generally considered to be negative politeness strategies that function to show respect and sensitivity to the addressee's need not to be imposed upon.

Coates analyzed parallel texts from two sources: a conversation between 5 women friends recorded in the author's home, and a spoken text from the Survey of English Usage of a conversation between 3 males who were old friends. Coates found that women used more epistemic modals than men. These modals occurred in discussions about sensitive topics involving self-disclosure, where the style was cooperative rather than competitive. They gave the speaker a way to retreat from a proposition if it turned out to be unacceptable to other participants in the conversation. Thereby the speaker could protect his or her own positive face. There appeared to be an implicit assumption that you do not come into open disagreement with others, that you avoid making outright assertions, and that you thereby allow room for further discussion and modification of view. In Coates's study epistemic modals tended not to occur in narrative portions of conversation but rather in discussion sections. There, they helped facilitate a more open discussion by not imposing one viewpoint on another.

It is Coates's contention that women use epistemic modals not because they doubt the truth of their propositions, but to show respect for the face needs of the addressee or to protect their own face needs. Epistemic modals occur more frequently when talk is personal, topics are sensitive, and self-disclosure is intimate. As a consequence, if the talk of women is often more personal than that of men (this literature is discussed in chapter 6), women's frequent use of epistemic modals may have to do with the nature of the conversations being studied. The norm that speakers cannot come to open disagreement may be more true for female conversation than male conversation, which would also account for women's greater use of epistemic modals.

Functional Analyses of the Use of "you know" A language form that is sometimes included in sets of qualifying phrases is *you know*. Lakoff and others assumed *you know* expresses the speaker's uncertainty, and they included it along with expressions like *sort of, kind of, I guess,* and *I think.* Unlike *I guess* or *I think,* which are speaker oriented, or *kind of* and *sort of,* which are content oriented, *you know* is always addressee oriented.[71] A functional analysis of *you know* suggests that this form may serve many functions, and its inclusion in an index indicative of uncertainty is highly problematic.

Janet Holmes points out that *you know* is syntactically mobile like *I think* and can appear at the beginning, middle, or end of an utterance.[72] Both the intonation and syntactic position of *you know* make a difference in its interpretation. At the beginning of an utterance of a speaker's turn, *you know* serves to claim attention—for example, "*You know* I find that diet food is really boring."[73] At the end of an utterance preceded or followed by a pause it may be a floor-yielding device or an invitation for feedback. It can be a verbal filler or fumble, giving the speaker time for planning. It can be used to emphasize or intensify the strength of a speech act, usually with a falling intonation in the final position in an utterance—for example, "It's very good really *you know* it's a real experience."[74] The use of *you know* to express uncertainty or lack of confidence is only one of its many functions.

Holmes studied *you know* in a 50,000-word corpus of men's and women's spontaneous speech. Twenty thousand words came from formal contexts such as television and radio interviews, 30,000 from informal, relaxed contexts in homes, often at mealtime. Holmes identified and analyzed 207 instances of *you know*. There were no overall gender differences in the use of the phrase. *You know* was found to occur primarily in informal conversation, and only 12 instances were found in formal contexts. Holmes categorized *you know* by function into two broad categories—expressions of *certainty* and expressions of *uncertainty*—and found *you know* to be used more frequently by men to convey uncertainty and by women to convey certainty. Men used *you know* more often than women to communicate awareness that their utterance was not encoded precisely enough—for example, "The money seems to be going for basics rather than for things like, *you know*, extra equipment."[75] Women used *you know* more often than men to emphasize, intensify, or boost the strength of a statement, as in "it's worse than eating, *you know*" spoken with a falling intonation.[76] They also used it to express certainty about the validity of their proposition or confidence that the addressee knows what is meant, as in, "They obviously thought he was a bit stupid, *you know*."[77] Thus, *you know* should not be taken universally as a hedge, indicative of uncertainty and lack of confidence by women, nor is it true that women use *you know* more frequently than men to express uncertainty.

Holmes further noted:

> *You know* seems to occur most frequently in sections of relatively sustained narrative or accounts of the speaker's personal experiences intended to amuse, amaze, or, at least, retain the interest of the addressee. *You know* occurs much less often in sections of discussion, argument, planning or "phatic" talk, for instance, where there is more frequent speaker-change.[78]

Thus, the more frequent use of *you know* by women may reflect their attention to engaging the addressee in their speech.

Support for this interpretation comes from Fishman in her previously discussed study of informal conversation among heterosexual couples in their homes.[79] Fishman found that women used *you know* five times as often as men—not as a reflection of insecurity, but rather in places where they were unsuccessfully trying to pursue topics. *You know* appeared to be an attention-getting device by which speakers checked to see if their partner was listening and following what they were saying. It was concentrated in long turns at talk, often after pauses in women's speech in places where their partners might have responded but didn't, and it was an attempt to resolve the conversational trouble. Thus, *you know* in this context had a facilitative function; it was used to express solidarity or positive politeness and to maintain conversation.

Sex Composition of the Group Research reveals no clear pattern of gender differences in the use of modals or qualifying words when comparisons are made of interaction in all-male, all-female, and mixed-sex groups. Results are difficult to compare from study to study because the measures are not identical and because behavior is assessed in task groups in one study[80] and in informal conversation in dyads in another.[81] Modal constructions may serve a different function when two people are getting acquainted than when they have a task problem to solve.

Some evidence suggests that women use more qualifying words in task groups with men than they do in single-sex groups. Julie McMillan and her colleagues found women used more modal constructions in mixed-sex than in single-sex groups working for an hour to solve a murder mystery. With men, women may have attempted to "be polite and permit others to have different perspectives or desires about the event."[82]

Similar results are reported by Linda Carli.[83] Carli studied 26 mixed-sex, 30 all-male, and 30 all-female dyads discussing a topic for 10 minutes on which they disagreed. In mixed-sex task groups women used more disclaimers than men preceding their statements—for example, "*I'm no expert, I may be wrong, I'm not sure, I don't know, I suppose, I mean* and *I guess.*"[84] However, there were no gender differences between the single-sex dyads in the use of disclaimers. Thus, women were more likely to use these speech forms in the presence of men. Carli recognizes the use of disclaimers as an indirect influence strategy. These speech forms may reflect women's greater politeness and reluctance to impose a viewpoint on men—behaviors consistent with the gender role norms that dictate that men should take the lead. In fact, Carli found the use of disclaimers to be functional for women in mixed-sex groups. Women who used disclaimers more frequently had greater influence over their male partners.

Summary Gender differences have not been consistently found in the use of qualifiers and hedges; gender differences vary with the age of the participants, the nature of the conversation content, and the sex composition of the group. Research on the individual speech forms like *I think* and *you know* demonstrates that each speech form can be used to serve different functions. While Lakoff assumed that qualifications in women's speech are indicative of uncertainty, uncertainty is not their sole, or even their most frequent, function. Similar to the findings for tag questions, it is men, rather than women, who more frequently use forms like *I think* and *you know* to express uncertainty. Women use these forms more frequently than men to convey certainty and to give emphasis and weight to their propositions. They do this more often in formal contexts in which men may be assumed to have greater competency and women need to establish themselves as competent. Women may also use qualified speech with men as an indirect influence strategy. If women violate sex role norms by being too assertive with men, their contributions are less likely to be accepted.

Epistemic modals like *perhaps* or *probably* occur when talk is personal and sensitive; they function to soften or attenuate speech and to protect the face needs of both speaker and addressee. Women's more frequent use of modals or hedges in some research may be due to the more personal content of conversations between women. What has been taken to characterize female speech may be a style of speech that occurs during discussion of personal and sensitive material.

Back-Channel or Minimal Responses

Starkey Duncan noted that in face-to-face conversations, listeners do not remain mute but utter a variety of vocalizations such as *m-hm* and *yeah*.[85] These behaviors have been labeled back-channel responses. Duncan identified a group of behaviors that he took to constitute back-channel responses: sentence completions, brief requests for clarification, brief restatements, head nods and shakes, and minimal responses like *m-hm, yeah, right,* and *yes*. These responses provide feedback to the speaker as the turn progresses.

Minimal responses, or back channels, have drawn the attention of language researchers, and although definitions vary from study to study, women have been found in many studies to use more minimal responses than men.[86] Some researchers have found the gender differences in back channels to be affected by the sex composition of the group[87] or the extent to which speakers are in agreement or disagreement.[88] Other researchers have found no gender differences in the frequency of use but have found differences in the timing and placement of minimal responses.[89]

The Timing and Placement of Minimal Responses Minimal responses are generally taken to be signals to the speaker of the listener's continuing interest and coparticipation in topic development. Don Zimmerman and Candace West noted the effect of delayed minimal responses on speakers in mixed-sex dyads.[90] They found examples in 3 of their 10 mixed-sex transcripts of a series of delayed minimal responses bringing a topic to a close. Zimmerman and West suggested that the delayed response may be taken to signal lack of understanding and inattention to current talk, as well as lack of support for continued topic development.

Pamela Fishman also found that minimal responses take on different meanings depending on their placement in a conversation.[91] In her study of the conversations of heterosexual couples in their homes, Fishman found that both males and females used minimal responses, but males did not use minimal responses to encourage women to elaborate on a topic. Minimal responses by men tended to occur after a lengthy remark by a woman to fill a turn that needed to be filled. Fishman believed these were attempts to discourage interaction. Women, on the other hand, inserted minimal responses throughout streams of talk rather than placing them at the end as men did. Thus, when used by women, minimal responses signaled continuing attention and interest, whereas for men they signaled lack of interest.

Nature of the Conversation The frequency and usage of minimal responses is affected by the type of conversation. Carmelina Trimboli and Michael Walker studied 6 all-male, 6 all-female, and 6 mixed-sex dyads.[92] Each dyad held two cooperative conversations (i.e., friendly chats about similar views) and two competitive conversations (i.e., arguments about topics on which they held opposing views). Subjects were free to discuss any topics they wished. Trimboli and Walker found no gender differences in the use of back channels, but they did find more back-channel responses to occur during cooperative conversations than during competitive ones. In friendly conversations back channels signal support and continued interest in topic development. Their decreased presence in competitive conversation signals lack of addressee support for continued topic development. Some researchers have found minimal responses to occur more frequently in all-female conversations than in all-male or mixed-sex conversations, suggesting that a greater element of competitiveness may be present when men are part of a conversation.[93]

Stage of the Conversation   Jennifer Coates found that minimal responses were placed differently in conversation by women depending on the stage of topic development that the conversation had reached.[94] In her analysis of personal conversation in a women's group, Coates found that there were opening monologues in which a speaker introduced a topic by sharing a story. These narrative portions were followed by discussion sections in which many speakers joined the conversation. Coates noted that in the interaction-focused discussion sections of conversation, minimal responses occurred frequently, inserted in speech without interrupting the speaker's flow and indicating active attention and speaker support. Minimal responses occurred less frequently in the narrative portions, and they occurred at the end of a summary or the end of a topic introduction to signal that the listeners had taken the point, agreed with the summary, and accepted it as a topic. Thus, women do not insert *m-hm* or *yeah* continually throughout speech; they vary the use depending on the interaction process.

Power and Dominance   The use of minimal responses does not vary consistently with the power or dominance of participants in a conversation.[95] Peter Kollock and his colleagues studied homosexual and heterosexual couples whom they categorized as power balanced and power imbalanced based on who had more say in decisions.[96] In mixed-sex couples where one member held more power in the relationship than the other, there were no significant differences in the rate of back-channel responses used by the less powerful and the more powerful person.

In a study of colleagues at work, Nicola Woods found no relationship between power and back-channel responses for women, but she did find them to be related for men. Woods recorded conversation in the workplace among triads of single-sex and opposite-sex colleagues of differing occupational status.[97] She found that females did not use more minimal responses when they were in the role of subordinate than when they were in high-status positions. She did, however, find minimal responses to be used more frequently by male subordinates than by males in high-status positions.

Helena Leet-Pellegrini conducted a study in which one partner was given greater expertise at a task than the other partner. Nonexperts used more assent terms (e.g., *yeh, uh-huh*) than experts did in single-sex dyads and in dyads where a male expert was paired with a female nonexpert. But female experts used more assent terms than their male nonexpert partners.[98] Female experts were more likely than male experts to repeat the words and complete the thoughts of their nonexpert partners.

Derek Roger and his colleagues carried out two studies looking at dominance and use of back-channel responses in dyads.[99] In both studies subjects were assessed for dominance on the dominance scale of the Edwards Personal Preference Schedule and assigned to one of four types of pairs: 2 high-dominance subjects; 2 low-dominance subjects; a high-dominance female and low-dominance male; and a high-dominance male and low-dominance female. Subjects were given 10 minutes to convince their partner of their own point of view about topics on which they disagreed. In both studies women were found to produce more back-channel responses than men. In neither study were there differences in the rate of back-channel responses used by high- and low-dominance individuals in high-low dominance pairs.

These studies suggest that the overall frequency of use of back-channel responses has no consistent relationship to the power and dominance of the speakers, but rather that gender interacts with the power of the speaker. Males appear to use more back-channel responses in subordinate roles than in powerful roles, but power has less effect on the use of back-channel responses by women. Gender differences have been found to occur in the use of back-channel responses even when status has been controlled. Differences may also exist in the way back-channel responses have been used by high- and low-dominance speakers that have not been examined in these studies.

Summary Taken together, research studies suggest women are more often found to use back-channel responses than men, but gender interacts with other variables. Back-channel responses are used more frequently in cooperative than competitive talk, and they occur most frequently in interaction-oriented rather than narrative portions of personal conversations. Back-channel responses may carry different meanings depending on their timing and placement in conversation. When inserted in streams of speech, these speech forms show active attention, support, and continued interest in topic development. When they occur after a lengthy remark, they signal the listener has taken the point or agreed with the summary. When they occur after a delay, they may signal lack of understanding or interest in continued topic development. While Fishman found men were

more likely than women to use minimal responses at the end of nar-
ratives and suggested they were signals of disinterest, Coates also
found women placed minimal responses at the end of narrative portions of conversations and inserted them in streams of talk only during interaction-focused discussion sections. Some evidence suggests
that women may be more likely than men to insert back-channel
responses throughout streams of talk in discussions, but there is not
sufficient research evidence controlling for timing, placement, and
type of conversation to draw clear conclusions about gender and the
use of back-channel responses. Minimal responses do not appear to
be consistently associated with power or dominance.

Intensifiers and Exaggerations

Mary Key claimed that women used intensifiers such as *so, such,
quite*, and *vastly* more frequently than men,[100] and her ideas gained
support from Robin Lakoff. A number of empirical studies provide
evidence in support of these claims.[101] The set of intensive adverbs
that are considered in the speech of men and women differs from
study to study, and yet the results appear to be consistent across a
variety of settings that women use more intensifiers than men. These
results were found in informal and task-oriented conversation in single-sex and mixed-sex groups;[102] in descriptions of landscape photographs;[103] and in in-class speeches in a communication studies
class.[104]

Lakoff suggests that the use of the intensive *so* is an attempt to
hedge strong feelings, "a device you'd use if you felt it unseemly to
show you had strong emotions, or to make strong assertions, but felt
you had to say something along those lines anyway."[105] However,
these linguistic forms may also indicate the speaker's emotional
involvement with his or her statements.[106] As is the case with the
other language forms discussed in this chapter, intensifiers may not
carry a single meaning and may serve different functions in conversation. Intensifiers have not been well studied, and in future research
we need to classify them by function to better assess their meaning
in conversation.

Personal Pronouns

A final language form that has received some attention from
researchers is the use of personal pronouns. The research is consistent in finding that women use personal pronouns—the self-referent

I and the plural form *we*—more frequently than men in speech.[107] Research results come from a variety of interaction settings: individuals getting to know one another,[108] discussing assigned topics,[109] solving problems in single-sex and mixed-sex groups,[110] describing landscape photographs,[111] talking about an interesting or dramatic life experience,[112] answering reflective, open-ended questions in interviews,[113] and asking questions in a question-and-answer session at a professional conference.[114]

A study of in-class public speeches from a communication studies class stands alone in the finding that men used more first-person singular pronouns than women.[115] This study suggests that personal pronouns, like all other language variables, may serve a different function when used in different contexts and when used in a monologue rather than in a conversation. All but one of the studies that find that women use more personal pronouns than men were based on language samples from interaction rather than monologues,[116] and this may in part have accounted for the contrasting results.

The more frequent use of personal pronouns is likely to be related to the conversation content (which I discuss in chapter 6). The use of personal pronouns would be expected to be greater when conversation content is personal. However, even in settings where the information shared is not personal and intimate in nature, or the topic is controlled, women are more likely to make their comments personal.

Marjorie Swacker found that during the question-and-answer sessions at a professional conference, women were more likely than men to introduce their questions with reference to themselves—for example, "I would like to ask if . . . ," "It seems to me that . . . ," or "I wonder if. . . ."[117] Rather than overtly challenging or rejecting the speaker's ideas, women may use the reference to self as a form of politeness to show respect for the face needs of the speaker. Consistent with Carli's findings on disclaimers discussed earlier,[118] the use of the reference to self may be an indirect influence strategy used by women due to their subordinate status in this context.

Topic Initiation and Change

An important aspect of conversation management is control of the topic: initiation of the topic, topic development, and topic change. A change of topic or lack of topic development denies the speaker the opportunity for continued evolution of his or her thoughts. Although the research is limited in this area, it suggests that men do less work than women in maintaining conversations and more frequently cut off the development of women's ideas than women cut off men.

Research on married couples by Fishman, discussed earlier, revealed that women raise more topics than men and work harder to develop those topics.[119] Fishman found that women raised 62% of the topics. While all the topics raised by men produced conversations, only 38% of the topics raised by women were successfully developed. Men thus did less work in interaction to develop topics than women did. Fishman's study has been widely cited, but there have been no follow-up studies that attempt to replicate her results.

Candace West and Angela Garcia had 5 male and 5 female unacquainted students relax and get to know each other in mixed-sex dyads.[120] West and Garcia audiotaped 12 minutes of conversation from each dyad and analyzed topic changes. They identified 33 cases of possible topic change, from 3 to 10 per conversation. Men were responsible for initiating more changes of topic than women (64% versus 36%). West and Garcia then divided topic changes into two categories: *topic extinctions*—topic changes preceded by silences between speaker turns and/or a series of unsuccessful attempts to generate topical talk; and *topic closure*—topic change preceded by collaborative topic-bounding activity, conclusion drawing, or offers of assessment. Forty-two percent of the topic changes were preceded by collaborative topic-bounding activities by both parties, whereas 30% were preceded by topic extinctions. There were no gender differences on topic closures or topic extinctions.

The remaining 27% of the topic changes could not be considered to be either topic extinctions or topic closures. They were unilateral shifts by a single party. All of these shifts were initiated by men. In these cases the man did not acknowledge or agree that the turn was concluded—he just shifted immediately to a new line of talk. These unilateral shifts in topic often occurred in the wake of potential "tellables," things about which more could have been said if the topic had been pursued. Men refrained from asking when there were grounds for asking. They tended to sigh or were silent, followed by a unilateral topic change. Women would have been more disclosing had they not been curtailed by men.

Another laboratory study of interaction between strangers looked at six 2-person conversations.[121] In contrast to the West and Garcia results, this study found no gender differences in the number of topics initiated for discussion or the number of topics developed.

In summary, there has not been a great deal of research directed to the analysis of topic initiation, development, and change, but the limited evidence that exists suggests that women may do more work in personal conversations to facilitate talk. Men, on the other hand, do not always pursue topics that have potential for further development. Attention to topic development is a sign of positive politeness—an attempt to make the speaker feel valued and respected by encouraging the development of his or her thoughts.

The research studies by Fishman and by West and Garcia focus on personal conversations between men and women. The lack of attention by men to the development of topics initiated by women reflects an underlying devaluation of women's concerns, and it supports the contention that men and women do not engage in these interactions as status equals. The degree to which men and women are willing to work to develop a topic may be related not only to gender but also to the topic matter itself. We need further research to determine whether there are contexts in which women exceed men in topic extinctions and men exceed women in topic development.

Female Language, or the Female Register

Many researchers have examined gender differences in language by forming combinations of the speech characteristics just discussed into indices of "women's language," or the "female register." They have then compared men and women on these indices. Combining occurrences of a range of disparate language features is problematic because multiple occurrences of a single language feature are not functionally equivalent. The combination of diverse language features that serve different functions into a single index leads to a measure whose functional meaning cannot be determined.

For example, Linda Carli constructed an index of tentative language by summing qualifiers, hedges, and tag questions.[122] In a study of male, female, and mixed-sex dyads, Carli found that women used tentative speech more than men overall, and that women used it more in mixed-sex dyads than men did. The problem here is the assumption that this index in fact is a measure of tentativeness. These language forms can be used to serve a variety of functions, and a functional analysis of the use of these language features might yield a different interpretation. A second problem with these indices is that generally researchers count each occurrence of "women's language"—be it a hedge, a tag question, an intensive adverb, or the like—and add them together. Thus, it is possible that a frequent use of tag questions may account for a high score on the index for one subject, and a frequent use of hedges may account for a high score

on the index for another subject. The same index then carries different meanings not only from one instance to another but from individual to individual.

Social Powerlessness

The most widely cited example of this combination form of research
was carried out by William O'Barr and Bowman Atkins, who found
no clear gender differences in the use of "women's language" but
did find that use of these language forms varied with societal
roles.[123] They recorded 150 hours of trials over 10 weeks in a North
Carolina superior criminal court. All lawyers for these trials were
male, but both sexes were equally represented as witnesses. O'Barr
and Atkins defined "women's language" based on Lakoff's propositions to include hedges, superpolite forms, tag questions, intensifiers, empty adjectives, hypercorrect grammar and pronunciation,
lack of a sense of humor, direct quotations, special lexicons (words
like *magenta*), and question intonation in declarative form. O'Barr
and Atkins noted that a high frequency of usage of one language feature was not necessarily associated with a high frequency of usage
of another. They found some women spoke with these features, but
that there was considerable variability in the degree to which women
used "women's language." Those women who frequently used
"women's language" were housewives, while those who used it less
frequently were of higher social status and were well-educated, professional women. Those men who used "women's language" most
frequently held subordinate, lower status jobs or were unemployed.
Thus, O'Barr and Atkins argued that "women's language" may have
more to do with social powerlessness than with gender.

Task and Social-Emotional Roles

Bent Preisler in his study of single-sex and mixed-sex discussion
groups found women to use more "tentative" speech than men, but
he also found this type of speech to be related to the roles participants played in groups.[124] Preisler's definition of tentative speech
was based on 30 linguistic features "generally acknowledged to have
a bearing on the expression of tentativeness,"[125] which included
forms like tag questions and hedges. Again, these language forms
were assumed to express tentativeness, but they do permit other
interpretations.

Preisler then linked this index with interaction scores based on

Interaction Process Analysis. He divided group members into two types. Task-persons were defined as individuals with relatively high scores in the categories comprising "attempts answers" and low scores in other IPA categories. Social-emotional-persons were defined as individuals with low scores in the categories for "attempts answers," and high scores in other IPA categories, particularly "positive reactions." Social-emotional-persons used more tentative speech than task-persons. Thus, he associated tentative speech with both gender and role.

As pointed out in chapter 2, Interaction Process Analysis considers an opinion or suggestion to be social-emotional behavior if even an element of interpersonal feeling is present. It is quite possible that what Preisler took to be tentative speech, such as tag questions and hedges, in fact was a form of "positive politeness" and was used to show support for other speakers.

Preisler's sample was stratified to include professionals, non-manual workers, and semiskilled and unskilled workers. It is interesting to note that among the professionals, tentative speech correlated with task roles and was particularly frequent in the speech of female task-persons.[126] These results raise further questions about the assumption that this index is a measure of tentativeness. It is possible that professional women used these forms as task leaders either to facilitate talk or to add weight and authority to their propositions. They may also use these speech forms because competent women will be better received and more influential when they do.[127]

Finally, Faye Crosby and Linda Nyquist in a series of three studies examined the impact of role and status on the differential use of the female register by men and women.[128] Their research suggests that gender differences in the use of the female register are not universal but depend on the situational context and the role of the speaker. They did not find high- and low-status speakers to differ on use of the female register. Gender differences were more likely to occur when speech was informal than when it was governed by more well-established rituals, as it was at an information booth. Dede Brouwer and her colleagues similarly found no gender differences in language at an information booth.[129]

The limitation of these studies is that it is not possible to determine the meaning of these indices of "women's language." Language forms that serve a variety of functions have been added together, and as O'Barr and Atkins noted, a high frequency of occurrence of one speech feature in the index was not correlated with that of another. Because indices of "women's language" differ from study to study, it is difficult to compare results across studies. A reanalysis of the data from these studies in which speech forms were categorized according to their function would reveal more information about the meaning of these gender differences in language.

Combinations of Language Variables That Differentiate Male and Female Speakers

There are a number of studies that have used a statistical procedure called discriminant function analysis to determine whether the speech of men and women can be distinguished based on the frequency of usage of a variety of speech forms. Anthony Mulac and his colleagues in a series of studies have demonstrated that a combination of language variables can be used to accurately discriminate between the speech of men and that of women.

Mulac and his associates transcribed 15 male and 15 female speeches given in a communication studies class.[130] One-minute portions were selected at random from the beginning, middle, and ends of the speeches. When asked to identify the sex of the speaker from these samples, subjects could not do so accurately. Mulac and his colleagues then carried out a discriminant analysis using 35 language variables to predict the sex of the speaker. Ten language variables were found to be indicative of male speech, and 10 variables to be indicative of female speech. By using a weighted combination of these 20 variables, the computer could reclassify the transcripts by sex with 100% accuracy.

The study provides impressive evidence for gender differences in the language use of males and females. The actual speech features that so accurately discriminated the speech of men and women in this study are surprising, however. Few of the speech features for men have been widely held to be characteristic of male speech.[131] Men used more first-personal singular pronouns and more references to people in their speeches—characteristics of speech usually associated more with female speakers. The category references to people, however, included references to *some people* or *anybody*, which were not personal references. The one speech characteristic that has been found to characterize male speech in a number of studies that was among the predictors of male speech in this study was the use of more vocalized pauses (e.g., *uh, ah*).[132]

The speech features Mulac and his colleagues found to predict female speech showed greater consistency with past research. Women used more fillers (e.g., *ok, like, well*), more intensive adverbs (e.g., *so*, *really*), and more references to emotion. However, as was the case for males, many of the predictors for females have not generally been associated with female speech.[133]

In a following study Anthony Mulac and Louisa Lundell again found a combination of variables to discriminate accurately between male and female speakers, but the lists of variables for each sex in this study was quite different from the previous study.[134] Mulac and Lundell audiotaped 40 speakers ages 11 to 64 describing landscape photographs to either a male or a female researcher. The subjects were sixth graders, undergraduates, graduate teaching assistants, and older residents from the adjacent town. When asked to correctly guess the sex of the speakers, a separate group of 42 subjects was unable to do so accurately.

Mulac and Lundell coded the transcripts for 31 linguistic variables. A discriminant analysis revealed that 17 variables in combination could predict the sex of the speaker with 87.5% accuracy. Eight variables were more indicative of male speakers. Again, these speech characteristics have not been widely held to characterize the speech of men.[135] Fillers, which were found to be a marker of speech for females in the previous study, were now found to be a marker of speech for males. None of the markers of male speech in this study were found to predict the speech of men in the previous study.

In regard to women, three of the language features found to be markers of female speech in this study had been found to characterize the speech of women in previous research: tag questions, intensive adverbs, and personal pronouns. Four language features distinguished the speech of women in this study and the previous one by Mulac and his colleagues.[136] The final three features of female speech have not often been found to mark female speech in other research.[137]

The data cannot be interpreted to mean that a single variable is indicative of speaker sex, but rather that a particular combination of variables is able to predict speaker sex. Mulac and Lundell note that "the high degree of accuracy of gender reclassification (87.5%) was possible only when a substantial number of variables were differentially weighted and combined by the computer."[138] The data also make clear that the situational context in which the speech sample is drawn will determine the features that distinguish between men and women. Mulac and Lundell point out:

> The extent and form of language similarity or overlap, and its converse, gender distinguishers, is likely to differ from situation to situation. When

we compare the results of the present discriminant analysis to tho⌄e of two earlier studies assessing discriminating clusters of variables, we find evidence of this changing or 'fluctuating' nature of the linguistic overlap.[139]

In the previous two studies by Mulac and his colleagues, speech samples were drawn from noninteractive speech rather than from speech in actual interaction. Mulac and his colleagues extended this line of research to speech in conversation.[140] They formed 12 all-male, 12 all-female, and 24 mixed-sex dyads with undergraduates who were instructed to work in a cooperative atmosphere to discuss issues such as the five most common problems university students face in finding suitable housing. The groups were given 20 minutes for their discussions. Samples of 300 words were taken from the discussions for transcription, and 12 linguistic variables were coded. Discriminant analyses were carried out to distinguish between male and female speakers. A weighted combination of eight variables was found to predict the sex of the speaker.

Three variables were indicative of male speech: interruptions, directives (i.e., telling the other what to do), and conjunctions/fillers to begin a sentence (e.g., *okay, and another thing, well let's see*). Five variables were found to be indicative of female speech: questions, justifiers (i.e., justification is given for a previous statement), intensive adverbs, personal pronouns, and adverbials beginning sentence. The results are consistent with previous research for the majority of variables that discriminated the speech of men and women.

Mulac and his colleagues then looked at the effect of the sex composition of the group to determine whether gender differences in language would be greater in single-sex or in mixed-sex groups. They found that men and women could be differentiated on the basis of language more accurately in single-sex than in mixed-sex groups. That finding suggests that language behavior is less sex role stereotypical in discussions with opposite-sex partners. Reasons why the speech style of men and women may converge in mixed-sex conversation are discussed in a later section.

The series of studies by Mulac and his colleagues suggests that only a few linguistic markers of speech may consistently discriminate between men and women. Out of 35 language variables studied, the majority were found either to predict gender differences in only a single study, or to predict one sex in one study but the opposite sex in another study.[141] The greater use of intensive adverbs and personal pronouns by women in at least two of the studies is consistent with the research cited previously, as is the greater use of directives by men. It is interesting to remember that subjects were unable to accurately guess the sex of the speakers in these studies, and only a combined weighting of speech characteristics by the computer was able to classify speakers accurately by gender. The majority of the variables that Mulac and his colleagues studied tended to be situationally dependent. Gender differences in language use are mediated by variables such as the role and sex of the participants and the setting and topic of the conversation. Let us focus briefly on such mediating variables.

The Setting and Topic of Discussion

As the studies by Mulac and his colleagues demonstrate, the linguistic features that distinguish the speech of men and women differ depending on whether samples are taken from in-class speeches in a communication studies class, from descriptions of landscape photographs, or from problem-solving discussions in dyads. Thus, speech features that discriminate male and female speech vary with the particular speech setting.

Several studies demonstrate that gender differences are diminished in public settings that call for informational or ritual use of language. Gender differences in speech were not found in utterances produced by people buying a train ticket[142] or in interactions at an urban municipal center information booth.[143] This is a situation where speech is more formal and informational.

William Soskin and Vera John also found that gender differences were reduced in social settings calling for informational language as opposed to private settings of greater intimacy.[144] Soskin and John offered a married couple a vacation without cost at a resort in exchange for having each partner carry a radio transmitter so that their conversation could be tracked by the experimenter from a half mile away. The greatest gender differences occurred when the couple was in private in intimate social contexts. Here the wife used more expressive messages. Gender differences were reduced in social settings that called for a relatively heavy reliance on informational language—objective statements about oneself and the world.

The frequency with which gender differences occur in speech depends on the nature of the discussion—whether participants are in agreement about a topic or whether they disagree with one another. Research by Angus McLachlan shows no gender differences in back channels to occur when participants disagree about a topic, but women use them more than men when they agree with their partners.[145] Speech features that have been associated with "women's language" such as tag questions, qualifiers, epistemic modals, minimal responses, and personal pronouns occur more frequently when talk is cooperative and personal. These speech features may have more to do with the content of the conversation than the gender of the speakers.

Status and Role

Because gender is related to status and power in this society, with males assuming positions of higher status and power than women, some researchers have argued that gender differences in language may be accounted for by differences in status and power. Persons with high power, for example, have been found to use less politeness than persons with low power.[145] Requests to superiors (e.g., orders, suggestions, questions) are more mitigated than requests to subordinates.[147] Group leaders and group members with more status use more directives than other group members.[148] Clients requesting information or aid at a police station use more female speech features than police personnel.[149] Individuals who have higher social status, who are well educated and professional, use "women's language" less frequently than those who are unemployed, are housewives, or hold subordinate lower status jobs.[150]

Studies have found gender differences in language to be mitigated when status was controlled. Cathryn Johnson found that gender differences were less salient in determining language use than differences in authority.[151] Regardless of gender, subordinates had higher rates than managers of back channels and qualifiers—speech features associated with women. When males and females were assigned to identical management roles, Samuel Moore and his colleagues found no gender differences in the use of tag questions, disclaimers, fillers, qualifiers, self-references, *we* references, or references to others.[152] When men and women were assigned to a more expert or more novice role in comparison to their partners, Lynda Sagrestano found power rather than gender to predict the use of direct influence tactics.[153]

Gender differences in speech cannot always be fully accounted for by status differences. While in many studies the language of low-status persons is marked by speech forms more commonly used by females, this is not consistently true and depends on the particular speech form under consideration and the gender of the speaker.

Nicola Woods found assent terms (*umm, yeah, yes, right*) to be used more frequently by male subordinates than by males in high-status positions, but status did not affect the use of back channels by females.[154] Helena Leet-Pellegrini found experts to use assent terms less than nonexperts except in the case of a female expert in interaction with a nonexpert male partner.[155]

When women attain positions of power or status over men, they have violated traditional sex role norms. Their persistence in the use of patterns of language characteristic of low-status roles may be due to the fact that women in positions of power are better received when they are friendlier and more group oriented.[156] When gender becomes salient in conversation, participants are more likely to display behavior consistent with gender role norms, which dictate that females should be more supportive and responsive and men more dominant and directive.

The same speech feature may be used to serve different functions when spoken by people who differ in power. Deborah Cameron and her colleagues examined interactions between speakers who differed in power.[157] Although tag questions in general have been associated with women and thus with a lack of power, facilitative tags were used by powerful speakers regardless of gender to get others to speak at length. They were not, however, used by powerless speakers. Modal tags, which express uncertainty or request information or reassurance, were more likely to be used by powerless than powerful speakers. Thus, the question is not simply whether the use of a particular speech form varies with status, but rather whether the use of a particular speech form to serve a specific function varies with status.

Sex Composition of the Group

The findings are not consistent as to whether gender differences in speech are greater in single-sex than in mixed-sex interactions. Results vary with the particular speech feature examined and from one study to another. There are some studies that show greater linguistic gender differences in single-sex than in mixed-sex groups.[158] Other studies find greater gender differences in mixed-sex than in single-sex encounters or find the results to depend on the particular gender of the speakers in combination with the speech feature under consideration.[159]

When members of two separate groups interact, such as men and women, their speech styles may converge and become more similar to one another, or they may diverge and remain distinct from one another. Speech accommodation theory accounts for the shifts we make in speech style during social interaction depending on our motives for social approval or distinctiveness.[160] Convergence in speech style is a strategy used to evoke social approval or to attain efficiency in communication. It can refer to attempts to move toward the other's actual speech style or toward a stereotyped belief about that person's speech style. Convergence may be mutual—when speakers match each other's styles— or nonmutual. Divergence is a strategy used to accentuate differences between self and others in order to maintain a separate social identity. Subordinates have been found to show convergence to the speech style of superiors.

Speech accommodation predicts that in mixed-sex groups men and women will accommodate and be mutually influenced by each other in order to attain social integration. But it also predicts that women, as lower status than men, would be likely to show more convergence than men. These predictions are not consistently borne out by research. To test speech accommodation theory carefully, however, we need to look more closely at the degree to which gender identity is salient in an encounter, as well as the interaction goals of the participants.

Summary, Explanations, and Conclusions

The literature on gender differences in language has been reviewed in numerous books and articles over the past 20 years. Early reviews included few empirical studies.[161] The field was comprised primarily of "speculations, untested hypotheses, and anecdotal observations."[162] A considerable interdisciplinary literature has now developed on gender and language, but controversy continues about whether gender differences in language are based more on stereotypes than on actual speech differences, and on how to interpret the data we have. Some researchers have concluded we lack evidence for consistent gender differences in speech—that stereotypes abound but research evidence is less clear—whereas others have concluded that there are reliable gender differences in speech.[163]

If we search the literature for evidence of significant gender differences in speech, we can find it in many studies using a variety of subjects, settings, methods, and measures. Women have been found to exceed men in expressions of positive politeness (making a person feel liked, respected, valued) through the use of more back-channel responses inserted in streams of speech, more facilitative tag questions, and the speech form *you know.* Women have been found to exceed men in expressions of negative politeness (not imposing upon or constraining a person) through the use of more imperative statements in question form and qualifications. Men, on the other hand, have been found to use more face-threatening speech forms like imperatives or directives. Research shows women use more intensifiers, personal pronouns, and the self-referent *I.*

When we take another perspective on these data and pay more careful attention to the methodological problems that plague many of the studies—the power, status, and roles of the participants and the contextual variability in the use of language forms—another understanding of the literature emerges. We see that gender differences in language are few in number. They do not appear consistently but are situationally variable depending on the setting, topic, role, status, and gender of the participants. Many studies report no gender differences. The magnitude of these gender differences has not been assessed. Researchers in the area of language have paid attention to statistical significance but not to effect sizes. Even if meta-analyses were carried out on language and gender, however, their results would be problematic given the methodological problems inherent in so many of the research studies.[164]

The Essentialist Position

Scholars have debated the existence and nature of "women's language" for over two decades. Those who take an essentialist position have argued that men and women differ in their use of language, that the differential socialization of males and females leads to the development of contrasting styles of communication that are persistent and can be seen across many contexts in daily life.[165] From an essentialist position, women are believed to acquire feminine traits (which include politeness, expressiveness, and an interpersonal orientation), and men to acquire masculine characteristics (which include assertiveness and directness)—traits that shape the way men and women express themselves in interaction. The essentialist position does not assume these gender differences are biologically based, but it does stress that gender differences represent traits or styles that are located within individual men and women.

The essentialist position has drawn on the argument put forth by Daniel Maltz and Ruth Borker that boys and girls in this society interact primarily in single-sex groups and thus grow up in two different sociolinguistic subcultures.[166] Boys and girls learn different assumptions about friendly conversation and learn to exaggerate differences with the opposite sex. Maltz and Borker suggest that the same speech features take on different meanings for males and females. For example, questions for women are vehicles for maintaining conversations; for men, they are merely requests for information. Women learn to acknowledge what is being said and to make a connection to it, whereas men learn no such speech convention.

Critique of the Essentialist Position and the Two-Cultures Approach

Within-Group Variability Essentialist models fail to address the diversity of experience and behavior found among members of the same sex. Through the lens of the essentialist model, members of the same sex are portrayed as a homogeneous group. The term "women's language" is used without regard to the fact that research on gender differences in language has focused primarily on white, middle-class subjects. Women who do not fit this pattern are rendered invisible. All women do not speak in a universal manner.

Nancy Henley and Cheris Kramarae point out that given the limitations to our research, we do not know whether the gender differences we have found are particular to members of a certain race, class, or ethnicity.[167] The communication patterns of African-Americans differ from those found for European-Americans,[168] but we know little about the interrelated influences of race and gender as they affect language use. Thus, what we take to be "women's language" may be only the language of white, middle-class women in some contexts.

Karen Tracy and Eric Eisenberg found that race had a significant effect on subjects' concerns about addressing the face needs of conversational partners.[169] They had 24 subjects (one third of whom were nonwhite) give criticism to a superior or a subordinate. Secondary analyses of the data revealed that whites were more concerned than nonwhites about face concerns (e.g., prefacing their criticism with initial positive statements about the other person's work and ability). Attention to the face needs of conversational partners is not universally characteristic of women's speech.

The "two-cultures" approach to the acquisition of different linguistic styles presumes that boys and girls interact primarily in single-sex contexts and thereby learn different linguistic styles. In a book on children's play in elementary schools, Barrie Thorne critiques the contrasting picture of the cultures of boys and girls and notes that "*a skew toward the most visible and dominant—and a silencing and marginalization of others—can be found in much of the research on gender relations among children and youth.*"[170] Thorne argues that many boys and girls are left out of the descriptions of the male and female cultures. We fail to notice the boys who are loners, shy, or afraid of sports, or the children who are not class privileged and white when we characterize male and female cultures. In addition, we have looked at average differences between groups of boys and girls and have tended to overlook the communalities between boys and girls and the variability within each of these groups. We have exaggerated the coherence of male and female cultures.

The two-cultures approach has minimized the importance of the fact that boys and girls have daily interactions with members of the opposite sex, with siblings, parents, relatives, friends in the neighborhood, or teachers at school. While people of different classes or racial groups may have little opportunity to interact with people outside their group, this is not true for males and females.[171] Although boys and girls tend to select same-sex peers as their primary companions, their daily interactions are by no means limited to people of the same sex.

Power and Status What the two-cultures approach has taken to be gender-related differences may be accounted for in many cases by power-related differences. For decades, feminist researchers have critiqued the essentialist approach by arguing that language reflects the hierarchical social structure of the larger society and helps to perpetuate it. The language differences we observe are produced in a context in which men hold positions of power over women. We cannot deal with women's language outside of a context of power relations; gender is not a matter of difference but a matter of dominance and power.[172] Women's language symbolizes their lack of power.

Language not only reflects gender divisions, it creates them as well. Barrie Thorne and Nancy Henley argue, "Language helps enact and transmit every type of inequality including that between the sexes; it is part of the 'micropolitical structure' that helps maintain the larger political-economic structure."[173] Pamela Fishman, in reviewing her findings on conversations between married couples, concluded that there is a division of labor in conversations, and that it is women who do the routine maintenance work.[174] She recognized women as the "shitworkers" of interaction.[175] We relegate to women the job of doing the support work necessary to help maintain and continue conversations; women do what needs to be done.

The power/status approach has been critiqued for its failure to explain gender differences between men and women who are status equals in single-sex encounters. Cheris Kramarae, though, argues that because gender places everyone in a hierarchical ordering, it shapes single-sex interaction as well. "Men are *men* because of their insistence upon the subordinate category *women*; much of their understanding of their behaviours and power (whether they are together in the corporate boardroom or on the street corner) comes from their constantly reiterated *otherness* from women."[176]

Once we take men's greater power and status into consideration, we can see women's greater use of politeness, tag questions, qualifications, and hedges as signs of indirectness and deference—behavior that is consistent with their less powerful social position. Functional analyses show that earlier characterizations of women's speech as more uncertain and "tentative" than men's were incorrect. Instead, there is evidence that women do more work in personal conversations than men to facilitate conversation, to show support, and to offer solidarity with the addressee. Can the greater emphasis by women on politeness and on supporting and facilitating the speech of conversational partners likewise be explained by their greater powerlessness?

In mixed-sex conversation, when women use facilitative tags, ask more questions, or insert more minimal responses in the course of speech, they may be using indirect forms of power—the only forms of power open to them—to keep conversations going about topics men are not eager to pursue. Women continue to use these speech forms more than men even when they are assigned to comparable positions of power, because women in positions of power violate sex role norms for behavior. The use of these language features may make women less threatening and more acceptable to men, and it may be the only way they can have their ideas considered. Men and women both use the strategies that will be most effective in meeting their interaction goals.

The Association of Speech Styles With Men and Womem　It is problematic to assign a gender to styles of speech. For example, Eleanor Maccoby suggests that males develop a constricting or restrictive style, whereas females develop an enabling style:[177]

> A restrictive style is one that tends to derail the interaction—to inhibit the partner or cause the partner to withdraw, thus shortening the inter-

action or bringing it to an end. . . . Enabling or facilitative styles are those, such as acknowledging another's comment or expressing agreement, that support whatever the partner is doing and tend to keep the interaction going.[178]

In a similar vein, David Bakan distinguished between two fundamental modalities—agency and communion.[179] Agency manifests itself in self-assertion, self-expansion, and separation, whereas communion manifests itself in connection and cooperation. He suggests that agency is more characteristic of men, communion of women.

The characterization of men as either agentic or restrictive is consistent with the data that men make less use of facilitative tags and more use of unilateral topic changes, minimal responses after a delay or after long streams of speech, and directives. The depiction of women as communal or enabling is likewise consistent with the data that women show greater use of politeness, facilitative tag questions, and back-channel responses. However, the characterization of women as enabling or communal and men as restrictive or agentic tends to polarize and exaggerate the differences in language reviewed in this chapter. Bakan, in fact, notes that agency and communion characterize both men and women.[180] Likewise, enabling and restrictive styles are used by both men and women depending on the situational context and their interaction goals.

The question we need to address is whether a particular style is more characteristic of people in certain roles or statuses, engaged in certain types of conversations, or trying to achieve particular goals than it is of different genders. Tag questions, qualifiers, epistemic modals, minimal responses, and personal pronouns occur more frequently when talk is cooperative and personal and are more rarely found in competitive conversations. They are more likely to occur in discussion portions of conversations than in narrative portions. Gender is but one determinant of linguistic behavior, and it plays a relatively small role in many situational contexts.

The Situational Context The essentialist position, by locating gender differences within individuals, cannot adequately account for the fact that the appearance of gender differences in speech is situationally variable, that men and women use the speech forms associated with the opposite sex in certain roles and contexts (e.g., male talk-show hosts, teachers, and interviewers use tag questions frequently), and that no gender differences in speech occur in some contexts. Gender differences in speech are less likely to be found in public settings that call for informational language and objective statements, and they are most likely to occur when talk is personal. The literature suggests that men and women do not have invariant styles across conversations. Research by Mulac and his colleagues, for example, shows a different set of linguistic variables to distinguish the speech of men and women from one setting to another.

Individuals may express themselves differently from one situational context to another depending on the degree to which gender is salient in interaction. There will be contexts in which other roles or norms override gender role norms. Women and men are most likely to use language differently when gender becomes salient in interaction—when there are concerns about self-presentation as masculine or feminine and about the consequences for violations of gender-related expectations.

There are few reliable gender differences in speech that occur across situational contexts. In fact, our perceptions about gender differences in speech are at odds with actual speech differences; stereotypes of speech depict men and women as more distinct in their language use than they actually are.[181] These stereotypes about the speech of men and women are discussed in chapter 7.

Methodological Problems

Earlier conclusions about gender differences in language use have been marred by faulty methodology, incorrect assumptions about the meaning of the language features studied, and failure to take situational context into account. We cannot assume a priori that a speech feature holds a single meaning; we need to consider the functional use of a speech form in context.

Research demonstrates that Lakoff was incorrect in her assumption that tag questions and qualifiers express tentativeness and uncertainty, and that the language of women is more tentative than that of men. When tag questions and forms like *I think* and *you know* are used to express uncertainty, men use them more frequently to serve this function than women. Women more frequently use these speech forms to express certainty, to facilitate speech, or to soften the force of a proposition. They use language forms like *I think* and *you know* more often in formal contexts to add weight and authority to what they are saying. This may again be related to issues of power—to expectations of men's greater performance competency and the need by women to establish their competency.

Future Directions for Research

Debate began over the existence and nature of gender differences in language use in the 1970s and continues today. Over the years, an increasing body of research evidence has accumulated, but the same evidence yields many truths and has been used to support opposing arguments. It is likely that further comparative studies of the speech of men and women will not settle the issue. Although the argument has been made in this chapter that there is no such essentialist phenomenon as "women's language," the same data could also be used to support the case for gender differences in speech.

The situational variability of language suggests that our understanding of gender and language will not be furthered by continued studies using sex as the independent variable. We must build contextual variables into those analyses.[182] We must study interaction contexts rather than the relative use of language features independent of social situations. Are there particular linguistic features that are used in specific settings, by people in certain roles, in discussions of specific topics or in discussions governed by certain norms? Gender cannot be understood apart from these contextual variables.

By focusing our research on comparative studies of the speech of men and women, we employ a methodological approach that is set up to identify gender differences. The data from these studies can easily be mistaken to suggest that gender is the cause of any differences we find.[183] By studying the use of speech of people in different roles and interaction contexts, by contrast, we employ a methodological approach that locates gender within the interaction itself—an approach that is set up to better illustrate that in some roles and contexts people display masculine behavior, in other contexts, feminine behavior. What we take to be masculine and feminine behavior is a way of describing what people do in particular roles and interaction contexts that have become linked with gender.

Linguistic variables do not operate independently, but rather in combination. The combinations formed by many researchers, however, have not been meaningful. They have been constructed by adding together a variety of speech forms taken to be indicative of female speech under the mistaken assumption that these speech forms serve a single function. It would be more meaningful to investigate a particular communicative strategy by adding together only those instances of linguistic forms that expressed that particular strategy. For example, we might take the facilitation of talk to be the linguistic strategy and identify those speech features that are used to facilitate speech.

Researchers now must focus on the function of speech forms— the goals speakers are trying to achieve through the use of a variety of speech forms. Because functional analyses run the risk of reflecting the biases of the researchers, though, researchers might consider including the perspective of the speakers in addition to the observers of the interaction when they make assessments.

6

The Content of Conversation

In the previous four chapters I have explored gender differences in the communication styles of men and women, focusing on various dimensions of the form or manner in which men and women communicate. I shift now from a focus on the interaction process to a focus on interaction content, to a consideration of what men and women choose to talk about in conversation.

Folk wisdom has denigrated women's talk as "idle chatter," "gabbing," and "gossip." When Cheris Kramer examined the beliefs held by high school and college students about the speech of males and females, she found students were more likely to associate gossip, talk about trivial topics, and gibberish with female than with male speakers.[1] The study of gender differences in conversation content suffered for many years from the tendency to devalue what was considered to be female talk. However, in recent years, feminist scholars have recognized female talk as different from men's talk and reconceptualized it on its own terms.[2]

Deborah Jones, for example, suggested that women's "gossip" is a language of intimacy, that it provides emotional sustenance. "Gossip is a staple of women's lives, and the study of gossip is the study of women's concerns and values, a key to the female subculture."[3] What, then, is women's talk and to what extent does it differ from the talk of men?

Overall Gender Differences in Conversation Content

Before embarking on an examination of gender differences in conversation content, I should note that research studies have found talk to be more important to women's relationships than to men's.[4] Mayta Caldwell and Anne Peplau asked 98 undergraduates to choose whether they would rather do an activity or just talk to their same-sex best friends.[5] Twice as many men as women preferred to do an activity; three times as many women as men preferred to talk. When asked to name the three most important factors that contributed to forming the basis for a friendship relationship, more women than men mentioned talk.[6]

Leslie Baxter and William Wilmot had 58 students keep diary records monitoring day-to-day encounters in two relationships — one same-sex relationship and one opposite-sex relationship.[7] They then examined the proportion of encounters that involved "talk for talk's sake" as opposed to some social activity. Encounters just to talk were more frequent for females than for males (75% versus 64%). Elizabeth Douvan and Joseph Adelson, in a large-scale survey of adolescents, found talk to be more central to the friendships of girls and shared activity to be more central to the friendships of boys.[8]

Adelaide Haas and Mark Sherman asked a sample of 276 adults to report on the importance of same-sex conversation. They found more women than men felt their same-sex conversations to be important (38.4% versus 24.4%) or necessary (24.4% versus 13.3%).[9] Women pointed to empathy and depth as what they especially valued. In a study of female friendship, Fern Johnson and I found talk to be the most central element of the friendship.[10] Talk provided mutual support and enhancement of self-worth and contributed to personal growth and self-discovery.

Not only has talk been found to be more important to women's relationships than to men's, but the talk of women has been found in many studies to be more personal than the talk of men.[11] Definitions of what constitutes personal talk vary from one study to another, but they include disclosure about one's self, feelings, personal relationships, personal and family problems, doubts, and fears. The finding that females talk more personally than males comes from studies using a wide variety of methodologies: laboratory groups of strangers and friends,[12] interview studies of close friendship,[13] questionnaire self-reports of friendship and other relationships,[14] unobtrusive observation of conversations in public places,[15] and diary records of interaction.[16]

Meta-analytic Findings

Although many studies show women to talk more personally than men and women to be more highly self-disclosing, Kathryn Dindia and Mike Allen, in a meta-analysis of self-disclosure covering 205 published studies and 51 dissertations and a total of 23,702 subjects, conclude, "Whether the magnitude of sex differences in self-disclosure is theoretically meaningful and practically important is debatable. . . . It's time to stop perpetuating the myth that there are large differences in men's and women's self-disclosure."[17] Dindia and Allen found women to be more self-disclosing than men overall, but they found the effect size to be small ($d = .18$).

How do we reconcile the many research findings that talk is more important to women's relationships and more personal in women's relationships with the meta-analytic findings that show gender differences in self-disclosure to be quite small in magnitude? First, although statistically significant differences are found in the importance of talk, or in conversation content, we must also address the magnitude of the differences. For example, while Baxter and Wilmot found women more often get together to talk for talk's sake, women did this in 75% of their encounters, men in 64% of their encounters. In other words, we must be cautious not to polarize the difference. Men quite often got together with others to talk and not to do social activities. Likewise, to say that women speak more personally than men cannot be taken to imply that men do not talk personally; they may do so but to a lesser degree than women do.

There are a variety of additional factors that account for the discrepancy between the results of the meta-analysis and the many findings that the conversations of women are more personal in content. While the meta-analysis is extremely comprehensive, the majority of studies covered by it use the Jourard Self-Disclosure Questionnaire (JSDQ), the most widely used instrument to assess self-disclosure. Many studies that report the talk of women to be more personal than that of men have used other instruments or methodologies, and they are not all included in the meta-analysis. Thus, we must look in more detail at the JSDQ to account for the meta-analytic findings that there are no meaningful gender differences in self-disclosure.

The Jourard Self-Disclosure Questionnaire

In 1958 Sidney Jourard and Paul Lasakow published a questionnaire for measuring both the amount and content of self-disclosure

made by individuals to a variety of other persons.[18] The questionnaire contained 60 items covering six general categories of information about aspects of the self: attitudes and opinions, tastes and interests, work (or studies), personality, money, and body. Three hundred
subjects were asked to report the extent to which they had talked
about each item with mother, father, a male friend, a female friend,
and a spouse. Jourard and Lasakow found that total self-disclosure
was higher for females than it was for males, and they replicated this
result on another sample.[19] Jourard attributed this gender difference
to the male role that requires men to be "objective, striving, achiev-
ing, unsentimental, and emotionally unexpressive."[20]

Numerous reviews of the self-disclosure literature have been carried out over the years.[21] All have found the relationship between
gender and self-disclosure to be more complicated than it was originally portrayed by Jourard and his colleagues. Many studies have
found women to be more self-disclosing than men, but some have
found no gender differences. The inconsistent findings have been
attributed to a variety of mediating variables.[22] The extent to which
men and women differ in self-disclosure is affected by the topic of
disclosure, the sex of the person to whom one discloses, the relationship between the speakers, and the characteristics of the disclosing person. Charles Hill and Donald Stull suggest:

> Self-disclosure is far more complex than anyone realized when this
> research was begun. The original prediction that traditional male-role
> expectations inhibit men's disclosure is too simple because it does not
> take into account the many situational factors that affect disclosure. We
> now know what many of these factors are, but we still cannot specify
> how these factors interact with one another and with gender. Future
> studies need to incorporate these situational factors and test hypotheses
> about interactions among them.[23]

Let us look more carefully at these mediating factors that affect gender differences in self-disclosure.

Situational Factors Affecting Self-disclosure

Topic of Self-disclosure

The meta-analysis by Dindia and Allen summarizes gender differences in self-disclosure based on overall scores on a self-disclosure
scale. It does not look at the extent to which gender differences may
be mediated by the topic of self-disclosure. Items on the Jourard

Self-Disclosure Questionnaire (JSDQ) cover six topic areas. Some items involve intimate information about the self (e.g., facts about a person's present sex life, things one feels ashamed and guilty about, feelings about personal shortcomings), whereas other items are nonintimate (e.g., favorite foods, tastes in clothing, likes and dislikes in music). Total self-disclosure scores are summaries across the entire range of topics and mask information about whether men and women differ in disclosure about intimate topics. A high self-disclosure score can be produced by frequent self-disclosure about all nonintimate topics.

In a study of self-disclosure patterns in 167 women students to a male friend, female friend, and romantic partner using the JSDQ, Donna Sollie and Judith Fischer found that the greatest self-disclosure occurred on topics with the lowest intimacy, and the least disclosure occurred on topics of high intimacy. They found 15% of the variance in self-disclosure scores were accounted for by the intimacy level of the topic.

Research shows females to be more disclosing than males on intimate topics, but it shows no gender differences in self-disclosure about nonintimate concerns. Brian Morgan gave 64 subjects a 25-item version of the JSDQ and scaled the items for intimacy.[24] Subjects rated self-disclosure to mother, father, best male friend, and best female friend. Males and females were found to be equally disclosing when all items were combined into a single score and to be equally disclosing on low-intimacy topics. But males were found to be less disclosing than females on high-intimacy topics. Similarly, A. George Gitter and Harvey Black gave 260 subjects the JSDQ and had them rate a best friend and slight acquaintance.[25] No gender differences were found on the nonintimate topics, but females were found to disclose more information on the high-intimacy topics.

In tandem with this result, researchers using methodologies other than the JSDQ have found females to be more disclosing than males about intimate concerns, but equally disclosing about nonintimate concerns. The results are similar whether findings come from laboratory conversations involving self-disclosure to strangers[26] or from interviews of adults about self-disclosure to same-sex friends and spouses.[27] Some researchers have found no gender differences in intimate self-disclosure.[28]

The inconsistency in results may be accounted for by the fact that each study has included a different set of topics, a different definition of high-intimacy topics, and a different set of persons to whom the self-disclosure is made. Thus, findings are not directly comparable from study to study. However, while some studies find no gender differences in intimate self-disclosure, none find men to be more disclosing of intimate information about the self than women.

Relationship Between the Speakers

Gender differences in self-disclosure may depend on the relationship between the speaker and his or her conversational partner—usually referred to as the "target" of disclosure. If we combine assessments of self-disclosure to strangers, acquaintances, and intimates into a single self-disclosure index, we mask the relationship between the speaker and the target. There may be differences in the degree to which males and females will be disclosing to strangers, close friends, or spouses.

In the initial stages of relationships there is greater breadth of disclosure across many topics, but as relationships develop and closeness increases, the depth or intimacy of topics shared increases while the breadth decreases.[29] Donna Sollie and Judith Fischer found female subjects were most highly self-disclosing to romantic partners, were less disclosing to female friends, and were least disclosing to male friends. Overall, the relationship to the target person was an important predictor of self-disclosure, accounting for 32% of the variance in self-disclosure scores.[30] The data suggest that greater self-disclosure occurs in relationships with a greater depth of involvement.

We might expect men and women to be equally disclosing in less intimate relationships where there is greater breadth of disclosure, and women to be more disclosing than men at later stages of relationships when the depth and intimacy of topics increases. The data on self-disclosure to strangers is difficult to assess because males report levels of self-disclosure to strangers equal to females, but observations of self-disclosure to strangers show females to disclose more than males.[31]

When we examine the literature on the close friendships of men and women—that is, relationships that are more intimate—there is consistent evidence that women are more disclosing of personal information than men to same-sex friends. The literature on adolescent same-sex close friendship shows females to be more self-disclosing about personal topics than males. Caldwell and Peplau had college students list the three topics they typically discussed with best friends.[32] Women listed personal topics twice as often as men. Other questionnaire studies of college students report similar results.[33] In an interview study of 14- to 16-year-olds, Douvan and Adelson found that boys' friendships do not attain the depth of intimacy that girls' friendships do.[34]

It is important to note that these gender differences do not mean that adolescent males do not have intimate conversations with their close friends, but merely that these types of conversations occur more frequently between female friends. Fern Johnson and I found that nearly half the males in our college sample talked frequently with their best friends about doubts and fears (46%), personal problems (46%), and intimate relationships (51%).[35] Because these topics were talked about frequently by over 75% of the females with their best friends, the differences were statistically significant, but they should not be taken to mean that some males do not frequently share intimacies with their best friends.

In a compilation of data from 8 studies of over 1,000 adolescents ages 12 to 19, James Youniss and Jacqueline Smollar found that 40% of male friendships involved mutual intimacy and 33% involved a lack of intimacy altogether.[36] These latter male friendships were characterized by nonunderstanding, absence of intimacy, and guardedness or defensiveness; males were unable to report their true feelings and described themselves as dishonest or insensitive with their close same-sex friends. Note, though, that this pattern characterizes only a third of the males in their sample and must not be taken as descriptive of the relationships of men in general.

The literature on same-sex adult friendship reveals similar findings. Women disclose more about personal matters than men, but they disclose equal amounts on more topical matters. In an interview study of 100 adults ages 18 to 35, Lynne Davidson and Lucile Duberman found no gender differences in conversations about topical content (i.e., politics, movies, current events), but women reported having more personal conversations involving feelings about themselves and their private lives and about the friendship relationship.[37] In an interview study of 120 adults ages 25 to 50, Jeanne Tschann found no gender differences in less intimate disclosure, but she did find women to disclose more on more intimate topics and problems.[38]

In a questionnaire study of 136 adults with an average age of 50, Fern Johnson and I found no gender differences in talk about nonintimate topics, but we did find that women spoke more frequently about personal problems, doubts and fears, family problems, and intimate relationships.[39] It is not that men never discussed these more personal topics, but rather that they discussed them less frequently than women did. Twenty-six percent of the men reported that they frequently discuss family problems with their close friends. Although this contrasts with reports by women (47% of women discussed family problems frequently), it is interesting to note that family problems were not a frequent topic of conversation by the majority of close friends of either sex. To take another example, talk about one's intimate relationships were a frequent topic of discussion for 8% of the men versus 26% of the women. Again, three quarters of the adults did not discuss their intimate relationships frequently. In fact, no single intimate topic was talked about frequently by even half of the women.

When we look at meta-analytic findings on self-disclosure that are based on measures combining self-disclosure scores across many targets, both intimate and nonintimate, and across many topics, both intimate and nonintimate, we find gender differences to be quite small. The effect size most likely underestimates the extent of gender differences that are found on intimate topics discussed between best friends of the same sex.

Sex of Target

According to the literature on close same-sex friendship discussed previously, women talk more frequently than men about personal and intimate matters. Because these findings are based on single-sex interactions, it is possible to conclude that the sex of the conversational partner contributes to the overall finding. In other words, women may disclose more to their best same-sex friends because their best friends are female; men may disclose less because their best friends are male. Comparisons need to be made of the self-disclosure by men to male and female targets, and by women to male and female targets.

Men have been found to talk at greater length to women than to men when talk is informal[40] and to be more self-disclosing to women than they are to other men.[41] For example, I conducted a study of 2 all-male, 2 all-female, and 2 mixed-groups of strangers.[42] The groups met for five 1 1/2-hour sessions with the task of getting to know each other. Five minutes of the discussions were transcribed every half hour, and a computer-aided content analysis was carried out on the conversation. Overall, women in all-female groups talked more about themselves, their feelings, their homes and families, and their personal relationships with friends and lovers than men did in all-male groups. Males in all-male groups were more concerned about where they stood in relation to each other, and they engaged more in dramatizing and storytelling. However, in mixed-sex groups the male themes of aggression and competition gave way to more personal talk by males about themselves and their feelings.

Similar findings have been reported by other researchers in studies of strangers and of friends using a variety of methodologies, interviews, laboratory interaction, and daily recording of interactions. In a study of 60 college males, Mirra Komarovsky found that males disclosed more to female than male friends because of competition with male friends.[43] These men saw confiding in a male friend as childish and contrary to their need to be reassuring and strong.

Valarian Derlega and her colleagues paired 96 subjects with a stranger or a close friend of the same sex or the opposite sex.[44] They were given a list of nine topics—three masculine, three feminine, and three neutral—and asked to select three to write about to their partner. Males showed a greater willingness to write about feminine content (e.g., "when you feel childlike," "how sensitive you are to what others think of your appearance"[45]) with female partners than with male partners, and they showed less preference for sharing masculine content with female friends than male friends. In a follow-up study, Derlega and her colleagues found males made more intimate self-disclosures in written self-descriptions for a partner who was female than one who was male.[46]

When subjects are asked to keep daily records of interaction, men are found to share more personal information with females than with males. Harry Reis and his colleagues had 54 subjects keep interaction records for 4 days, completing records for every interaction lasting longer than 10 minutes.[47] Males reported their interactions with females to be more intimate than their interaction with males.

Susan Shimanoff had college students tape their conversations for a full day.[48] The sample included 13 same-sex dyads and 13 opposite-sex dyads. Males used more affect words (references to positive and negative internal states like love, happiness, and sadness) when speaking to females than to males.

Not all studies, however, have found males to be more self-disclosing to females than they are to males.[49] Helen Hacker, in an interview study of friendship pairs, found no difference in self-disclosure for men to male and female friends.[50]

Overall, the studies show a tendency for males to be more self-disclosing to female than to male partners, although we have no assessments of the size of this effect. Are women likewise more self-disclosing to female than to male partners? The data for women are quite contradictory from one study to another. Some studies have found little effect of the sex of the target for women.[51] When self-disclosure to romantic male partners is compared to disclosure to female friends, women are found in some studies to be more disclosing to males: women are found to be more disclosing to romantic male partners,[52] to spouses,[53] and to opposite-sex romantic friends[54] than they are to same-sex best friends. Some women, however, report that they share more intimacies with close female friends than they do with their husbands.[55]

Do men and women disclose equally to each other in mixed-sex interaction? The meta-analysis by Dindia and Allen reveals that females disclosed slightly more in mixed-sex interaction to men than men did to women, with an extremely small effect size ($d = .08$). It is important to note that these findings represent summaries of studies using a range of targets from strangers to intimates and are assessments of overall self-disclosure rather than intimate self-disclosure. Thus, the overall results would not be expected to match those findings based only on intimate self-disclosure in intimate relationships.

Gloria Mulcahy found that male and female high school students were equally self-disclosing to opposite-sex friends.[56] While some studies of married couples have found wives are more disclosing than their husbands,[57] others have found no differences in self-disclosure between husbands and wives.[58] Helen Hacker interviewed 44 female, 26 male, and 56 cross-sex pairs of friends about their relationships.[59] She found that in cross-sex pairs there were no gender differences in levels of self-disclosure.

In sum, the sex of the target mediates gender differences in self-disclosure. Overall, the highest levels of self-disclosure are found between females, the lowest level between males, and opposite-sex self-disclosure falls in between.[60] The meta-analysis by Dindia and Allen shows gender differences to be greater in single-sex ($d = .31$) than in mixed-sex interaction ($d = .08$), but the effect size is extremely small for mixed-sex interaction. Males are more highly self-disclosing to females than they are to other men.

Some have explained these results on the basis of reciprocity.[61] Reciprocity occurs when the self-disclosure of one partner influences the other to match his or her level of disclosure. If women disclose more than men, men and women will reach an intermediate level of disclosure in mixed-sex interaction, each matching the other's level of disclosure. Women's greater self-disclosure will influence men to increase their level of self-disclosure over levels they will express with other males.

Characteristics of the Disclosing Person Affecting Self-disclosure

The literature reviewed previously suggests that situational factors affect gender differences in self-disclosure (specifically, the topic of self-disclosure, the relationship between the speakers, and the sex of the target). While some researchers have focused on the situational context, others have tried to determine whether there are characteristics of the disclosing person that affect self-disclosure by men and women.

Some researchers hold that a person's sex role orientation should be a good predictor of self-disclosure. Sex role orientation is an assessment of the degree to which people perceive themselves to possess traits and characteristics considered to be stereotypically masculine or feminine. In this construction, masculinity and femininity are reflected by two distinct orientations toward interaction— one active-instrumental, the other nurturant-expressive. Characteristics like being active, assertive, controlling, and instrumental are associated with masculinity, whereas characteristics like being expressive, understanding, and emotionally responsive are associated with femininity.

Researchers have determined scores on masculinity and femininity by using the Bem Sex Role Inventory (BSRI) and then combined the scores to create four types of individuals.[62] Masculine sex-typed individuals score high on masculinity and low on femininity, feminine sex-typed individuals score high on femininity and low on masculinity, and androgynous individuals score high on both masculinity and femininity.[63] Undifferentiated individuals score low on both masculinity and femininity. This approach to the study of gender as a personality variable became quite popular for a decade beginning in the mid-1970s. Critics have since raised questions not only about measurement issues, but also about the very assumption behind these measures that masculinity and femininity are stable internal dispositional qualities that may be predictive of behavior from situation to situation. This approach continued to be widely used even after it was abandoned by its original proponents, Sandra Bem and Janet Spence.[64]

Self-disclosure requires both masculine and feminine characteristics; it may require a willingness to take risks and to be assertive, as well as a willingness to be expressive and intimate.[65] Many studies using the BSRI have found androgynous men and/or women to be more highly self-disclosing than those who are sex-typed or undifferentiated,[66] but contradictory findings have been reported as well.[67] A study by Donna Sollie and Judith Fischer found significant differences between androgynous and sex-typed women on self-disclosure, but they found that sex role orientation accounted for less than 1% of the variance in self-disclosure scores. Thus, knowlege of a person's sex role orientation is of little use in predicting self-disclosure scores, whereas situational factors have much more predictive utility. As mentioned earlier, knowledge of the target of self-disclosure accounted for 32% of the variance in that study.[68]

Some researchers have not used the four fold classification of subjects available from the Bem Sex Role Inventory but have simply used the masculinity and femininity scores to predict self-disclosure. Joseph Stokes and his colleagues found masculinity to be predictive of high disclosure to strangers and acquaintances, whereas high scores on both masculinity and femininity were necessary to predict high disclosure to intimates.[69] However, Stokes and his colleagues found that knowledge of a person's sex role orientation was no more useful in predicting self-disclosure scores to strangers and acquaintances than knowledge of their gender alone, and that knowledge of either gender or sex role orientation had little utility in predicting self-disclosure. In terms of self-disclosure to intimates, sex role orientation had slightly better predictive utility than gender: subject gender accounted for 1% of the variance, whereas knowledge of subjects' gender and BSRI scores accounted for 7.4% of the variance.

Research suggests that masculinity and/or femininity may be related to self-disclosure, but they have limited predictive power. In a study of strangers, Barbara Winstead and her colleagues found that masculinity accounted for 11% of the variance in disclosure intimacy for males to males, but neither masculinity, femininity, nor their combination accounted for a significant amount of variance in self-disclosure for females or males with female partners.[70] In studies of self-disclosure in intimate relationships, researchers found that femininity but not masculinity was predictive of self-disclosure.[71]

These studies suggest that when individuals do not know each other well, masculine assertiveness may make it easier to disclose, whereas in more intimate relationships between friends and family members, these masculine traits play a less important role and feminine expressiveness is more important. However, masculinity and femininity used singly or in combination as predictors of behavior account for only 1% to 11% of the variance in self-disclosure.

In summary, the studies of sex role orientation suggest that while conceptually compelling, sex role orientation has not been found to be a major factor in accounting for gender differences in self-disclosure. The percentage of variance explained by gender role orientation is far less than that explained by other mediating variables such as conversation content or relationship to the target. The possession of masculine traits may facilitate disclosure to strangers and acquaintances, whereas the possession of female traits may facilitate disclosure to intimates, but overall masculinity, femininity, or their combination as measured by the BSRI explain very little of the variance in self-disclosure.

Assessment and Explanation of the Findings

Many studies find women talk more personally and are more self-disclosing than men, but gender differences in conversation content are affected by the situational context in which the conversation occurs. Women are more disclosing about intimate topics, but there are no gender differences in self-disclosure about less intimate concerns. Men are less disclosing than women in same-sex relationships, but men are much more highly self-disclosing to women than they are to men.

The greatest gender differences in self-disclosure are found in intimate self-disclosure to same-sex friends. The talk of women friends is frequently more personal than the talk of male friends. Women share more about their feelings about themselves, their intimate relationships, and their doubts and fears with their close female friends than the men do with their close male friends. It is important to note, however, that when men and women were asked to come to the laboratory and have an intimate conversation with their same-sex best friend—to discuss something important and to reveal thoughts, feelings, and emotions—Harry Reis and his colleagues found no gender differences in self-disclosure.[72] Nor was there any difference in how meaningful men and women felt these conversations to be. Thus, males are capable of sharing intimately and can be induced to do so when conditions are created that make it desirable to do so. Some men share intimately with wives or intimates and with same-sex friends; some do not.

We must be careful not to polarize the differences that have been found between the talk of males and females by portraying men as universally inexpressive and women as expressive. Many men and women are equally disclosing to same-sex best friends.[73] Men have been found to talk more frequently than women about matters peripheral to the self such as sports, sports figures, hobbies and shared activities, and entertainment-oriented events.[74] These data should not be taken to mean that men primarily talk about sports. In the study Fern Johnson and I conducted on conversation between adult same-sex close friends, 45% of males compared to 18% of females talked about sports frequently.[75] Thus, sports was a frequent topic of conversation for less than half of the males. Talk about sports is characteristic of only some males. Forty-one percent of the women never talked about sports, whereas only 14% of the men never talked about sports. Thus, 59% of the women discussed sports with their best friend, although infrequently. Sports is a topic of conversation that is more likely to come up between males and to come up frequently between some male friends.

Men are less self-disclosing to other men than they are to women. One explanation that has been put forth to account for this phenomenon is reciprocity; males may be influenced to match the greater level of self-disclosure of their female partners. Another explanation comes from the literature on gender differences in language. In chapter 5 we saw that females use tag questions, back-channel responses, and questions to facilitate interaction in personal conversations. Thus, females may help facilitate self-disclosure in conversations with men by showing interest, attentiveness, and encouragement. In conversations between men such listener support may not be as forthcoming. A third explanation comes from the literature on dominance and hierarchy discussed in chapter 3. Men place greater emphasis on displays of dominance and hierarchy in interaction with men than with women. The more competitive nature of male interactions may make the expression of personal vulnerabilites more difficult for some men in their relationships with other men. It is not that men are inexpressive and nondisclosing, but rather that normative expectations discourage men from being self-disclosing with other men.

Personality

Jourard found men to be less disclosing than women and attributed his findings to the male role in this society, which requires men to be objective and emotionally unexpressive. Men develop personalities that suit them for the roles they must fill in society. Jourard's explanation is not sufficient to account for the individual and situational variabilility that we find in self-disclosure, and for the small magnitude of the gender differences in self-disclosure in some contexts.

The findings for self-disclosure reveal that we should not conceptualize it as a personality trait.[76] Men are more self-disclosing to women, for example, than they are to men. We need an explanation of self-disclosure that can account for differences in levels of self-disclosure depending on the relationship to the target (strangers, acquaintances, intimates), the gender of the target, and the intimacy of the content of disclosure.

Social Roles

Conversation content and the importance of talk is shaped by the larger social context—by the nature of sex role differentiation and male-female relations within society. Gender differences in conversation content have been attributed to the sexual division of labor in society and the different roles assigned to men and women. We would expect that the stronger the sexual division of labor and sex segregation in a society, the greater the differences in the conversation content of men and women. Susan Harding, for example, studied a small agricultural village in northeastern Spain where men's work centered in the fields, women's work in the home.[77] Women's talk concerned people and their personal lives, family, health, family welfare, and the needs and feelings of others. Men kept more private and talked about the land, crops, weather, prices, wages, inheritance, work animals, and machinery. On the side they also discussed hunting, playing cards, and sports. The study provides a good example of the ways in which differences in the conversation content of men and women reflect the extent to which they move in separate spheres.

We might expect gender differences in self-disclosure, then, to be affected by social class. Where roles are more clearly differentiated by sex, as they are in the working class, gender differences in conversation content should be greater in magnitude.[78] Although the majority of the literature on conversation content has not looked at social class, Helen Hacker categorized her subjects as working class, lower-middle class, or upper-middle class. In same-sex friendships she found the highest self-disclosure rates in working-class women and the lowest self-disclosure rates in working-class men.[79] Thus, gender differences in self-disclosure were more pronounced among working-class individuals than among lower-middle- and upper-middle-class individuals.

To what extent is the talk of males and females attributable to differences in the social roles and situations in which men and women find themselves rather than to their gender? Deborah Jones points out that talk between women takes place in the private and personal domain. Women get together more frequently with friends just to talk, whereas males prefer activities.[80] Jones suggests:

> Women are an occupational group of a special kind, and our occupation and training as wives, girlfriends and mothers are reflected in the topics of gossip. We are expected to be knowledgeable in our field: housework (cooking, cleaning, sewing, interior decoration, etc.); childrearing; the wifely role (sexuality, appearance, psychological expertise).[81]

Housetalk for women can be taken to be equivalent to shoptalk for men. It is an exchange of information and resources by women connected to their unpaid occupation as homemakers. Women in paid occupations engage in shoptalk just as men do. One might expect the talk of men to resemble more closely the talk of women if men were the homemakers and the primary caretakers of young children. Women talk more about family matters because it is women who have been assigned primary responsibility for family affairs. Their talk reflects their place in society.

7

Gender Stereotypes and the Perception and Evaluation of Participants in Interaction

Many psychologists have argued that the locus of gender differences is in the eye of the beholder.[1] We immediately recognize each participant in conversational interaction as a male or a female. To the extent that we hold stereotyped beliefs about men and women, these beliefs can lead us to form different expectations about what male and female participants are like and how they will behave. In this chapter I examine the nature of gender stereotypes and their influence on our perception, evaluation, and response toward participants in interaction. I look at the extent to which we bend our perceptions in the direction of sex role stereotypes and perceive gender differences that may not even be present. I also examine the way gender stereotypes cause us to evaluate males and females differently or to respond to them differently, even when their behavior is identical.

To begin, we need to know what is meant by a stereotype. A stereotype is a set of beliefs about the characteristics presumed to be typical of members of a group. Stereotypes distinguish one group from another—for example, men from women, or blacks from whites. Stereotypes can be positive or negative, accurate or inaccurate. To the extent that they are accurate, stereotypes provide information that is useful in forming expectations to help guide behavior. To the extent that they are overgeneralizations, exaggerations, or inaccurate depictions of group members, stereotypes can lead to prejudiced perceptions, evaluations, and responses to individuals.

Stereotypes of the Personality Traits and Interaction Styles of Men and Women

Stereotypes are held by individuals, and thus stereotyped beliefs about men and women vary from one individual to another. To what degree is there broad general agreement across individuals about the characteristics presumed to be typical of men and women? There are no clear criteria for determining "general agreement." We could say there is general agreement about masculinity and femininity if 60% of the people questionned agree, or if 75% agree, or if 90% agree. Inge Broverman and her colleagues took a 75% level of agreement as their criterion to identify gender stereotypes, and they demonstrated that across groups varying in age, educational level, marital status, and religion there is a broad consensus about the differing personality traits considered to be characteristic of males and females.[2]

Men are described by a cluster of instrumental traits: as leaders, as dominant, aggressive, independent, objective, and competitive. Women are described by a cluster of affective traits: as emotional, subjective, tactful, aware of the feelings of others, and as having their feelings easily hurt. In David Bakan's terminology, masculinity is associated with agency or self-assertion, femininity with communion or concern with others.[3] Although there is a broad consensus about the characteristics of masculinity and femininity, it is important to remember that particular definitions of manhood or womanhood varied from one individual to another.

People hold stereotypes about men and women as communicators. When Cheris Kramer had high school students rate the speech characteristics of male and female speakers, she found gender differences on 36 of 51 speech characteristics.[4] Male speakers were believed to be loud, dominating, forceful, authoritarian, aggressive, straight to the point, blunt, militant, to show anger rather than conceal it, and to use slang and swears. Female speakers were believed to be gentle, friendly, open and self-revealing, enthusiastic, emotional, and polite, to talk a lot, to use many details, and to show concern for the listener. Their speech was seen as gossip—talk about trivial topics and gibberish.

Michael Burgoon and his colleagues had students respond to whether they would expect a male or female to be most likely to use 17 different persuasive strategies.[5] Two strategies that were verbally aggressive were seen almost unanimously to be used by males: threat and aversive stimulation. Less verbally aggressive strategies like promise, positive moral appeal, or altruism were perceived almost unanimously to be strategies used by females.

Paula Johnson had students rate the likelihood an influencer using different types of power was a male or a female.[6] More indirect influence strategies were associated with women (e.g., personal reward and sexuality); more direct strategies with men (e.g., coercion, power based on expertise, information, and legitimacy).

Studies of college students reveal that there are widely held beliefs about the speech features used by men and women. When students were asked to rate sentences containing either strong assertions, modified assertions, or tag questions for degree of likelihood that they came from a male or a female speaker, David and Robert Siegler found that tag questions are more often attributed to women and strong assertions to men.[7] Katherine Hawkins assessed expectations about interruptions and found that respondents expected males but not females to interrupt.[8] James Orcutt and Lynn Harvey presented several groups of undergraduates with a description of the Zimmerman and West[9] study of interruptions in mixed-sex groups and asked them to guess the results.[10] Regardless of their gender, more students believed males would interrupt females than the reverse (although the majority did not hold this belief), and more students thought males would interrupt females than that there would be equality in interruptions in mixed-sex dyads.[11] Taken together, these studies provide evidence for normative expectations about gender differences in interaction and speech.

Stereotypes about language begin in childhood. Carole Edelsky presented a list of sentences including 12 language variables to first, third, and sixth graders, and to adults, and asked them to indicate whether a man, a woman, or both men and women would be more likely to say each of the sentences.[12] Among adults there was a high consensus (defined as 70% or more subjects rating the sentence as indicative of one sex) that women use *adorable, my goodness,* and *oh dear,* whereas men use *I'll be damned.* By sixth grade, children's ratings agreed with adult ratings on all but one variable.

H. Thompson Fillmer and Leslie Haswell studied 121 children in grades one to five in an inner-city school.[13] Children read sentence pairs that were identical except for a single word or phrase. They then had to choose the one that would be more likely to be said by a man or a woman. On 15 of the 20 items that focused on language, over 50% of the children chose the answer that matched stereotypes of speech. Swearing and aggressive speech were associated with males; tag questions, intensifiers, and specialized vocabularies were associated with the speech of women.

Young children's awareness of the cultural prescriptions for the speech of males and females has been demonstrated by Elaine Andersen using a very different methodology.[14] Andersen studied 24 children ages 4 to 7 engaging in play with three puppets. Children were told they were going to "play family" at bedtime and were given a mother, father, and young child puppet. Mothers used more hints and more polite speech than fathers; fathers used more direct imperatives than mothers. Thus, children understood fathers' speech to be more straightforward and forceful, mothers' to be less direct and more polite.

Stability of Stereotypes Over Time

Gender stereotypes have changed relatively little over the last 20 years despite the considerable changes that have occurred in the status of women in society. Paul Werner and Georgina LaRussa replicated a 1957 study of gender role concepts 21 years later and found that 62% of the adjectives used to describe men and 77% of the adjectives used to describe women remained unchanged.[15] No adjective used to describe men or women in 1957 was used to describe the opposite sex 20 years later. Men continued to be seen as more dominant, aggressive, forceful, industrious, and outspoken; women as more emotional, submissive, warm, sympathetic, and sensitive.

Similar results are reported by David Bergen and John Williams, who gave 50 male and 50 female college students 300 items from an Adjective Checklist and asked them to decide whether the adjective was more frequently associated with men or with women.[16] They gathered their first data set in 1972 and repeated the experiment in 1988 with another sample. A high degree of similarity in sex role stereotypes existed over the 16-year period.

T. Joan Fecteau and her colleagues[17] had 600 students rate 303 items for how masculine and feminine they were on a 7-point scale to see if notions of masculinity and femininity had changed over the 20 years since the development of measures like the Bem Sex Role Inventory[18] and the Personal Attributes Questionnaire.[19] While overall the majority of items were seen as only slightly masculine or slightly feminine, more extreme stereotypes persisted on items pertaining to interaction style. Characteristics such as "acts like a leader," "aggressive," "dominant," and "forceful" were more highly associated with masculinity, whereas "does not use harsh language," and "eager to soothe harsh feelings" were more highly associated with femininity.

Accuracy of Stereotypes

Research shows that people hold stereotyped beliefs about the personalities, interaction styles, and speech of men and women, and that these stereotypes have remained relatively stable over time. Years ago, Philip Smith cautioned that many of these stereotypes are not reliable markers of gender.[20] Tag questions are associated with female speech, but gender differences in the frequency of use of tag questions were shown in chapter 5 to be quite inconsistent from study to study.

Janet Swim tested the accuracy of people's beliefs about gender and leadership against actual meta-analytic findings. She found that the perceived effect size for leadership emergence by males was quite large ($d = 1.04$), whereas the actual meta-analytic findings were significantly smaller ($d = .49$).[21] Men are expected to interrupt, but the data on interruptions reviewed in chapter 4 do not support this stereotype. Gender stereotypes are not always consistent with actual behavior; they may portray certain characteristics to be more prevalent than they actually are for members of each sex.[22]

The Impact of Stereotypes on the Perception of Speakers

Stereotypes have the power to define listeners' perceptions of and predispositions toward speakers. Listeners may actively seek to confirm their own expectations.[23] If actual speech does not conform to preconceived stereotypes, listeners may hear what is not present or overlook or reinterpret features that were not expected.[24] Thus, the same speech can be perceived differently depending on whether it is attributed to a male or to a female speaker.

Philip Smith had subjects listen to tape-recorded voices of 1 of 4 male and 4 female speakers, each reading the identical prose passage.[25] Subjects were asked to rate the speakers on 10 characteristics to show their impressions of what the speaker was like as a person. Ratings on being neat, expressive of emotions, nagging, sensitive, and feminine were combined into a single scale representing femininity, whereas ratings on being arrogant, aggressive, coarse, dominant, and masculine were combined into a rating of masculinity. Male speakers were rated higher on masculinity than female speakers; female speakers were rated higher on femininity than male speakers.

A number of interesting studies demonstrate how our expectations or preconceived notions about a speaker can influence our perceptions of that person. Jitendra Thakerar and Howard Giles had undergraduates listen to a tape containing two 30-second passages spoken by a male talking about an intelligence test task.[26] After listening to the tape, subjects were asked to rate the speaker. Subjects were then given written descriptions of the speaker, identifying him in one of three ways—as a person of high status, low status, or status unspecified. Subjects then listened to another speech sample that they believed to be a continuation of the same speaker, and they completed the rating scales a second time. Thakerar and Giles found that the high-status speaker was perceived as having spoken at a faster rate with a more standard accent and as being more competent than the control and low-status speakers. Subjects changed their personal impressions of the speaker and their perceptions of the speaker's speech style in the direction of expected characteristics.

While Thakerar and Giles looked at the power of stereotypes about status in shaping perceptions of speakers, others have demonstrated similar effects for gender. Nora Newcombe and Dianne Arnkoff had subjects listen to tape recordings of conversation in which male and female speakers used tag questions and qualifiers equally.[27] Subjects perceived females to use tag questions and qualifiers more frequently than males.

Even when men and women contribute equal amounts of speech to a conversation, they may be perceived as contributing different amounts. Anne Cutler and Donia Scott selected four excerpts from plays.[28] In the mixed-sex dialogues, the female was judged to be talking more than the male even when they spoke an equal number of words. In single-sex dialogues, both sexes were judged to be speaking equally. Thus, while perceptions were accurate in single-sex conversations, subjects biased their perceptions in the direction of the belief that women talk more than men in informal mixed-sex conversation. Cutler and Scott took the speech samples in this study from plays. It is possible that if they had taken the excerpts from mixed-sex task groups, the perceptions of amount of speech might have been biased in the opposite direction—subjects might have perceived men to have talked more than women.

These studies point to the importance of gender stereotypes in shaping our perceptions of speakers. Sex is one of the powerful categories that affect our perceptions of and responses to the world. In everyday conversation we have knowledge about the sex of the speakers based on discernible visible cues. These cues trigger gender schemas, or cognitive structures that represent our knowledge about gender. Given the complexity of incoming information, we rely on schemas and stereotypes to organize and guide our interactions. Associations to people based on their sex become automatic. We have social schemas for the behaviors we expect of men and women and for the traits they will possess. These influence the way we encode new information. If speech does not conform to stereotypes, the discrepancies between schemas and objective behavior may not reach our awareness, and we may hear speakers in a way that conforms with our stereotyped beliefs.

Richard Street and Robert Hopper suggest that as listeners we first transform the actual message we hear into a perceived message.[29] Our evaluative response is then triggered by this perceived message. The actual message and the perceived message may not be identical, and the perceived message is more important than the actual message in our evaluation of speech.

The Evaluative Component of Stereotypes

Each characteristic that comprises our stereotypes of men and women may be seen on a continuum from socially desirable to socially undesirable. Stereotypes of men and women contain some characteristics that are socially desirable and favorably evaluated, and some that are undesirable and negatively evaluated. For example, we see masculine traits like dominance, independence, and forcefulness as highly socially desirable and evaluate them positively, whereas we see masculine traits like being boastful or hardheaded as unfavorable. We evaluate feminine traits like being warm, understanding, and sympathetic favorably, but we evaluate traits like being submissive, emotional, and weak unfavorably.[30] Thus, stereotypes have both a descriptive and an evaluative component.

Twenty-five years ago research showed that stereotypically masculine traits were considered to be more socially desirable than stereotypically feminine traits.[31] In the mid-1980s Werner and LaRussa found that although stereotypes have changed little over time, there has been a change in our evaluation of the two sexes.[32] We have come to evaluate the stereotype of women more favorably.

In line with these findings, a study by Alice Eagly and Antonio Mladinic assessed attitudes toward the sexes and found that stereotypically feminine characteristics have come to be much more highly valued.[33] When men and women were rated on expressive qualities, women were evaluated more favorably than men. When women and men were rated on instrumental qualities, however, men were evaluated more favorably than women. Thus, women are not globally viewed as inferior to men; their expressive qualities have come to be more highly valued over time. However, people still hold negative stereotypes about women's instrumental competence. If instrumental competence is more highly valued in the professional world than expressive behavior, women may be seen as "very good people,"[34] but this will not be enough to overcome prejudice against them in the instrumental sphere.

Isolation and Assessment of Stereotype Effects

The studies I have just reviewed suggest that men and women can be perceived differently when they display the same behavior. The researchers who examined this question carried out laboratory studies in which they carefully controlled for the behavior of men and women and asked subjects to evaluate male and female speakers displaying the identical behavior. The results of these studies may not be applicable to ongoing interaction outside the laboratory where actual gender differences in behavior may be present.[35] When actual gender differences are present, it is difficult to determine whether people evaluate men and women differently because of actual behavioral differences, or because of gender stereotypes. For example, when Kevin Lamude and Tom Daniels had 86 superior-subordinate pairs from 23 organizations rate each others' communication competence, female superiors were rated as less competent than male superiors, and female subordinates as less competent than male subordinates.[36] It is impossible to determine from this study whether subjects perceived women to be less competent because of actual deficiencies in their communication styles, or whether we can attribute the results to stereotype effects.

In a carefully crafted study, Anthony Mulac and his colleagues separated the effect of naturally occurring gender differences in language from the effect of gender-based language stereotypes in the perception of speakers.[37] Mulac and his colleagues collected language samples from college graduates who were asked to describe two landscapes orally. Speech was tape-recorded and 12 transcripts were developed to form four language/stereotype conditions:

1. *Language effect only* (naturally occurring gender differences in language). The sex of the speaker was not identified in the transcript.

2. Language effect plus stereotype effect. The correct speaker sex was included at the top of the page on the transcript (i.e., the speech was correctly attributed to either "a man" or "a woman").
3. Stereotype effect only. Speech was attributed to either "a man" or "a woman," but in only half the cases did the labels correctly identify the sex of the speaker; in the other half speech was assigned to a speaker of the opposite sex.
4. Language effect versus stereotype effect. Transcripts that said "a man" were originally spoken by a woman; those that said "a woman" were originally spoken by a man.[38]

Students and older nonstudents then rated transcripts from one of the four conditions using the Speech Dialect Attitudinal Scale, a 12-item semantic differential. This instrument has consistently been factor analyzed to produce three factors: *socio-intellectual status* (high social status, white collar, rich, literate), *aesthetic quality* (pleasing, nice, sweet, and beautiful), and *dynamism* (strong, active, aggressive, and loud).

Mulac and his colleagues found that based only on naturally occurring speech differences between males and females, subjects associated female speech with higher social status and saw it as more pleasing, whereas they saw male speech as stronger and more aggressive. Knowledge of the gender of the speaker produced the same perceptions of speech, but the combination of naturally occurring gender differences in speech and stereotype effects was significantly greater on aesthetic quality and dynamism than either operating alone. Thus, differential perceptions of naturally occurring speech differences are further heightened by knowledge of the sex of the speaker. The ratings based on the language effect and the stereotype effect shared 86% of the variance in common. The results were similar regardless of the sex or the age of the subjects.

Stereotypes biased perceptions in the direction of expectations. When subjects believed the speaker was a female, they saw the speech to be more pleasing, and when they believed the speaker was male, they saw the speech as stronger and more aggressive, regardless of whether that speech was produced by a man or a woman, or whether there were actual speech differences.[39] The study demonstrates the influence of gender stereotypes on the perception of speech, and it suggests that even if men and women were to change their language, the stereotype effect would to some degree counteract actual changes in behavior.

The Elusive Nature of Stereotype Effects

The results of the study by Mulac and his colleagues provide convincing evidence that speech will be perceived differently regardless of whether actual gender differences in speech occur. The study was followed up and extended by Christopher Zahn[40] and by Samuel Lawrence and his colleagues,[41] who found either little evidence or more qualified evidence for differences in the perception of male and female speakers. While Mulac and his associates used monologues as speech samples, Zahn transcribed eight segments from audiotaped conversations. Six of the transcribed segments came from naturally occurring conversations, two from interactions in a laboratory setting. Segments included interaction from same-sex and mixed-sex dyads. Speaker names were placed on the transcripts at each speaking turn to identify the sex of the speaker. The actual sex of the speaker and the attributed sex of the speaker (male, female, or unspecified) served as independent variables. That is, either male speakers were correctly identified as males, they were identified as females, or their sex was unspecified. Subjects were unable to identify the sex of the speaker at a better than chance rate.

Students and adults were asked to evaluate the speakers on a semantic differential that produced three factors: superiority (including educated, intelligent, literate, upper-class, white-collar, organized, fluent, clear, competitive, rich), attractiveness (warm, nice, pleasant, friendly, good-natured, considerate, sweet, kind, likable, good), and dynamism (aggressive, talkative, enthusiastic, and active). These three factors are similar to those used by Mulac and his colleagues.

Zahn found the actual language used by men and women to be quite variable from one individual to another and from one conversation to another and no evidence for the stereotype effect. Subjects did not rate speech differently on superiority, attractiveness, or dynamism when it was attributed to a male or to a female. One explanation for the discrepancy in findings between the study by Mulac and his colleagues and that of Zahn is that when asked to evaluate "a man" or "a woman," these labels trigger stereotypes to a greater extent than the use of names does on a transcript. In both studies, with the absence of visual and vocal cues, it is possible that gender stereotypes were not fully evoked, and this may be true to an even greater extent in the study by Zahn.

Lawrence and his associates extended the work of Zahn by using both audiotaped presentation and transcripts, and by making conversational content an independent variable to determine whether the stereotype effect remains stable across two different conversations. In a first study, they examined four independent variables: the actual sex of speaker, the attributed sex of speaker, the mode of presentation (audio recordings or transcripts), and the conversation (40-minute segments from two naturally occurring mixed-sex conversations were used with two versions of each: male and female actors spoke lines produced originally by members of their own sex, or the male actor spoke lines originally produced by a woman, and the female actor spoke the lines produced by a man).

One hundred students listened to or read transcripts of conversation and were asked to evaluate the speaker on the same instrument that was used by Zahn. The actual speech of men and women was perceived differently. Men's speech was rated higher than women's on dynamism and socio-intellectual status and lower on attractiveness. It is puzzling to note that the speech of females was found to be higher on socio-intellectual status by Mulac and his colleagues, but was found to be lower by Lawrence and his colleagues. When speech was attributed to a female, speakers were rated higher on dynamism—the reverse of the stereotype expected—and there was no effect on attractiveness or socio-intellectual status. Thus, there was little support for the notion that stereotypes about speaker's sex activate different perceptions of male and female speakers. It is difficult to account for the discrepancy between the presence of stereotype effects in the study of Mulac and his colleagues, and the absence of stereotype effects and steretoype effects in a contrary direction found by Lawrence and his colleagues.

Lawrence and his colleagues then carried out a second study using a greater variety of conversational material and a broader sample of subjects from noncollegiate populations. Stimulus conversations were based on four mixed-sex dyadic conversations, two from the first study plus two from a professional work setting. Students and nonstudents served as subjects. Again, the actual speech of males and females was rated differently. Men's speech was rated higher on dynamism, and there were no gender differences on attractiveness or socio-intellectual status, but men's speech was rated as more dynamic than women's in only a single conversation. Lawrence and his colleagues found evidence for the stereotype effect. Speakers believed to be male were rated higher on dynamism than speakers believed to be female, but they found the stereotype effect for only two of the four conversations.

What is particularly interesting about these results is that stereotype effects have a great deal of similarity to naturally occurring gender differences in speech. Stereotype effects, like actual gender differences, vary in their degree of salience from one conversation to another. They appear in some conversations but not in others, depending on the conversational context. The speech of men and women differs in some contexts but not in others, and the tendency to bend perceptions in the direction of sex role stereotypes occurs more readily in some contexts than in others.

When speech was attributed to a male, speakers were rated as more dynamic than when it was attributed to a female, but perceptions of attractiveness and socio-intellectual status were not affected. When the actual speech of females was attributed to females, female speakers were seen as less dynamic than when the speech of males was attributed to females, or than when male speakers used female speech. Thus, if men use women's speech, they are not evaluated as negatively as if women use women's speech. The lowest ratings on dynamism were produced by speakers thought to be female using female speech, whereas the highest ratings on dynamism were produced by speakers thought to be male using male speech.

Conclusions

We can draw several conclusions from these studies. The studies reveal that the actual speech of females is rated lower on dynamism than that of males; that is, women's speech is seen as less active and aggressive than men's. But whether men's speech is seen as higher on dynamism depends on the specific conversational context. If women use men's speech, they will not be evaluated equivalently to men; women using male speech are seen as less dynamic than men using male speech. If men speak like women, they will not be evaluated as negatively as women using women's speech; women using women's speech are evaluated as lower on dynamism than men using the same speech. The data also reveal that gender stereotypes may be evoked to varying degrees depending on the particular context and content of the conversation. Gender-based stereotypes have much in common with naturally occurring gender differences. The appearance of either depends on the situational context. Gender stereotypes have a greater impact on the perception and evaluation of speakers in some contexts than in others—leading male speakers to be seen as more active and aggressive—but the nature of those contexts has not yet been well understood.

The Evaluation of Speakers Who Use Stereotypically Female Speech

Many claims have been made over the years about gender differences in speech; for example, women are believed to use more tag questions and qualifications, men are believed to interrupt more. As shown in chapters 4 and 5, research findings are actually inconsistent; some studies find gender differences consistent with these claims, some find no gender differences, and some find gender differences opposite to expectation. Many researchers believed that the negative evaluation of women on the dimension of power and competence derived from the speech features that they used. Researchers set out to determine whether speakers who used the speech features Lakoff claimed to characterize women's speech (like tag questions and hesitation forms) were more negatively evaluated along the dimension of instrumental competence than speakers who did not use these speech features. If these speech features are used more frequently by women in some situations and are evaluated negatively, then the use of these features can have a negative impact on how competent women appear to be in those situations.

Methodological Considerations

We need to address one issue before reviewing this research. In chapters 4 and 5 I have shown that speech features like interruptions, tag questions, or qualifiers do not carry a single meaning; they may be used to serve very different functions. Interruptions may convey power or may convey support, and although interruptions have been stereotypically associated with power, they often are not used to serve this function. Likewise, tag questions may convey uncertainty or may be used to facilitate speech. Stereotypically, tag questions are seen to convey uncertainty, but this is not necessarily their most frequent function.

In the studies that follow, researchers have tended to overlook the multiple meanings of speech features. For example, they have examined the evaluation of speakers when using speech forms like tag questions, but they have not made the distinction between tag questions that are used to convey uncertainty and tag questions that are used to facilitate speech. In addition, in many studies researchers combined many language forms (e.g., tag questions, hedges, intensifiers, and polite forms) that carry multiple meanings into a single index of "women's language." It is impossible to determine from these studies whether a single speech feature, several of them, or a particular combination of them affected the evaluation of speakers. Given the limitations to the research, the studies discussed next cannot be taken to be complete assessments of the impact of these speech forms on the evaluation of speakers.

Studies that address the evaluation of speakers who use female speech vary methodologically. In some studies subjects are asked to evaluate speakers based on tape recordings of speech. In other studies subjects evaluate speakers based on written transcripts. In only one study were subjects asked to rate speakers with whom they actually interacted. The benefit of this last approach is that it comes closer to the kinds of assessments we actually make of speakers outside the laboratory in everyday conversation, where we are both listeners and participants at the same time. Some studies focus on evaluations of "women's language" as characterized by a combination of speech features; other studies focus on the evaluation of single speech features like tag questions. Regardless of the methodology used, however, the results of this body of research are consistent. Speakers using speech features stereotypically associated with women are viewed as less competent and powerful than speakers who do not use these speech features. We should not conclude from this research, however, that these speech features convey a single impression—for example, that speakers who use tag questions will always be viewed as less competent than those who do not. When we extend the research to distinguish between speakers who use tags to facilitate speech and speakers who use tags to express uncertainty, we might find different results.

Sex of the Rater

A question that researchers asked in many of these studies is whether there are differences in the evaluations of male and female raters; that is, do men bring a different evaluative bias to speakers using female speech than women do? Research shows that the perceptions of male and female raters are not always the same,[42] but the particular biases of males and females are not consistent from one study to another. In some studies members of one sex give higher ratings than members of the opposite sex; for example, female raters may attribute greater warmth to speakers than male raters do.[43] In other studies there is an interaction between the sex of the rater and the sex of the person rated (i.e., males and females rate the same behavior by members of the same and the opposite sex differently), or there is an interaction of sex of rater and characteristics of the speaker.[44] For example, Linda Carli found that female subjects rated assertive speakers as more trustworthy than tentative speakers, whereas male subjects rated assertive speakers as less trustworthy than tentative speakers.[45] Inconsistencies between studies are difficult to interpret, and it is likely that the particular biases we bring because of our gender will depend on the setting and the conversation content.

Studies of "Women's Language"

There are a number of studies that assess listeners' perceptions and evaluations of speakers who use "women's language." Definitions of "women's language" differ from study to study, but they are usually based on some combination of speech characteristics identified by previous research as representing the speech of women. Because there is no universal definition of women's language, it is difficult to compare results across studies. Two other limitations to these studies should be noted. They combine speech features, so that we cannot determine whether effects are produced by particular components of "women's language" or by their combination. In some studies contrived speech samples have been so saturated with "women's language" that they may not come close to actual spoken language.

Bonnie Erickson and her colleagues used tape recordings of court trials as a basis to create two versions of a script.[46] They created a powerless version by taking a sample speech that included frequent use of such features as hesitation forms, hedges, intensifiers, question intonation, polite forms, and formal grammar. They created a powerful version by removing most of these features. Erickson and her colleagues then created four scripts varying the sex of the witness and using powerful or powerless speech. They presented each version in both written transcript form and orally, using actors to tape-record the script.[47]

Subjects rated their impressions of the witness on a series of 11-point semantic differential type ratings. The scales were factor analyzed to produce three factors: credibility in court (including being convincing, trustworthy, and competent), attractiveness (including being strong, likable, active, intelligent, and powerful), and masculine-feminine. The same effects held for both written and oral speech—regardless of the sex of the speaker, subjects found those speakers who used powerful language to be more credible and attractive than speakers who used powerless language.

Similar types of studies have also shown that when more features of women's language are present, speech is evaluated more negatively. William O'Barr and Bowman Atkins had students rate on a wider range of variables the same tapes or transcripts that were used by Erickson and her colleagues.[48] Whether the evaluations were based on tapes or transcripts, the results were the same—subjects judged speakers of either sex who used a high frequency of powerless features as less convincing, truthful, competent, intelligent, and trustworthy.

Linda Carli had male and female actors tape-record a persuasive message in support of charging a fare for use of the college bus system.[49] A tentative version was created by adding tag questions, hedges, or disclaimers. Subjects heard one of four versions of the tape—a male or female speaker using tentative or nontentative language—and rated the speaker. Regardless of speaker sex, subjects judged speakers who used tentative language to be more tentative, less confident, less powerful, less competent, and less intelligent than speakers using assertive language.[50] Thus, if women use "women's language" more than men do, their use of language will have a negative impact on how competent, intelligent, and knowledgeable they appear to be.

A number of studies have created two versions of short transcripts—a powerless/women's language version based on some combination of Lakoff's speech forms and a powerful version marked by their absence. They have found that regardless of the gender of the speaker, subjects view powerless language more negatively on most dimensions. They perceive powerful speakers as being more powerful, active, and competent,[51] more aggressive, more likely to succeed and be accepted,[52] and as having higher status/competence and dynamism.[53] They perceive speakers who use powerless/women's language as being more submissive, less assertive, less willing to take a stand, less believable but more caring,[54] less competent but higher on social warmth,[55] and less dominant but more competent.[56] Women's speech is associated with greater social warmth and caring, but these female traits may not make up for the lack of the highly valued male traits of competence and power.

The studies reviewed here all rely on contrived speech. Differential evaluation of male and female speech features may be more clearly demonstrated because researchers have manipulated speech to be as different as possible in the powerless/women's language version from the powerful/male language version. When the naturally occurring speech of males and females is used, effects are present but are less dramatic.

Anthony Mulac and Torborg Lundell assessed the degree to which speech characteristics could be used to predict the evaluation of speakers. They audiotaped 40 speakers describing landscape photographs.[57] The audiotapes were transcribed and coded on 31 linguistic variables (e.g., tag questions, hedges, intensive adverbs, personal pronouns). A combination of 17 of these variables were found to discriminate the speech of males and females with 87% accuracy. Mulac and Lundell also had subjects rate the communicators "as a person" without knowledge of their sex on socio-intellectual status, aesthetic quality, and dynamism. They then determined the degree to which the speech features that differentiated male and female speech could be used to predict the judgments of speakers on socio-intellectual status, aesthetic quality, and dynamism. Mulac and Lundell found that the linguistic variables had moderate ability to predict attributional judgments made of speakers.[58]

In sum, studies of the perception and evaluation of women's speech show that speakers of either sex who use "women's language" are evaluated as warmer and more caring but are viewed more negatively on the dimension of credibility, competency, and intelligence than speakers who do not use women's language. Research shows that the effects are strongest when speech is contrived and saturated with tag questions, qualifiers, and disclaimers, but it is unlikely that speech so constructed mirrors the speech of most women in most contexts. When studies are based on naturally occurring speech differences, which are themselves much more minimal, effects are found to be more minimal. The other complicating factor in the interpretation of these studies of "women's language" is that we cannot isolate which speech feature or speech features may have been most salient in affecting the evaluation of speakers.

Studies of Individual Language Features

While some researchers have examined the impact of "women's language" on the perception of speakers, others have tried to isolate the effect of particular speech features. Tag questions and qualifications, which have been held to characterize women's speech, are the speech features that have been of particular interest. Several researchers have found that speakers' use of tag questions and qualifiers leads to a lower evaluation of them on intelligence, assertiveness, and authority.

David and Robert Siegler had 96 subjects rate sentences with either tag questions, strong assertions, modified assertions, or no speech feature added.[59] Tag questions were associated with the least intelligence; strong assertions were associated with the highest intelligence.

Nora Newcombe and Diane Arnkoff had students listen to segments of conversation recorded by people who simulated conversation on the telephone.[60] Speakers using either tag questions or qualifications were seen as less assertive than those who did not.

James Bradac and Anthony Mulac had subjects rate the extent to which an interviewee was able to create the type of impression he or she desired.[61] In half the cases, subjects were told the interviewee wished to appear authoritative, in the other half, the interviewee wished to appear sociable. Subjects read segments taken from responses of job interviewees using different language forms. When the interviewee wished to appear authoritative, subjects found that tags and hedges took away from the desired impression.

Finally, John Wright and Lawrence Hosman had subjects read a transcript of testimony describing a traffic accident.[62] Witnesses using few hedges were perceived as more attractive (a factor defined as powerful, active, dominant, and strong) than those using many hedges. Taken together, these studies demonstrate that the use of tag questions, hedges, or qualifications causes speakers to be seen as less intelligent, assertive, authoritative, and powerful.

Research shows that speakers who interrupt are viewed as more powerful and assertive, but less social and reliable than those who are interrupted. Mary Wiley and Dale Woolley designed a one-page transcript of a conversation between a male and a female vice president of a national corporation in which one speaker interrupted the other three times. They also varied the sex of the interrupter and the person interrupted.[63] They had subjects read the transcripts and rate the speakers. Regardless of speaker sex, subjects rated interrupters higher than interrupted speakers on job success and saw them as more driving (aggressive, competitive, ambitious, independent, confident, convincing) and less companionable (friendly, likable, warm, honest, open-minded) than interrupted persons. They rated interrupters lower on social acceptance and saw them as less reliable (responsible, trustworthy, neat, loyal, intelligent) than interrupted persons, but they saw women, regardless of interruptions, as more reliable than men.

Laura Robinson and Harry Reis distinguished between interruptive questions and interruptive statements in the way they affected the perception of speakers. They developed a transcript based on a mixed-sex dyad in conversation on two topics, and they interjected

10 interruptions into the speech of one conversant.[64] They created three versions of the transcript: one using interruptive statements, one using interruptive questions, and one using no interruptions to serve as a control. Subjects listened to one of the audiotapes and rated both participants. Subjects saw both male and female interrupters as less sociable and less feminine than controls, as well as more assertive and masculine. The type of interruption had no effect. They saw interrupted persons as less assertive, more emotionally vulnerable and in need of emotional support, more feminine, and less masculine. Being interrupted and not interrupting—characteristics associated with female speech—are associated with being less driving, less assertive, and more emotionally vulnerable and companionable.

Comparisons of Men and Women Who Use Female Speech

Research findings show that speakers using language features associated with women's speech are more negatively evaluated on intelligence, power, and competency than those who do not use these forms of speech. A question we need to ask is whether women using women's language are more negatively evaluated than men using women's language. Do these speech features universally convey the impression of lower intelligence and competency, or do they take on a different meaning depending on the sex of the speaker? Does the evaluation of a speaker depend on an interaction between the sex of the speaker and the actual speech feature used?

A number of studies show the negative effect of women's language features to be greater for female speakers than for male speakers. The most striking study was carried out by Patricia Bradley, who had participants in an interaction evaluate each other at the conclusion of the discussion.[65] In the research studies reviewed earlier, subjects read or overheard conversations; they were not listeners and participants at the same time. Bradley ran 24 groups, placing a male confederate in half the groups and a female confederate in the other half. The confederates posed as subjects, but they were trained by the experimenter to behave in a specific manner. The confederates argued for a position contrary to the views of the other group members. In half the groups confederates advanced arguments with support—giving evidence, factual data, and statistics. In the other half of the groups confederates simply advanced their assertions without proof. Half the confederates in each condition introduced arguments with tag questions and disclaimers, half did not. Groups were composed of 2 male and 2 female subjects, along with the confederate. Groups had 30 to 40 minutes to arrive at consensus about the truth or falsity of the statement that there is nothing wrong with moderate drinking of alcoholic beverages. Subjects filled out ratings of other group members following the conclusion of the discussion.

Bradley found that male confederates who used no supportive arguments were viewed as more intelligent, knowledgeable, and influential than females who advanced arguments without support.[66] Females who used tag questions and disclaimers were seen as less intelligent, less knowledgeable, and less dynamic than males who used them. While responses to males hardly varied if they used tag questions and disclaimers, women were perceived as less dynamic, knowledgeable, and intelligent when using them. The study by Bradley provides evidence to suggest that when men adopt women's language they do not suffer the same negative evaluation that women do in the realm of competence.

Other studies have also found women to be evaluated more negatively than men when using female speech. Wright and Hosman found that women who use many hedges are seen as less credible than men who use many hedges, but women are seen as equally credible when they do not use hedges.[67] Lawrence and his colleagues found that when males use female speech, they are evaluated as more active and aggressive than when females use female speech.[68] Mary Glenn Wiley and Arlene Eskilson found that male job applicants who used powerless speech were seen as more aggressive than females using powerless speech.[69] Carli found that men were viewed as equally knowledgeable when using tentative or assertive speech, but women were viewed as less knowledgeable when using tentative speech than when using assertive speech. In addition, males were viewed as more knowledgeable than female speakers regardless of the speech they used.[70]

Thus, while speech forms themselves contribute to the impression a speaker makes, their effect depends on the sex of the speaker. Evaluation of speech is based both on speech forms and on stereotypes evoked by the sex of the speaker. As noted earlier, researchers have not directly assessed the evaluation of speakers when they use speech forms to serve different functions. It is highly likely that the evaluation of speakers using particular "female" speech forms will depend on the function for which these speech features have been used (e.g., people using tags to facilitate speech will be viewed differently than people using tags to express hesitancy).

The Evaluation of Females Who Adopt Stereotypic Male Behavior

Research suggests that women may not gain equality with men by adopting male behavior. Many studies provide support for this proposition, showing that when women use language, or enter into roles, or exhibit behaviors stereotypically associated with men, they may be evaluated more negatively than men in performing those roles or exhibiting those behaviors. When women adopt the speech features of men, they are still evaluated differently than men. Subjects rated women interrupters as more driving than men who interrupt.[71] Female applicants using powerful speech were seen as more aggressive than male applicants.[72] Being driving and aggressive are characteristics that are acceptable for men but violate the norms for femininity. They carry negative connotations when applied to women.

Alice Eagly and her colleagues conducted a meta-analysis of gender and the evaluation of leaders.[73] The meta-analysis covered 61 studies in which subjects were asked to evaluate descriptions of males and females performing the identical managerial behaviors. Overall, there was a very small tendency for female leaders to be evaluated less favorably than male leaders ($d = .05$), but the tendency for males to be evaluated more favorably than females was more pronounced for roles that are occupied primarily by men ($d = .09$)—and particularly for leaders using an autocratic style ($d = .30$). In other words, as women departed from sex role expectations and assumed roles held primarily by men and used masculine leadership styles, they were evaluated more negatively:

> Thus, gender roles appear to restrict the options of female managers in the sense that they "pay a price" in terms of relatively negative evaluation if they intrude on traditionally male domains by adopting male-stereotypic leadership styles or occupying male-dominated leadership positions.[74]

Similarly, Michael Burgoon and his colleagues found that women who violated expectations for femininity and used verbally aggressive persuasion strategies like threat and aversive stimulation were seen as less persuasive than women who used female strategies like altruism and positive moral appeal. Males who used aggressive persuasion strategies, however, were seen as more persuasive than those who used less aggressive strategies.[75]

These studies demonstrate that masculine behavior may convey a different meaning when displayed by a woman than a man because it violates gender role expectations when performed by a woman. When women exhibit behavior that goes against expectations for femininity, they are evaluated more negatively than men who perform the identical behavior. When women use language stereotypically associated with women, they are viewed as lacking in instrumental competency; when they use language stereotypically associated with men, they are viewed as aggressive. Women are thus caught in a double bind. They face a difficult task in trying to establish themselves as being equally as competent as men.

Gender Stereotypes as Self-fulfilling Prophecies for Behavior

The differing attributions and evaluations we make of men and women can become self-fulfilling prophecies for behavior. Interaction is guided by perception. We form expectations about individuals in interaction based in part on gender stereotypes, and these expectations may guide and influence our interactions with those individuals. Our perceptions serve as the basis of our responses to others, generating behavior in others that in turn validates our own perceptions.

Mark Snyder and his colleagues provided a clear demonstration of this phenomenon.[76] Male subjects were led to believe they were going to interact with either an attractive or unattractive female partner. Knowledge of the partner's attractiveness was influential in the formation of first impressions about that partner before the encounter began, and males interacted differently with their partners based on these initial perceptions. Different behaviors were elicited from women consistent with the initial stereotypes of the perceivers. Thus, stereotypes became self-fulfilling prophecies for behavior.

Mark Zanna and Susan Pack also demonstrated the power of the sex role stereotypes in determining the behavior of others.[77] When female subjects expected to have an intimate encounter with an attractive male partner, they presented themselves in accordance with the expectations they believed their partner held for the ideal woman. In other words, they portrayed themselves in line with what they believed to be their male partner's stereotypic view of women.

Robert Rice and his associates in a study of West Point cadets also demonstrated that the attitudes males in a group hold toward women can affect the behavior of women leaders.[78] Almost a year previous to the study, subjects were tested on the Attitudes toward

Women Scale,[79] a measure of the degree to which they held traditional or liberal attitudes toward women's roles in society. Cadets were assigned to 4-person groups composed of 3 male followers and a male or female leader. Subjects were assigned to groups such that in half the groups followers held traditional attitudes about women's roles, in half they held liberal attitudes. Group members were strangers and did not know each other's attitudes. The data reveal that the attitudes male followers had toward women were manifested in behavior that led women leaders to initiate more structure and play a more important role in the groups of male followers holding more liberal attitudes. Women leaders' potential to lead was impeded in groups where men held traditional attitudes.

The attitudes male followers had toward women influenced their perception of leaders: male followers with traditional attitudes toward women rated male leaders higher than female leaders on initiating structure, whereas those with liberal attitudes toward women rated women leaders higher than men. Female leaders felt they played a less important role in the group when males held traditional attitudes than when they held egalitarian attitudes. For male leaders, the opposite pattern emerged. Taken together, these studies demonstrate the power that stereotypes have to induce behavior that fulfills the initial stereotype.

Beliefs about task-related competence may be a powerful determinant of how people are treated. Research shows that people who are believed to be less competent are treated with less respect and more hostility. Because stereotypes about women carry negative evaluations about women's competence, women are often assumed to be less competent than men in task-oriented groups and may consequently receive more negative treatment than men do.

Bernice Lott compared the behavior of males interacting with a male or a female partner on the task of building a domino structure, which may be considered to be a "masculine" task. Males followed advice less frequently with female than with male partners, suggesting they judged female partners to be less competent and behaved accordingly.[80]

Patricia Bradley carried out an interesting study of interaction that revealed not only that low-competence group members were treated with more hostility, but also that low-competence females were treated with more hostility and more dominance than low-competence males.[81] Bradley formed 5-person groups, each including 4 males and a male or a female confederate whose role was to argue for a deviant position. Groups held 45-minute discussions

about the penalty to be assigned to a journalism major who had plagiarized a paper. Half the confederates were shown to have task-
related ability, half to have no such ability. Statements directed to
females low in competence were more dominant and more hostile
than those directed to low-competence males. Competent females
were not treated with greater dominance or hostility than high-competence males. Thus, when female competence was demonstrated
prior to the beginning of an interaction, it mitigated the effects of
gender stereotypes. Females may argue a contrary position if they
are competent, but competent females pay a greater price than competent males for violating rules of politeness and equity.[82]

Conclusions

We are always aware of the sex of participants in interaction, and
knowledge of their sex leads us to form different expectations for
them, for the traits they will possess, and for the type of speech and
interaction styles they will display. Our perceptions are not always
accurate representations of reality. The research reviewed in this
chapter reveals clearly that men and women may be perceived differently even if they display identical behavior. Research evidence
shows that we bend our perceptions in the direction of expectations.
Listeners may not attend to certain speech features and may create
ones that are not present. What people feel they hear based on
speech stereotypes may be more important to their experience than
what actually occurs in speech.[83]

Stereotype effects appear to be much like gender effects themselves. They may be evoked to a different degree depending on the
situational context, and they are not evoked in all situations. They
are more strongly felt when gender is a more salient issue in an
interaction than when it is not. The magnitude of stereotype effects
has not been assessed. It is likely that the effects, like gender effects,
are statistically significant but not large. Just as gender effects are
greatest in short time encounters and are mitigated over time,
stereotypes may also have a larger impact in shaping expectations
and perceptions of speakers as an interaction begins. Speech perception studies give raters a few pages or a few minutes of speech to
evaluate. Although stereotype effects are found in this context, we
need further research to determine the extent to which they may be
mitigated over time. The impact of stereotypes may be different in an
initial encounter among strangers than among people who are more
intimate.[84] Social psychological research has found that as more

personal information about an individual becomes available, there is less reliance on stereotypes.[85]

There are a number of reasons why gender stereotypes should cause us concern. First, stereotypes do not always provide an accurate guide to perceiving reality. As was demonstrated in earlier chapters, in some situations men talk more than women, interrupt more, and use more tag questions; in others, women talk more than men, interrupt more, and use more tag questions. There are also many situations in which men and women do not differ on these characteristics. In many situations gender stereotypes evoke inaccurate expectancies that are not always easily overcome by speakers. Schemas have been found to resist change and to persist in the face of disconfirming evidence.[86] If a man or a woman does not fit our gender-based expectations, we develop a subtype of men or women to cover the isolated case. Subtyping, however, allows us to "fence off" certain types—to label them as atypical—and to keep overall stereotypes in place.[87]

Second, gender stereotypes play a powerful role in shaping behavior. Gender stereotypes are prescriptive and dictate how men and women *should* behave. Although all stereotypes have both descriptive components (indicating what group members are like) and prescriptive components (indicating what behavior is appropriate for group members), gender stereotypes have a stronger prescriptive component than other stereotypes.[88] In many situations there are norms and expectations for behavior appropriate for each sex, and there are pressures to conform to these sex role demands to avoid real or imagined social sanctions.[89] People who do deviate from traditional sex role norms pay a price. Women who violate norms for the display of femininity and talk or act like men in male roles are more negatively evaluated than men displaying the same styles or speech. Women using powerful language are seen as more aggressive and driving than men using the same language. Thus, as women move into positions of power traditionally held by men, they face biases that work against their equality with men.

Stereotypes have a critical effect on the evaluation of speakers. Gender stereotypes create a bias favoring male speakers on the dimension of instrumental competency. While research shows that speech forms believed to characterize the language of women carry many negative evaluations, women using these speech forms are more negatively evaluated than men using the same language. Women may be more negatively evaluated than men on the dimension of competency not because of actual differences from men, but because of stereotype effects. Actual gender differences in behavior are not the sole cause of discrepancies in the way men and women are evaluated.

Finally, stereotypes have the power to shape behavior by serving as self-fulfilling prophecies. Research shows that people who are believed to be less competent are treated with more dominance and hostility. To the extent that gender stereotypes depict women as less competent than men, they will be treated differently than men in interaction, and this differential treatment has been shown to make women less effective as leaders.

We must also put gender stereotypes into context. It is important to keep in mind that gender stereotypes have more impact on the perception and evaluation of speakers in some settings than in others, and that they are only one among a host of cognitive structures that influence perceptions of speech. They should not be taken to be either the most important or the sole determinant of perceptions. Gender is not salient in all situations. The evaluation of male and female speakers is mediated by the effect of other variables such as social class, occupation, race and ethnicity, and political ideology.[90] Because of gender inequalities in status, differential perceptions and evaluations of men and women may be based on status as well as on gender.

8

Conclusions, Explanations, and Implications

The research reviewed in this book could be used to make a strong case for differences between the interaction styles of men and women. The same general findings emerge across many different subject populations, settings, and research methodologies. Men show a greater task orientation in groups, women a greater social-emotional orientation; men emerge more often as leaders in initially leaderless groups; men interrupt more; women pay more attention to the face needs of their conversational partners; women talk more personally with their close friends. People have drawn on this research evidence to popularize the view that men and women think differently, interpret the world differently, and interact differently. These ideas have had widespread appeal. Many people feel these depictions of men and women capture their own experience; the research findings mirror gender differences they see in their daily lives.

I have argued, on the other hand, that the research evidence on gender and conversational interaction permits multiple interpretations—that the "facts" do not yield a single "truth." I have gone back through the research literature to demonstrate that the data reveal the similarities between men and women to be far greater than the differences, and that knowledge of a person's gender will give us little ability to accurately predict how a person will behave in many situations. Let me review the questions that have been raised throughout this book—questions that have been raised in scholarly journals and articles by feminist researchers over the past two decades but that have not had a major impact on popular conceptions about men and women.

189

Limitations to Current Interpretations

Generalization From White, Middle-Class Samples

The notion that men and women have primarily different styles of interaction is based overwhelmingly, although not exclusively, on studies of individuals who are white and economically privileged. We must exercise a great deal of caution in extending these findings to "men" and "women" in general. We cannot talk about "men" differing from "women" when our findings pertain only to selective groups of men and women.

Neither men nor women in this society form a homogeneous social group. Members of each sex differ from one another in race, class, ethnicity, and sexual orientation—variables that make a profound difference in people's life experiences, their identities, and their patterns of interaction.

Gender has not been identified as the primary issue of importance for research on the lives of racial or ethnic minorities, so that relatively few studies have been carried out comparing gender differences in white, middle-class samples to samples that differ in race and ethnicity. It is quite likely, however, that the gender differences that characterize white, middle-class samples do not hold for men and women of different races or classes. Latina women[1] and African-American women[2] have been found to endorse more masculine qualities than white women. When blacks and whites were interviewed about the communication styles that characterized their friendships with people of their own race, terms like confrontive, quick-tempered, and skeptical were included in descriptions of self and others for black friends; for white friends, terms included nonconfrontive, withdrawn, and tactful.[3] What we hold to be true about the behavior of "women" based on studies of white women may not hold true for "women" in other racial and ethnic groups.

A Focus on Group Rather Than Individual Differences

Characterizations of men and women as groups exclude from our view the behavior of many men and women. The study of gender differences over the years has been a study of group differences— how men as a group differ on average from women as a group. Because there is considerable variability in behavior in any situation from one man to another, or from one woman to another, many men and women deviate from our characterizations for members of their sex.[4] For example, while Strodtbeck and Mann found men to be more task oriented than women, they also noted that there were many instances in which women devoted more of their interaction to task behavior than men did. Although women have been found to talk more personally to same-sex best friends than men, there are men in the samples studied that talk just as personally as women do. Many men and women do not fit the norm. In our efforts to characterize men and women as groups, we have given more credence to group than to individual differences.

In the introduction to his bestseller *Men Are from Mars, Women Are from Venus*, John Gray reports that sometimes couples and individuals reveal that they relate to his examples but in an opposite way; men relate to his depiction of women, and women to his depiction of men.[5] Gray labels this phenomenon role reversal and suggests that readers seek out the examples that fit them and ignore the others. In so doing, Gray diverts attention from individual differences; they are removed from view. As Eagly points out, "These individual differences are only of tangential relevance to the task of integrating research on sex differences, because sex-difference findings are group comparisons—aggregate female versus male comparisons that do not take these individual differences into account."[6] We gain a different perspective on gender differences when we attend more closely to individual differences.

Polarization of Differences

In emphasizing group differences, we tend to polarize the differences between men and women. A statistically significant finding can result even when there is considerable overlap between the distributions for men and women and only a very small average difference between the groups. A small difference is often misrepresented to be a more mutually exclusive difference. For example, many studies have found statistically significant gender differences in task behavior, but these findings have been exaggerated to convey the impression that men are task oriented and women are not. The findings actually show that both men and women are highly task oriented in groups, but men devote from 8% to 15% more of their behavior to task activity than women do.

When research studies find men are more dominant and inexpressive than women, there is considerable overlap between the distributions for men and women. There are, of course, men and women who fall at the extreme ends of the distributions—men whose styles are primarily dominant and inexpressive, women whose styles are primarily emotionally expressive and supportive. These individuals provide confirming evidence for our stereotypes about gender. But there are men and women who fall at the opposite extremes of the distributions—women whose styles are dominant or inexpressive and men whose styles are emotionally expressive and supportive. Gender generally accounts for less than 10% of the variance in behavior in most studies. When we look at the magnitude of the gender differences that have been found, gender differences tend to be small to moderate. Meta-analyses reported in this book pertaining to the relationship between gender and verbal interaction show effects that never exceed the moderate range, with a 67% overlap in the distributions for men and women.[7] Many effects are small, with an overlap of 85% in the distributions for men and women.

Failure to Recognize Situational Variability in Behavior

Gender differences emerge in some situational contexts but not in others. The characteristics of the participants (e.g., sex, age, race, class, ethnicity), their relationship to each other, the interaction setting, the topic of conversation, and the length of the encounter all have a major influence on the degree to which gender differences emerge in interaction. Men are not always more task oriented than women. Gender differences in task behavior are mitigated in more intimate relationships, in groups that meet over time, or when the roles participants must enact require instrumental behavior. Similarly, men do not always assume leadership in groups. Men are more likely to emerge as leaders in initially leaderless groups, but this is particularly true when people meet as strangers in short encounters and when the task they must perform draws on skills or interests that are more typically associated with men. When women have been assigned to the leadership role—or to roles that demand stereotypically masculine behavior (persuasiveness, assertiveness, autocratic leadership)—and given equal power, competence, or legitimacy, there are few gender differences in leadership behavior.

Gender is more likely to be salient in initial encounters between strangers when people notice gender and have little information to draw on to form expectations about each other. Gender may be less important when groups meet for an extended period, when other roles provide clear prescriptions for behavior, when social settings call for informational language, when men and women interact who have equal power and authority, when topics are of equal interest to men and women, and when task skills do not favor one sex. We will never be able precisely to define those situations in which gender differences appear and those in which they do not, because gender may become salient in any of these situations. As long as people hold different beliefs about and attitudes toward the attributes and abilities of men and women, gender can become salient because of the differential evaluation and treatment of men and women.

Inaccuracy of Perception

Research on gender stereotypes suggests that many gender differences reside in the eye of the beholder,[8] that our perception of gender differences can be greater than actual behavioral differences. We expect men to be leaders, but our expectations exceed the extent to which men actually take the lead in groups. There are widely held stereotypes about the interaction styles of men and women that shape our perceptions of speakers. We attribute masculine characteristics like intelligence and competence to men, and feminine characteristics like friendliness and sincerity to women, even when the behavior of men and women is identical. We bend our perceptions in the direction of stereotyped expectations; for example, we perceive women to use more tag questions and qualifiers than they actually do. We expect and notice behavior that is gender stereotypic; it provides further confirmation for our beliefs. We give less salience to behavior that does not fit our stereotypes, or we develop a subtype of men and women to cover the exceptions, thereby keeping overall stereotypes in place.

We have a pervasive tendency to attribute behavior to individual dispositions and to underestimate the importance of the situational context in shaping behavior. This tendency has been labeled the "fundamental attribution error." We perceive gender differences in our daily lives because we see men in social roles and statuses that differ from those held by women,[9] and we attribute the differences in their behavior to their gender rather than to their status or role. The interpersonal sensitivity we attribute to women is associated with people in subordinate roles, just as the dominance we attribute to men is associated with people in more powerful roles. When men and women are placed in the same role or given the same status, many gender differences in behavior are mitigated. Research has shown that women assigned to leadership roles and other stereotypically masculine roles will display the same behavior as men.

As we study men in roles that have been traditionally assigned to women—men who are primary caretakers of young children or who are nurses and nursery school teachers—we are likely to find that these men display "feminine" behavior just as women in organizational settings display "masculine" leadership behavior (although they may be perceived, treated, or evaluated differently).[10] Thus, what we perceive to be gender differences may not be gender differences at all; they may be differences due to role or status.

Explaining Gender Differences in Behavior

How can we best explain the pattern of gender differences that has emerged through our research? We need to account for differences between individual men and women, for variability in the magnitude of gender differences from one situational context to another, and for the small to moderate magnitude of the differences overall. Explanations of gender differences offered throughout this book locate the source of the differences either at the individual level (in the personalities of individuals), at the interpersonal level (in norms, stereotypes, expectancies in ongoing interaction), or at the sociostructural level (in the division of labor or in hierarchies of status and power).[11] It is useful to review these explanations and to draw them together to reach a fuller understanding of gender and communication.

The Individual Level

We can begin to explain gender by examining the construction of gendered personalities through socialization. As noted earlier, we are raised in a society in which gender is an important social category. Knowledge about gender is acquired early in life. By the age of 2 or 3, children acquire gender identity and can categorize themselves as males or females. Children learn the cultural expectations for appropriate behaviors and roles for members of their sex, and they learn the consequences for deviating from those prescriptions for behavior.[12]

A popular explanation of the acquisition of gender differences is the cultural approach provided by Daniel Maltz and Ruth Borker.[13] Maltz and Borker draw on the widely documented finding that beginning at the age of 3, children tend to sex segregate in their play groups[14]—a pattern that continues on through childhood. They argue that men and women grow up in different subcultures that have different rules for speaking. Because males and females interact in separate and different social contexts, they learn different norms for engaging in and interpreting conversation. "Members of each sex are learning self-consciously to differentiate their behavior from that of the other sex and to exaggerate these differences."[15] The different cultural rules for conversation acquired by males and females come into conflict when "women and men attempt to talk to each other as friends and equals in casual conversation."[16] Deborah Tannen built on this argument in her bestseller *You Just Don't Understand: Women and Men in Conversation,* in which she argues similarly that men and women have developed different rules for communicating and fail to properly interpret the meaning of each other's communications and intentions.[17]

I recognized the two-cultures approach to be quite compelling in my 1987 review of the literature on gender and communication, but I have come to see the limitation of this explanation. First, it fails to recognize the importance of sexual inequalities at a societal level.[18] The two-cultures approach postulates that problems arise when men and women talk together "as equals" in casual conversation. An implicit assumption is made here that men and women are equals, but men are accorded greater power, status, and privilege in society than women are—they are paid more for the same work. Even when husbands and wives both hold jobs outside the home, it is women who carry out the vast majority of the childcare and housework.[19] When a husband and wife come together in a conversation, they cannot be assumed to come together as equals. If a woman is financially dependent on her husband, holds a lower status job, or gets paid less than her husband, she does not enter the interaction as an equal. The two-cultures approach does not recognize that many of the differences between the styles of men and women are associated with power differences.[20] Gender differences cannot be understood without putting them in the context of gender inequalities in society.

Second, the theory holds that men and women have problems communicating because they have learned different cultural rules for conducting and interpreting conversation. How then do we account for the fact that research on communication in marriage shows that there are happily married couples who can resolve problems and express emotions and are accurate in interpreting each other's nonverbal communication? Although there are unhappily married couples who fail to communicate effectively,[21] evidence also shows that unhappily married couples can communicate well with other people and can communicate well when brought into the laboratory and asked to "fake" good communication.[22] Many men and women are able to understand each other well; failures to communicate cannot be adequately accounted for by gender.

The theory assumes that boys and girls grow up in separate cultures, but this assumption may be erroneous. People grow up in families, extended families, or institutions that are populated by both males and females. Although many individuals may have very little interaction with people outside their own class or race, men and women have daily encounters with members of both sexes.[23] Children have countless experiences communicating with members of both sexes. In her recent book on children's play, Barrie Thorne has argued that our characterizations of these two cultures are formed by focusing our attention on the most dominant and popular children in school and by exaggerating the coherence of same-sex interaction.[24]

Finally, the two-cultures approach predicts that gender differences will be more extreme in single-sex groups than in mixed-sex groups. If men and women come from two different sociolinguistic subcultures, the theory argues, these differences should be clearest when men and women interact with members of their own subculture. The research data, however, provide no clear support for this claim. In some studies gender differences are greater in single-sex groups; in other studies gender differences have been found to be greater in mixed-sex groups.

Sex role socialization does not add up to the creation of girls who are sex-typed feminine (e.g., supportive, expressive, or submissive) and boys who are sex-typed masculine (e.g., dominant, directive, and inexpressive).[25] We live in a heterogeneous society in which there is broad general agreement across individuals about the characteristics presumed to be typical of masculinity and femininity, but there is no single definition of the characteristics that comprise them. African-Americans, for example, have different conceptions of masculinity and femininity than Anglo-Americans.[26] There are diverse definitions of womanhood among people of color.[27]

Children are exposed to individuals of both sexes who present different models for what it means to be a man or a woman. They grow up in families that differ in the extent to which sex-typed behavior is encouraged. For example, some boys will be encouraged to be emotionally expressive, others will be discouraged from the display of emotional expressivity; some girls will be rewarded for the display of submissive behavior, others will be encouraged to become more dominant. Children also internalize their culture in unique ways. All children are aware of themselves as males or females, but there will be variability from one individual to another in how important gender may be to a person's definition of who they are, and in definitions of masculinity and femininity.

All children display a wide repertoire of behavior and learn that different behaviors are appropriate in different social contexts. Children exhibit different behavior depending on the age, sex, status of their partners in interaction, or the interaction setting; they choose the behavior that is appropriate for the particular situational context. Thus, both males and females display more masculine styles in some situations, more feminine styles in others. For example, the same boy or girl who takes the lead and is domineering with his or her younger sibling may be unassertive and a follower with an older friend.

We cannot adequately explain gender differences in interaction by attributing them to the acquisition of different personality traits or styles of interaction through socialization.[28] In a 1992 assessment of the literature on gender differences in personality, Susan Basow concludes that behavioral differences between men and women are less likely to be due to personality differences than to "situational factors, differential learning opportunities, or societal rewards."[29] Social behavior is a function of interaction between people. Our personalities are only one of many variables that explain how we will behave in a given situation.

Thus, although we acquire gender identity and knowledge of what is appropriate behavior for members of our sex, the expression of gendered behavior depends not only on our unique internalization of images of masculinity and femininity that we have experienced, but also on the interaction between our personalities and the demands of particular situations. To understand gender differences in behavior, therefore, we must look also to the interpersonal level of analysis—to gender-related norms and expectancies that operate in social interaction.

The Sociocultural Level

Before moving to the interpersonal level of analysis, we need to consider the larger social forces that shape norms and expectancies for behavior that operate at the interpersonal level. For more than two decades, feminists have pointed out that gender differences in social behavior co-vary with differences in power, status, and social roles.[30] Despite considerable changes in society, we still have a division of labor by sex, which assigns different work, activities, privileges, and responsibilities to men and women. Even though more women have entered the paid labor force, they are still paid less than men for the work they do and have lower status jobs. Also, women who work outside the home still spend more time doing housework and child-care than men do. Male dominance is built into the familial, eco-nomic, political, and legal structures of society.

Feminists have argued that gender relations are power relations in which men and masculinity hold elevated positions, and that gen-der must be seen as a question of power—of male supremacy over women. Cheris Kramarae, for example, contends that the study of gender is the study of hierarchies.[31] Roles, resources, and legitimate power are allocated differently to men and women, and as a conse-quence, "women and men will use different strategies to influence others and shape events."[32] If women are in powerless roles, they show dependent behavior not because of their gender, but because of their status. The same behavior is exhibited by men in powerless positions.

A great deal of evidence reviewed in this book reveals that gender differences vary with role and status. The dominance and leadership we attribute to men is displayed more often by high-status than by low-status individuals. The interpersonal sensitivity we attribute to women is displayed more often by low-status than by high-status individuals. Studies show these gender differences are mitigated when men and women are assigned to the same role or status. When dominance and leadership are legitimized for women—for example, when we study women leaders in organizational settings—the behavior of women is quite similar to that of men. Men who are unemployed or hold subordinate, low-status jobs have been found to use "women's language." Thus, role and status account for many gen-der differences in behavior.

Psychologists have not always given sufficient weight to the importance of the social, political, and economic context of men's and women's lives in their explanations of gender differences. The predominant research method in psychology, modeled after the nat-ural sciences, is the laboratory study. Laboratory studies require that people be taken out of their current roles and situational context; these studies "remove" the effect of such extraneous variables. To study behavior in the laboratory under conditions that strip that behavior from its usual context means we fail to attend to the social context that shapes those behaviors.[33]

The Interpersonal Level

Expectations About Gender At the interpersonal level of analysis, two theories discussed in earlier chapters—social role theory and expectation states theory—point to the importance of gender-related expectations in accounting for gender differences in behavior. Both theories connect the content of gender stereotypes to societal differences in the roles and statuses accorded to men and women, and both claim that these stereotypes may become self-fulfilling prophecies for behavior.

Social role theory, developed by Alice Eagly, addresses the way in which the division of labor in society shapes gender-related expectations about behavior.[34] Eagly argues that the distribution of men and women in different social roles in the family and in society leads to expectations that men and women possess different characteristics suited for the roles they occupy. Social role theory acknowledges the importance of status differences by recognizing that the roles assigned to men carry more power and status than those assigned to women. Men are assumed to be more agentic, independent, assertive, controlling, and instrumental because they fill occupational roles in society that require these skills; instrumental behavior is associated with high-status roles. Women are believed to be more communal and emotionally expressive because they play domestic roles and fill occupations like nursing, teaching, and being a secretary that require these traits; expressive behavior is associated with low-status roles. The distribution of men and women into different roles leads to the acquisition of different competencies and skills, which can translate into gender differences in behavior. In addition, these stereotypes or expectations about men and women have a prescriptive element, providing guidelines for how men and women should behave.

Eagly's theory stresses the importance of expectations in shaping the behavior of men and women—expectations that men should be dominant and that women should be nurturant and expressive. These norms do not allow women to be too dominant or men too expressive. People try to present themselves in a manner that will create valued social identities and bring social acceptance.[35] A requirement for social acceptance in many situations is the display of gender-appropriate behavior; men and women who violate those norms—who fail to comply with the prescriptions for gendered behavior—are negatively evaluated or face other forms of discrimination. As Alice Eagly points out, "People often conform to gender-role norms that are *not* internalized, because of the considerable power that groups and individuals supportive of these norms have to influence others' behavior through rewards and punishments of both subtle (e.g., nonverbal cues) or more obvious (e.g., monetary incentives, sexually harassing behavior) varieties."[36] Research shows that when highly dominant women are paired with low-dominance men, women are reluctant to assume leadership in the vast majority of the pairs. Men are expected to take the lead, and sex role norms are strong enough to override personality dispositions.

The second theory that addresses the importance of gender-related expectations in accounting for gender differences in social behavior is expectation states theory, developed by Joseph Berger and his colleagues.[37] Expectation states theory holds that in task groups, members form different expectations for each other based on external status characteristics like sex. Because men have higher status than women in society and are seen to possess greater dominance and prestige, they will be expected to be more competent at the task, will be given more opportunities to participate, and will find their contributions are more highly valued. If people value the male status more highly, then the same behavior coming from a male rather than a female will be more favorably evaluated on the dimension of competence and knowledgeability. Even when there are no actual differences in power or status among males and females in a group, males may still be granted higher status just because they are male.

The research reviewed in chapter 7 supports the contention that people hold negative stereotypes about women's instrumental competence. Studies conducted in the late 1960s and early 1970s showed that males were characterized by traits associated with instrumental competency, and that these traits were more positively evaluated than female traits (e.g., warmth and expressiveness).[38] Clinically trained psychologists, psychiatrists, and social workers judged women who fulfilled the stereotype of femininity to lack the characteristics required to be competent, healthy adults.[39] More than 20 years have passed since those studies were conducted, and the stereotype of women has come to be more favorably evaluated over time. Although women today are more favorably evaluated than men on expressive qualities, people continue to evaluate men more favorably than women on instrumental competence.

Research shows that even when men and women use the same style, women can be perceived to be less competent than men. To take some examples, when men advanced arguments without support they were seen as more intelligent and knowledgeable than women who displayed the same behavior; women who used tag questions and disclaimers were seen as less intelligent and knowledgeable than men who used them. When women used speech strategies associated with men, they were not found to gain status and position as men do, nor was the speech of men seen to convey uncertainty if they used speech features associated with women. Power relations between the sexes dictate the ways a speech style will be evaluated; it can be assigned a different meaning if used by a man or a woman.[40]

Expectation states theory holds that our expectations about the differential competency of males and females will become self-fulfilling prophecies for behavior, and these ideas find support in the empirical literature. For example, negative stereotypes about women have been shown to impede women from performing competently. Women leaders were less able to initiate structure and played a less important role in groups when male followers in those groups held traditional attitudes about the role of women in society than when male followers held more liberal attitudes toward women's roles.

When expectations are altered, gender differences are mitigated. Gender differences in leadership are less likely to be found when groups meet over many sessions. When a group has been working for many months, members have many opportunities to gauge each other's task-related abilities, and the competencies of individual members may override stereotypes in determining leadership. When the greater task competency of women has been demonstrated, women have been found to come out equal to men in influence, although they do not gain the advantage. They do not gain the advantage because changes in expectations in a single situation are not adequate to overcome long-term prejudices against women. When women believe they are more capable than men, gender inequalities in behavior are reduced. The more confident women are in their own ability and in the superiority of their ability in relation to a male partner, the more influential they will be in mixed groups.

In sum, knowledge of gender sets expectations for our own behavior and that of others, expectations that derive from the differential roles and status of men and women in society. Recognition of the gender of our conversational partners shapes the way we perceive, evaluate, and treat them. We monitor and evaluate our own behavior and that of others in regard to gender stereotypes. The fulfillment of gender-related expectations facilitates social acceptance;

those who deviate from these expectations pay a price in dislike, disapproval, and harassment.

The Situational Context At the interpersonal level of analysis we must take account not only of gender-related expectations, but also of the situational context that shapes interaction. Why is it that gender differences are found in some situational contexts but not in others? Social role theory provides one explanation. Eagly argues that gender-related expectations will dictate behavior in settings in which other social roles are relatively unimportant, but they will not be important determinants of behavior when other roles provide clear requirements for behavior. In other words, we would expect to find gender differences if we take men and women out of their ordinary roles and observe them in the laboratory, but we would not expect to find gender differences if we study men and women who hold the same job, because there are clear dictates for job performance.

Expectation states theory, likewise, provides an explanation for situational variability in display of gender differences. It predicts that gender differences are likely to occur if people enter a group with no knowledge of the relative competencies of group members, but that gender differences are unlikely to occur if women are believed to have equal task competency (e.g., when tasks draw on skills more often acquired by women). The research discussed in chapter 3 actually shows that women must have greater task competency than men to come out equal.

Kay Deaux and Brenda Major provide a very interesting and more extensive account, not previously discussed, for why gender differences will be displayed to a different extent in different situational contexts.[41] The interactive model of gender-related behavior stresses the importance of three factors that interact to predict behavior. First, the model recognizes the importance of the expectancies we bring to an interaction based on the gender of the participants. If activated, these expectancies shape our behavior toward others in ways that may influence their behavior. Second, the model recognizes the importance of our gender identities, or self-conceptions as masculine or feminine. If activated, they lead us to conform to the gender-related demands of the situation. Finally, the model places emphasis on the situational context. Situations may place strong or weak pressures on individuals for the display of gender stereotypic behavior.

According to this model, the emergence of gender differences in any interaction will depend on a complex interplay between the content of our gender-related expectancies, the extent to which concerns are aroused for self-presentation as men and women, and the nature of situational cues. Thus, there is considerable complexity in making predictions from this model for gender-related behavior. Deaux and Major argue:

> Because perceivers, individual selves, and situations all vary in the content and salience of gender-linked expectations, we expect a wide range in observed female and male behaviors, from virtual identity of the sexes in some circumstances to striking differences in others. The task of the investigator thus becomes one of specifying how each of these sources of influence will operate in a specified circumstance.[42]

This model contends that the greatest gender differences are found in situations where gender stereotypes have been activated. For example, in initial encounters when there are not clear role prescriptions, gender roles become more salient in guiding behavior. When women are in the minority in the group, their distinctiveness makes gender salient. Gender must be activated or salient to be important to interaction. If gender is activated, definitions of oneself as a man or a women become salient. People have knowledge of the behavior that is prescribed for their sex and thus have expectations for their own behavior and that of others. Men and women will adapt themselves to the demands of the immediate situation.

Like expectation states theory and social role theory, Deaux and Major's theory assigns a great deal of weight to the importance of gender-related expectations in providing prescriptions for behavior and in shaping responses to others that may become self-fulfilling prophecies. Like social role theory, the interactive model predicts that in situations in which behavior is highly constrained and there is clear consensus about the behaviors to be performed, gender differences will be mitigated. Like the personality approach, Deaux and Major's theory gives weight to the importance of the gender identities of the participants. The model draws on the interaction of factors at the individual and interpersonal levels of analysis, but it does not take into account questions of power, status, and role that shape expectancies about gender.

A Comprehensive Approach

The interaction of a complex set of factors produces gender differences in behavior, and we can understand them only by analyzing gender simultaneously at the individual, the interpersonal, and the sociostructural level. Our division of labor assigns different roles to men and women, and it accords greater power, status, and prestige to men. Because gender is such an important social category, individuals early in life acquire gender identities or a sense of themselves as male or female. Men and women behave in different ways because of their different placement within the social hierarchy, the different statuses and roles they fulfill, the different skills and abilities they acquire in these roles, their desire to display behavior to confirm their gender identities, and the consequences they face for violating expectations for gender-related behavior. When gender is salient, men and women adapt to the demands of the situational context and enact gender-appropriate behavior.

The enactment of gendered behavior creates the illusion that the differences between women and men are essential and enduring dispositions. However, as Candace West and Don Zimmerman have argued, "A person's gender is not simply an aspect of what one is, but, more fundamentally, it is something that one *does*, and does recurrently, in interaction with others."[43] Indeed, individuals develop a gender identity or sense of self as a male or a female that leads to the enactment of certain types of behaviors and styles in accordance with sex role norms in some situational contexts. But, as West and Zimmerman contend, "the 'doing' of gender is undertaken by women and men whose competence as members of society is hostage to its production."[44]

The Search for Gender Differences and Its Implications

For many researchers of gender and communication over the past two decades, the search for gender differences has been motivated by two desires.[45] The first was a desire to unveil and document male dominance. Researchers hoped that the recognition and acknowledgment of gender inequalities would lay the groundwork for social change and greater equality for women. Researchers sought to find out "*how* men *do* dominance."[46] The study of gender and language became a study of the ways men enact inequality.

The second motive for a search for gender differences was a desire to counter the negative valuation placed on that which is female—to identify and reinterpret women's experience and to find an authentic female language and distinctive female subculture that could be highly valued. Women had been defined in opposition to men, by their otherness from men, whereas men were taken as the standard. From this masculine perspective, women's interaction style and speech characteristics were often taken to be deficiencies, while the characteristics of men were highly valued. Women's talk, for example, was denigrated as "gossip." Their speech was seen to convey hesitancy and uncertainty, the speech of men to convey certainty and authority.

Feminist researchers set out to examine women's behavior through a new lens. The talk of women friends was reinterpreted to be an "on-going mosaic of noncritical listening, mutual support, enhancement of self-worth, relationship exclusiveness, and personal growth and self-discovery."[47] Signs of uncertainty in women's language were reinterpreted to be signs of mutual support and solidarity.[48] The identification of differences provided the opportunity to redefine and newly value that which was female.

The valuation placed on female characteristics has changed over time. More recent research on gender role stereotypes shows that women are more favorably evaluated than men on expressive abilities. Now men are viewed as lacking the newly valued strengths of intimacy, connectedness, and expressiveness that women possess. The view that women were deficient in comparison to men has been replaced by the view that men are deficient in comparison to women in the interpersonal realm. We have attained instead a "deficit" view of men, one that valorizes women's interpersonal relatedness. The place we have reached is problematic. We now misrepresent and devalue men just as women were misrepresented using masculine models, and we continue to define men and women in opposition to one another and to polarize differences.

The Use of Research Evidence

Regardless of their original motives and intentions, researchers produce findings that can be subject to different interpretations and put to different uses. Depending on our reading of the research evidence, we can emphasize or minimize gender differences. What motivates us to give more weight to one perspective than to the other?

An emphasis on gender difference can be used to sustain the status quo. We live in a society where men hold positions of power and prestige, where there are structural inequalities in the opportunities afforded to men and women, where greater resources are available to men, and where greater valuation is placed on men's efforts and points of view. If people believe that women are emotional rather than rational, submissive rather than dominant, dependent rather than independent, then they are likely to conclude that women are ill-suited for the positions now reserved for men in our society. The supportive, emotional, unselfish, and expressive characteristics of women, however, suit them well for domestic roles. If people believe that men are not nurturant, expressive, or supportive, it would be unwise for men to have primary responsibility for the raising of children, nursing the sick, or caring for the elderly. If men are task oriented, assertive, and directive, they are better suited to the demands of many high-status work roles.

Curt Hoffman and Nancy Hurst argue that widely held stereotypes about the different personality traits of women and men are "an attempt to rationalize, justify, or explain the sexual division of labor."[49] From the perspective of those who hold the more powerful positions in society, it is useful for men and women to assume different roles, and it is reassuring to believe that they do so because their personalities suit them for those roles. People can use gender differences in personality to explain the fact that men and women are assigned to such different roles. By assuming the differences between women and men are essential and enduring dispositions, we can see our current social arrangements as an accommodation to these naturally occurring differences.

The perpetuation of gender stereotypes helps to sustain current realities and to keep inequalities in place, because gender stereotypes provide prescriptions for how individuals ought to behave. Women are rewarded for the display of feminine behavior, but women who behave in a stereotypically feminine manner are poorly suited for opportunities afforded to men. Men are rewarded for the display of masculine behavior, but men who behave in a stereotypical masculine manner are poorly suited for the roles assigned to women. As a consequence of gender stereotypes, women remain less powerful and relegated to less valued types of roles and behavior.

We can use an emphasis on the greater similarity than difference between men and women and on the situational variability in the appearance of gender difference to question the legitimacy of social arrangements that sustain the unequal treatment of men and women. By focusing on the small magnitude of gender differences and on within-gender and situational variability in behavior, we can show that gender is not an expression of naturally occurring differences in the styles and personalities of men and women. From this perspective, differences in the behavior of men and women become the product of the allocation of different roles, resources, and power to men and women and the product of gender-related expectations and situational demands on the behavior of women and of men. Our evidence shows that when placed in the same social roles, given the same legitimate authority, and observed over time, men and women do not differ in leadership or task orientation. These findings provide strong arguments for why current social arrangements could be changed, why men are no more suited to the positions they now hold in society than women are. We can use the minimization of gender differences to make the case for social change—for the argument that roles would better be assigned based on individual abilities and attributes than on gender.

Approaches to Social Change

Numerous studies have been carried out over the last 25 years that document group differences between men and women. The research findings, however, permit different interpretations or understandings of why those differences exist. How we explain gender differences will have important implications for whether and how we go about trying to achieve greater equality between men and women.

If gender differences are taken to be inherent or biologically based differences, then many would argue that the status quo should be maintained, because it builds on characteristics that come naturally to males and females. There is no research evidence, however, that gender differences in conversational style are biologically based differences.

If gender differences are attributed to personality differences, to differences in the styles and dispositions acquired by men and women, then the inequalities women face are perceived to stem from limitations in their own personalities, and possibilities for change reside in the individual in counseling or therapy; more profound social change is not required. Men can learn to be more interpersonal and expressive, women to be more assertive and dominant. If a woman feels dominated by her husband, she can learn to stand up to him. If a man feels unable to be emotionally expressive with his friends, he can learn to display this behavior.

The data reviewed in this book suggest, however, that gender differences in behavior are not best accounted for by essential differences located in the personalities of men and women. As long as people hold expectations that men are more competent at a task than women, women will not be recognized equally with men regardless of their personal skills, knowledge, or task competence. Change at the individual level will not be sufficient to overcome inequalities in status and role or to escape from the gender role stereotypes that derive from these inequalities.

Men and women acquire different skills because they are represented disproportionately in different social roles.[50] One route to social change would be to dissociate roles from gender—to give men the opportunity to engage in roles requiring expressive skills now reserved for women, and to give women the opportunity to engage in roles requiring the display of dominance and leadership now reserved for men. Without going beyond popular conceptions that certain roles are best played by members of one sex or the other, women and men cannot have the same opportunities to learn the skills currently acquired by members of the opposite sex. Until roles currently reserved for men or women are fully legitimized for members of the opposite sex, people who enter these roles will be treated with suspicion, their motives and character will be questioned, and their behavior will be perceived and evaluated differently.

If gender differences are attributed to social forces outside the individual, then the possibilities for attaining greater gender equality will require profound social change, which is not easily accomplished. In her research on working-class families, Lillian Rubin reports that women who have entered the workforce enter family decision making in more forceful ways.[51] When women did not work outside the home, they felt they lacked the right to contradict their husbands; when women held jobs, they felt free to have their say and to make demands on their husbands to do housework and childcare. The difference in their behavior stemmed not from personality change, but from changes in their social roles that brought about changes in behavior. But even when wives are employed outside the home, it is the wives and not the husbands who do the majority of housework and childcare.[52] The dominant and subordinate status of men and women is not easily overcome.

Directions for the Future

A central question that faces scholars is what should be on the research agenda for the future. What kinds of questions should researchers be asking? Since the 1970s, feminists have raised questions about biases inherent in current conceptualizations of gender and in the focus of research.[53] The questions that research asks and the way it is designed to answer them play a major role in shaping our understanding of gender.

Studies That Focus on Within-Group Variability

Because group differences have been deemed important and variability within members of the same sex to be of only tangential relevance, little attention has been paid to within-gender variability. Researchers have conducted relatively few studies that address the interaction of gender with race, ethnicity, class, or sexual orientation. This has created the misconception that members of each sex form homogeneous groups. As Rhoda Unger has suggested, comparisons are needed of black and white women, heterosexual and lesbian women, and working-class women and affluent women.[54] Extension of research to diverse subject populations will highlight the variability in behavior among women and among men. Studies that are more inclusive of existing diversity among members of the same sex will center our attention more directly on the accuracy of traditional stereotypes of the behavior of men and women.

Avoidance of Sex as an Independent Variable Without Proper Controls

Sex of subject is not a variable that can be manipulated by the experimenter. Yet, when the behavior of men and women differs, the assumption is often made that sex was the cause of the difference. If men assume leadership more than women, an association exists between sex and leadership, but there may be other variables that co-vary with gender that are responsible for the gender difference in leadership. Some scholars have argued for years that we must be more cautious in our use of sex of subject as an independent variable. Some have even suggested that we stop using sex as an independent variable.[55] Studies comparing men and women without proper controls for confounding variables augment the conception that men and women speak and interact differently because they are essentially different.

Research has too often failed to look directly at the influence of variables that co-vary with gender like social role and status. We need more studies that compare the behavior of women and men in the same social role in natural settings—comparisons of fathers who are the primary caretakers of young children with mothers who are the primary caretakers of young children, male secretaries to female secretaries, male executives to female executives. Studies such as these enable us to examine the relative influence of role and gender on behavior, to see whether traditional gender differences are mitigated when status and role are controlled. They allow for an understanding of the other variables that play a role in the linguistic and interactive choices people make in specific contexts. Confounding variables need to be included in research as independent variables.

Studies of Gender That Examine Situational Influences

Gender differences in behavior are situationally variable. The exploration of situational variables can provide alternative explanations for gender differences that are found in our research.[56] Which contexts make gender salient and elicit gender stereotypic behavior and which do not? We need to build situational context into research as an independent variable; that is, we need to compare the behavior of women and men in contexts that are more likely to elicit masculine or feminine behavior to see the extent to which gender or situational context predicts behavior.

Avoidance of Single-Sex Studies

It is problematic in research on gender to restrict studies to subjects of a single sex. For many years, studies were conducted and theories were constructed in psychology based on data from samples of all male subjects.[57] The research findings were erroneously taken to characterize women as well as men without any supporting evidence. A reverse trend has now emerged in more recent research and theory. Studies are being conducted using only female subjects. However, the assumption is now being made that the results would not hold true for men, again without supporting evidence. Recent work on women by Carol Gilligan and or by researchers at the Stone Center at Wellesley College has made an enormous contribution to furthering our depth of understanding of relational capacities in women, focusing attention on aspects of behavior overlooked in previous research.[58] We cannot properly draw the conclusion, however, that the relational capacities found in women are exclusive to women without making a comparison of men and women.

Avoidance of Masculine and Feminine Labels for Behaviors

We need to raise questions about the assignment of gender to behaviors and the implications of doing so. Men and women are found to display both masculine and feminine behavior depending on the situational context. For example, support work in conversation is not feminine behavior. Teachers, group facilitators, and clinicians, be they women or men, all use support work in conversation to draw out other people's points of view. Social-emotional behavior is not feminine behavior. It has come to acquire this association because of the roles women have traditionally played in society, but it is a style of interaction used by both men and women. Social-emotional leadership is important to the productive functioning of any group and is displayed by both men and women.[59]

In an interview study, Janet Spence and Linda Sawin found that instrumental and expressive personality characteristics had little place in people's self-images of masculinity and femininity.[60] Initially, only 12% of the men mentioned instrumental traits or roles (e.g., being a leader, assertive, or a problem solver) as part of their self-image of masculinity, and another 12% of the men did so with further prompting. More men located their masculinity in their family and work roles (38%). None of the women initially mentioned expressive characteristics (e.g., a need/want to please, to make people happy) as part of their self-images of femininity, and 19% of the women did with further prompting. Again, more women located their femininity in their role as wife and mother (46%) than in expressive traits. Although instrumental and expressive characteristics have been taken to distinguish men and women, they did not play a central role in individuals' self-definitions of masculinity and femininity. "In describing themselves, what became most salient for many was their current roles and the characteristics they perceived to be demanded by those roles."[61] Although their plea is only beginning to be heard, Spence and Sawin argued that traditional conceptions of masculinity and femininity be discarded.

Contemporary feminist psychoanalytic therapists argue that the assignment of gender to many behaviors has important consequences for the experiences of men and women and can create dilemmas of the self.[62] When individuals violate the norms for sex-appropriate behavior, internally they may feel anxiety, "out of gender." As Muriel Dimen contends, "Sometimes one's gender resembles an ill-fitting garment."[63] Individuals are pressed to split off and disown parts of themselves that are not congruent with their gender.[64] In not doing so, they pay a price in disdain, disapproval, and discrimination. Our current labeling of behaviors as masculine and feminine is not descriptive of much of the behavior of men and women, does not coincide with their self-images of masculinity and femininity, and is costly to individuals when behavior deviates from these descriptions.

Studies of Gender Role Violations

One place to focus attention is on the forces that operate at the interpersonal level to keep the production of gender in place. We need
studies of the experience and treatment of individuals who violate
norms for sex-related behavior. The display of dominance or submissiveness is not equivalent for men and women because dominance and submissiveness are gender-related traits. A man and
woman will experience the display of dominant behavior differently,
and they will be responded to differently because dominance is gender appropriate for a man and gender inappropriate for a woman.
A man who stays home and is the primary caretaker of his young
children may display comparable behavior to a woman who plays
the same role, but his experience will not be equivalent because he
has violated gender-related prescriptions for behavior. He will be
viewed by many with suspicion. Studies of men and women displaying either traditionally masculine or feminine behaviors should
focus on their experience and treatment. Such a focus will provide
important information about the forces that keep men and women
hostage in the production of gendered behavior.

Conclusion

This book has concentrated on gender differences in conversational
interaction, but the issues raised throughout are pertinent to gender
differences in many other domains of behavior. To take one example,
an extensive literature exists on gender and nonverbal behavior, and
the identical issues have been raised in both research domains.[65]
Gender differences in nonverbal behavior mirror status differences
with men and high-status individuals showing similar behavior.
Nonverbal behavior, like verbal behavior, takes on different meanings depending on the situational context. The nonverbal behavior of
adult women—that is, their tendency to smile more, gaze more,
show more facial expressiveness—has been interpreted to reflect
weakness and subordination just as women's language has been
interpreted to reflect hesitancy and subordination. Meaning has
been assigned to the nonverbal behaviors, as to linguistic behaviors,
without direct evidence about their meaning. Gender differences in
nonverbal behavior, like those in verbal behavior, vary in magnitude
across situations and are greater in laboratory than in field studies.
As with gender differences in verbal interaction, the identical nonverbal behavior is evaluated differently if it is performed by a man or

a woman. Even when women use body postures associated with dominance, they are not rated as dominant as men.[66]

My goal in writing this book has been to call into question polarized conceptions of the interaction styles of women and men, to question conceptions of gender differences as attributes that reside within individuals, and to place gender back in a larger social context that shapes the expression of gendered behavior. Strongly held beliefs that men and women are essentially different in the way they think, interpret the world, and interact are problematic because they foster gender stereotypes, which help to sustain current realities and to keep inequalities in place. The stronger our beliefs that men and women are essentially different, the more firmly we will keep inequalities in place.

Notes

Chapter 1. The Elusive Truth About Men and Women

1. Tannen (1990a).
2. Gray (1992).
3. Gray (1992), p. 5.
4. Wood (1994).
5. Aries (1987).
6. Differences in the ways that men and women communicate will be referred to as gender differences rather than sex differences. The term sex difference is commonly used to refer to innate biological differences between males and females—that is, differences that do not vary across cultures or over time. The term gender differences, on the other hand, is used to refer to socially constructed differences between males and females, to cultural expressions of masculinity and femininity that are learned rather than innate. Gender differences may vary from one culture to another and from one historical period to another within the same culture. Differences in the interaction styles of men and women are a question of gender—that is, socially acquired differences—rather than sex or biologically based differences.
7. See, for example, Foss & Foss (1983), Henley & Kramarae (1991), Kramarae (1981), Pedersen (1980), Putnam (1982), Ragan (1989), Rakow (1986), Thorne & Henley (1975), and West & Zimmerman (1987).
8. See, for example, Bohan (1993), Grady (1979, 1981), Hare-Mustin & Marecek (1990), Maccoby & Jacklin (1974), O'Leary, Unger & Wallston (1985), Unger (1979, 1990), Unger & Denmark (1975), and Wallston (1981).
9. Scholars like Beall (1993), Bohan (1992), Flax (1990), Gergen (1985), Hare-Mustin & Marecek (1988, 1990), and Unger (1990) have brought the ideas of postmodern philosophy from the humanities into psychology. Jane Flax suggests that Jacques Derrida, Richard Rorty, Jean-Francois Lyotard, and Michel Foucault have been particularly influential post-

215

modern writers. For an encounter with their ideas, Flax suggests, for example, Bayes, Bohman & McCarthy (1978), Culler (1982), Derrida (1981), Foucault (1973), and Rorty (1979).

10. Hare-Mustin & Marecek (1988), pp. 455–456.

11. Flax (1990).

12 Culler (1982).

13. Strodtbeck & Mann (1956), p. 9.

14. The actual percentage of behavior by men and women that was task related was never directly reported by Strodtbeck and Mann, but it can be calculated from other findings that are reported.

15. Aries (1987).

16. Regardless of the set of behaviors being studied, there will be variability in the scores for men and for women; they form distributions that overlap. When we compare the behavior of men to that of women statistically, we calculate average scores for men and for women and use tests to determine whether the differences that occurred were larger than differences that might have occurred by chance variation alone if there were actually no differences between the behavior of men and women.

Whether the difference between the means for men and women turns out to be statistically significant depends on the sample size, the degree of variability among men and among women, and the degree of difference between the mean scores for men and women. The larger the sample size, the larger the differences between the means for men and women, and the smaller the variability within each group, the more likely a statistically significant result will be found.

17. Technically, the effect size is calculated by taking the difference between the mean scores for males and females and dividing that by the pooled within-group standard deviation.

18. Epstein (1988).

19. Eagly (1987), Hyde & Linn (1986).

20. Giles, Smith, Ford, Condor & Thakerar (1980).

21. A more detailed and technical discussion of meta-analysis can be found in Eagly (1987).

22. Studies using multiple dependent variables often find gender differences on only a few of those variables. The gender differences are highlighted, but the findings of no difference are rarely cited by later reviewers and get lost in the literature. In addition, many findings of no difference are considered to be unworthy of publication.

23. Cohen (1977).

24. Cohen (1977), p. 26.

25. Eagly & Wood (1991).

26. Eagly (1987).

27. Thomas & French (1985).

28. Oliver & Hyde (1993).

29. Hall (1984).

30. Linn & Petersen (1986).

31. Ashmore (1990).

32. Unger (1990).

33. Unger (1990), p. 115.

34. Abelson (1985), Prentice & Miller (1992), Rosenthal & Rubin (1979), Rosnow & Rosenthal (1989). For example, if a small effect cumulates over time, it becomes in essence a large effect (Abelson (1985), or if the outcome of the effect has life and death consequences, a small effect is important.

35. Kenkel (1963).

36. See Rosnow & Rosenthal (1989).

37. Basow (1992).

38. Mulac, Lundell & Bradac (1986).

39. Mulac & Lundell (1986), Mulac, Wiemann, Widenmann & Gibson (1988).

40. See critique by Ragan (1989).

41. Mulac et al. (1986).

42. Mulac & Lundell (1986).

43. Horner (1972).

44. Gilligan (1982).

45. See Larrabee (1993), Tresemer (1977), and Mednick (1989).

46. Youniss & Smollar (1985). Gender differences in self-disclosure are discussed in chapter 6.

47. See, for example, Henley (1973–1974), Kramarae (1981), Spender (1980), Thorne & Henley (1975), and Unger (1976, 1979).

48. Eakins & Eakins (1983).

49. Johnson (1994).

50. Risman (1987).

51. Parlee (1981).

52. Barnett, Marshall, Raudenbush & Brennan (1993).

53. Risman (1987), p. 28.

54. Early discussions of this issue can be found in Unger (1979) and Wallston (1981).

55. Frieze, Sales & Smith (1991).

56. These pressures to appear attractive hold not only for heterosexual individuals in relation to the opposite sex. Gay men have been found to be more highly preferred as a partner if they present a stereotypical masculine image (Bell & Weinberg, 1978).

57. Gilligan (1982).

58. Stack (1986).

59. Leik (1963).

60. Lakoff (1975).

61. Holmes (1984).

62. Bohan (1993), p. 13.

63. Dimen (1991), p. 348.

64. Harris (1994).

65. West & Zimmerman (1987).

66. You can find numerous accounts of these processes in textbooks on women and gender. There is an early discussion of these issues in a textbook by Unger (1979), and the issues are well discussed in recent texts by Basow (1992) and Unger & Crawford (1992).

67. The process of sex role socialization has been described in numerous textbooks and articles over the past two decades. For a recent summary of these issues, see Cross & Markus (1993).

68. Bem (1993), p. 125.

69. Bem (1993).

70. Goldner (1991).

71. Binion (1990), Harris (1994).

72. Ashmore (1990).

73. Transsexuals provide an interesting exception.

74. The importance of sex as a stimulus characteristic has been recognized for years. Early analyses of this issue can by found in Grady (1979) and Unger (1979). A more recent review can be found in Cross & Markus (1993).

75. Grady (1979).

76. Smith (1985).

77. John & Sussman (1984–1985).

78. Geis (1993), p. 13.

79. Cross & Markus (1993).

80. Berger, Cohen & Zelditch (1972).

81. Pugh & Wahrman (1983), Wood & Karten (1986).

82. Ross (1977).

83. Goldner (1991).

84. Carbonell (1984), Fleischer & Chertkoff (1986), Megargee (1969), Nyquist & Spence (1986).

85. Mischel (1968).

86. Deaux & Major (1987).

87. A further discussion of this issue can be. found in chapter 8.

88. Fiske (1993), p. 622.

Chapter 2. Task and Expressive Roles in Groups

1. Parsons (1955). Support for his claim came from research on 14 all-male problem-solving groups by Bales & Slater (1955), in which role differentiation in social interaction occurred along instrumental and expressive lines.

2. Bales (1950).

3. Bales (1970).

4. Bales (1950).

5. Kenkel (1963).

6. Bales (1970).

7. Ridgeway & Johnson (1990).

8. Bales (1970).

9. See, for example, Anderson & Blanchard (1982), Carli (1989), Heiss (1962), Piliavin & Martin (1978), and Strodtbeck & Mann (1956).

10. Bales (1970), pp. 154–155.

11. Strodtbeck & Mann (1956).

12. Strodtbeck & Mann (1956), p. 635.

13. See, for example, Aries (1982), Carli (1989), Craig & Sherif (1986), Johnson & Schulman (1989), Kenkel (1963), Mabry (1985), Nemeth, Endicott & Wachtler (1976), Piliavin & Martin (1978), and Taylor & Strassberg (1986).

14. Anderson & Blanchard (1982).

15. Strodtbeck & Mann (1956), p. 10.

16. For example, although Eleanor Maccoby and Carol Jacklin in their comprehensive review of research on gender-related differences found few differences between men and women, the differences they found have been traditionally stressed in introductory psychology textbooks rather than the many similarities (Maccoby & Jacklin, 1974).

17. Carli (1982).

18. The lower number is based on studies with known d, the larger estimate is based on all studies with d estimated at 0 for studies with unknown effect sizes (Carli, 1982).

19. Cohen (1977).

20. Wheelan & Verdi (1992).

21. Leik (1963).

22. Heiss (1962).

23. Levinger (1964).

24. Levinger (1964), p. 447. Levinger argues that there can be no social-emotional specialization when groups are reduced to only 2 people, only in larger groups.

25. See Bales & Slater (1955).

26. Wheelan & Verdi (1992).

27. Wheelan & Verdi (1992), p. 6.

28. Wheelan & Verdi (1992), p. 7.

29. Brehm & Kassin (1993).

30. For example, see Mabry (1985).

31. Yamada, Tjosvold & Draguns (1983).

32. Strodtbeck & Mann (1956).

33. Carli (1989).

34. Lockheed & Hall (1976).

35. McGuire, McGuire & Winton (1979).

36. Kanter (1977a).

37. Izraeli (1983).

38. Johnson & Schulman (1989).

39. Nemeth, Endicott & Wachtler (1976).

40. Conversion to percentages is found in Anderson & Blanchard (1982).

41. The data were converted to percentages by Anderson & Blanchard (1982).

42. Strodtbeck & Mann (1956).

43. See Anderson & Blanchard (1982) and Aries (1982).

44. Carli (1989), Piliavin & Martin (1978).

45. Piliavin & Martin (1978).

46. Groups held three discussions, but during the second discussion an operant conditioning procedure was used to encourage an initially quiet speaker to participate more. Thus, data from the second and third discussion periods are confounded by effects of the manipulation; I therefore discuss only data from the first time period.

47. Carli (1989).

48. Carli used the combined category "attempted answers" (including "giving suggestions, opinions, or orientation") as her measure of task behavior, scored agrees and disagrees as separate categories, and collapsed the positive and negative reactions into measures of positive and negative social behavior.

49. Carli (1989), p. 573.

50. Strodtbeck & Mann (1956).

51. Berger, Cohen & Zelditch (1972), Berger, Fisek, Norman & Zelditch (1977).

52. Expectation states theory has been criticized for its inability to account for behavior in single-sex groups. According to the theory, status characteristics like gender should only be activated when individuals differ by sex, or when gender is seen as relevant to the task and will lead to differential performance expectations for males and females. For an extension of this theory to behavior in single-sex groups, see Ridgeway (1988) and Ridgeway & Diekema (1992).

53. Meeker & Weitzel-O'Neill (1977).

54. Ridgeway (1982).

55. Snodgrass (1985, 1992).

56. Snodgrass (1985).

57. Snodgrass (1992).

58. Eagly (1987); see also Eagly & Karau (1991).

59. Bales (1970).

60. Bales (1970).

61. Rapp (1992).

62. Kanter (1977a).

Chapter 3. Dominance and Leadership in Groups

1. See, for example, Rosenkrantz, Vogel, Bee, Broverman & Broverman (1968) and Fecteau, Jackson & Dindia (1992).

2. See, for example, Aries (1976), Duncan & Fiske (1977), Eakins & Eakins (1983), Hilpert, Kramer & Clark (1975), Kenkel (1963), Kimble & Musgrove (1988), Lockheed & Hall (1976), Mulac (1989), Siderits, Johann-sen & Fadden (1985), Simkins-Bullock & Wildman (1991), Strodtbeck & Mann (1956), Willis & Williams (1976), and Wood & Karten (1986).

3. See, for example, Anderson & Blanchard (1982), Carbonell (1984), Craig & Sherif (1986), Eagly & Karau (1991), Fleischer & Chertkoff (1986), Lockheed (1985), Lockheed & Hall (1976), Megargee (1969), and Stake (1981).

4. Bales (1970).

5. Researchers have looked at the average duration of utterances, but this has been a less reliable measure of leadership and a less reliable marker of gender differences. Some studies find men take longer turns than women (e.g., Eakins & Eakins, 1983; Frances, 1979; Mulac, 1989); some find women take longer turns than men (e.g., Bilous and Krauss, 1988; Markel, Long & Saine, 1976). Some studies have measured both speaking time and duration of utterance and have found gender differences on one of these indicators but not the other (e.g., Bilous & Krauss, 1988; Markel et al., 1976).

6. This was noted early on by Mann (1959).

7. The review by Stein & Heller (1979) included 72 correlations. Measures of total verbal participation correlated very highly with general measures of leadership (mean correlation $r = .74$) and general measures of task leadership ($r = .84$); total verbal participation correlated highly with task behavior ($r = .69$) and with giving information and opinions ($r = .72$).

8. The analysis by Mullen, Salas & Driskell (1989) covered 25 studies of face-to-face interaction using measures of either general or task leadership. They found that higher participation predicts leadership emergence regardless of whether the measures of leadership were based on observer judgments (effect size $d = 1.398$) or member judgments (effect size $d = 1.306$).

9. Robert F. Bales and Philip Slater (Bales & Slater, 1955) originally advanced the theory that groups tend to have two complementary leaders, a task specialist and a social-emotional specialist, but later research (Bales, 1958; Bonacich & Lewis, 1973) and reanalyses of Bales and Slater's data (Lewis, 1972) suggest that task and social-emotional roles are independent.

10. Lockheed (1985).

11. James & Drakich (1993).

12. Eagly & Karau (1991).

13. Cohen (1977).

14. Denmark (1977).

15. See, for example, Henley (1973–1974), Kramarae (1981), Thorne & Henley (1975), and Unger (1976, 1979).

16. Eakins & Eakins (1983).

17. Strodtbeck (1951).

18. Strodtbeck & Mann (1956).

19. Kenny & Zaccaro (1983).

20. Fitzpatrick & Dindia (1986).

21. Carbonell (1984), Fleischer & Chertkoff (1986), Kaess, Witryol & Nolan (1961), Megargee (1969), Nyquist & Spence (1986).

22. Andrews (1984), Stake & Stake (1979).

23. Andrews (1984).

24. Stake (1978).

25. Spillman, Spillman & Reinking (1981).

26. Rogers & Jones (1975).

27. Megargee (1969).

28. Carbonell (1984), Davis & Gilbert (1989), Fleischer & Chertkoff (1986), Nyquist & Spence (1986).

29. Carbonell (1984) in a first study reported here used the same task as Megargee. Nyquist & Spence (1986) used the board game MasterMind as the experimental task. The task used by Fleischer & Chertkoff (1986) involved subjects arranging dominoes on a grid.

30. Carbonell (1984).

31. Nyquist & Spence (1986).

32. Fleischer & Chertkoff (1986).

33. Davis & Gilbert (1989).

34. Nyquist & Spence (1986).

35. Fleischer & Chertkoff (1986).

36. Davis & Gilbert (1989).

37. Research by Kaess, Witryol & Nolan (1961) similarly shows that scores on general activity, ascendance and sociability could be used to discriminate leaders from nonleaders for males in all-male or mixed groups, but they could not discriminate leaders from nonleaders for females in mixed groups. The authors did not study all-female interactions.

38. Bilous & Krauss (1988).

39. Fennell, Barchas, Cohen, McMahon & Hildebrand (1978).

40. Aries (1973, 1976).

41. Bales (1970).

42. Miller (1985).

43. Ellis (1982).

44. Rhoda Unger (personal communication).

45. McCarrick, Manderscheid & Silbergeld (1981).

46. Wood & Rhodes (1992).

47. Ellis & McCallister (1980).

48. Ridgeway & Diekema (1989).

49. Johnson & Schulman (1989), Martin & Shanahan (1983), Wolman & Frank (1975).

50. Bunyi & Andrews (1985), Crocker & McGraw (1984), Johnson & Schulman (1989).

51. Aries (1973).

52. See literature reviews by Lockheed (1985) and Stein & Heller (1979).

53. Eagly & Karau (1991).

54. Carbonell (1984).

55. Dovidio, Brown, Heltman, Ellyson & Keating (1988).

56. Wentworth & Anderson (1984).

57. Kimble & Musgrove (1988).

58. Siderits et al. (1985).

59. See, for example, Frances (1979), Hirschman (1973), Markel, Long & Saine (1976), and Martin & Craig (1983).

60. See, for example, Dabbs & Ruback (1984), Kimble, Yoshikawa & Zehr (1981), and Petzel, Johnson & Bresolin (1990).

61. Aries (1976).

62. Eagly & Karau (1991).

63. See, for example, Dovidio et al. (1988), Hilpert et al. (1975), Kimble & Musgrove (1988), Mulac (1989), and Simkins-Bullock & Wildman (1991).

64. Eagly & Karau (1991).

65. Spillman et al. (1981).

66. Schneier & Bartol (1980).

67. See Heiss (1962), which was discussed in chapter 2.

68. Kenkel (1963).

69. Hershey & Werner (1975).

70. Kollock, Blumstein & Schwartz (1985).

71. See, for example, Bilous & Krauss (1988), Jose, Crosby & Wong-McCarthy (1980), Hans & Eisenberg (1985), Markel et al. (1976), Martin & Craig (1983), McMillan, Clifton, McGrath & Gale (1977), and Shaw & Sadler (1965).

72. Eagly & Johnson (1990).

73. Baird & Bradley (1979).

74. See, for example, Bartol & Butterfield (1976), Eagly, Makhijani & Klonsky (1992), Jacobson & Effertz (1974), and Jago & Vroom (1982).

75. Lamude & Daniels (1984).

76. Snodgrass & Rosenthal (1984).

77. Results for gender differences in leadership effectiveness are parallel to results for leadership styles. Gregory Dobbins and Stephanie Platz (Dobbins & Platz, 1986) carried out a meta-analysis of gender differences in leadership that include laboratory experiments, laboratory simulations, and field studies. They found the results of laboratory studies to be more prone to bias in line with stereotypes: male leaders were seen as more effective in laboratory studies ($d = .25$) but not in field studies ($d = .04$).

78. See, for example, Bartol & Wortman (1979), Brown (1979), Chapman (1975), Day & Stogdill (1972), Dobbins & Platz (1986), Martin (1972), Ragins (1992), Rice, Instone & Adams (1984), and Shockley-Zalabak & Morley (1984).

79. Anderson & Blanchard (1982).

80. Moskowitz, Jung Suh & Desaulniers (1994).

81. Wyatt (1988).

82. Kanter (1977b).

83. Wyatt (1988), p. 168.

84. Carli (1989).

85. Klein & Willerman (1979).

86. Stitt, Schmidt, Price & Kipnis (1983).

87. Geis, Boston & Hoffman (1985).

88. These predictions derive from the theory of status characteristics and expectation states (Berger et al., 1972) discussed in chapter 2.

89. Wood & Karten (1986).

90. Leet-Pellegrini (1980).

91. Pugh & Wahrman (1983, 1985).

92. Foschi (1992). The data are relevant to other minorities and disadvantaged groups in interaction. Race, like sex, serves as an external status characteristic, and blacks, like women, are assumed to have less task ability. Studies of interracial groups of blacks and whites have found that when the greater competence of blacks has been demonstrated to both black and white group members, inequalities are reduced (Cohen & Roper, 1972).

93. Wagner, Ford & Ford (1986); see also Wagner (1988).

94. Stake (1981).

95. Maier (1970).

96. See Meeker & Weitzel-O'Neill (1977) and Ridgeway (1982). Their ideas are discussed in chapter 2.

97. Eagly (1987), see also Eagly & Karau (1991).

98. Swim (1994).

99. Bartol & Wortman (1979), Day & Stogdill (1972), Hollander & Yoder (1980), Kanter (1977b).

100. Eagly & Johnson (1990).

Chapter 4. The Function and Patterning of Interruptions in Conversation

1. Zimmerman & West (1975).

2. West (1979); reported also by West & Zimmerman (1983).

3. See, for example, Bohn & Stutman (1983), Eakins & Eakins (1983), LaFrance & Carmen (1980), McMillan et al. (1977), Mulac et al. (1988), Natale, Entin & Jaffe (1979), Octigan & Niederman (1979), West & Zimmerman (1983), and Zimmerman & West (1975).

4. See, for example, Bohn & Stutman (1983), Kennedy & Camden (1983), McMillan et al. (1977), Nohara (1992), West (1979), West & Zimmerman (1983), and Zimmerman & West (1975).

5. See, for example, Bilous & Krauss (1988), Carli (1990), Dindia (1987), Frances (1979), Johnson (1994), Jose et al. (1980), Kollock, Blumstein & Schwartz (1985), LaFrance & Carmen (1980), Leet-Pellegrini (1980), Marche & Peterson (1993), Martin & Craig (1983), Roger & Nesshoever (1987), Roger & Schumacher (1983), Rogers & Jones (1975), Simkins-Bul-

lock & Wildman (1991), Smith-Lovin & Brody (1989), Smith-Lovin & Robinson (1992), Smythe & Huddleston (1992), Trimboli & Walker (1984), and Willis & Williams (1976).

6. Sacks, Schegloff & Jefferson (1974).

7. Murray (1985).

8. Tannen (1983).

9. Coates (1988).

10. Duncan (1974).

11. See, for example, Johnson (1994), Kollock et al. (1985), Natale et al. (1979), Roger & Nesshoever (1987), Roger & Schumacher (1983), and Smith-Lovin & Brody (1989).

12. Murray (1985).

13. Shaw & Sadler (1965).

14. Natale et al. (1979), p. 877.

15. LaFrance & Carmen (1980); see also LaFrance (1981).

16. Kennedy & Camden (1983).

17. Dindia (1987).

18. Willis & Williams (1976).

19. Goldberg (1990).

20. See Dindia (1987) and Kennedy & Camden (1983).

21. Zimmerman & West (1975).

22. Smith-Lovin & Brody (1989).

23. Kollock et al. (1985).

24. See, for example, Bilous & Krauss (1988), Bohn & Stutman (1983), Carli (1990), Drass (1986), LaFrance & Carmen (1980), Nohara (1992), Roger & Nesshoever (1987), Roger & Schumacher (1983), and Trimboli & Walker (1984).

25. Natale et al. (1979).

26. Murray & Covelli (1988).

27. Dindia (1987).

28. Markel et al. (1976) found that when people are seated together more intimately for informal conversation the duration of simultaneous speech was greater than when they were seated at a more formal distance (3 feet versus 12 feet apart).

29. Coates (1988).

30. Bilous & Krauss (1988), Dabbs & Ruback (1984), Hirschman (1973), Markel et al. (1976).

31. Edelsky (1981).

32. Tannen (1983).

33. Nohara (1992).

34. Bohn & Stutman (1983), McMillan et al. (1977), Mulac, et al. (1988), Octigan & Niederman (1979).

35. McMillan et al. (1977), Smith-Lovin & Brody (1989).

36. Smith-Lovin & Brody (1989).

37. Smith-Lovin & Robinson (1992).

38. Beattie (1981).
39. Greif (1980), West & Zimmerman (1977).
40. West & Zimmerman (1977).
41. Eakins & Eakins (1983).
42. Woods (1988).
43. Kollock et al. (1985).
44. Johnson (1994).
45. Beattie (1981).
46. Irish & Hall (in press).
47. See, for example, Dindia (1987), McMillan et al. (1977), Octigan & Niederman (1979), Smith-Lovin & Brody (1989), Willis & Williams (1976), and Zimmerman & West (1975).
48. Beattie (1981), Frances (1979), Marche & Peterson (1993), Martin & Craig (1983), Simkins-Bullock & Wildman (1991).
49. Smith-Lovin & Brody (1989).
50. McMillan et al. (1977).
51. Dindia (1987).
52. Rhoda Unger (personal communication).
53. See, for example, Dindia (1987), Kennedy & Camden (1983), Nohara (1992), and Octigan & Niederman (1979).
54. Bilous & Krauss (1988), Hirschman (1973), Markel et al. (1976).
55. Zimmerman & West (1975).
56. Dindia (1987), Nohara (1992).
57. Nohara (1992).
58. Roger & Schumacher (1983).
59. Roger & Nesshoever (1987).
60. Drass (1986).
61. Ferguson (1977).
62. Rogers & Jones (1975).
63. Aries, Gold & Weigel (1983).
64. James & Clarke (1993).

Chapter 5. Language Use and Conversation Management

1. Bodine (1975).
2. Lakoff (1973, 1975, 1977).
3. Lakoff (1977).
4. Lakoff (1973).
5. Lakoff (1990), p. 205.
6. Cameron, McAlinden & O'Leary (1988).
7. Fishman (1983).
8. Philips (1980), pp. 534–535.
9. Brown & Levinson (1978).
10. Brown (1980).
11. Baxter (1984).

12. Holmes (1989).

13. Johnson (1976).

14. Sagrestano (1992).

15. Steil & Hillman (1993).

16. Lapadat & Seesahai (1978).

17. Preisler (1986).

18. Preisler (1986), p. 284.

19. Engle (1980), Gleason (1987).

20. Jones (1992).

21. There were an equal number of men and women present at the meeting, but the author failed to control for the amount of talk by men and women.

22. See, for example, Carli (1990), Hartman (1976), Holmes (1984), Holmes (1985), Mulac & Lundell (1986), and Preisler (1986).

23. See, for example, Cameron et al. (1988), Dubois & Crouch (1975), and Lapadat & Seesahai (1978).

24. See, for example, Baumann (1976).

25. See, for example, Holmes (1984), Holmes (1985), Cameron et al. (1988), and Kollock et al. (1985).

26. Dubois & Crouch (1975).

27. Hartman (1976).

28. Holmes (1984).

29. Holmes (1984), p. 153.

30. Holmes (1984), p. 153.

31. Holmes (1984), p. 153.

32. Holmes (1985).

33. Cameron et al. (1988).

34. Cameron et al. (1988), p. 84.

35. Coates (1988).

36. Coates (1988), p. 116.

37. Coates (1988), p. 117.

38. Holmes (1984), p. 172.

39. Fishman (1978, 1980, 1983), McMillan et al. (1977), Simkins-Bullock & Wildman (1991).

40. Johnson (1980).

41. Johnson (1980).

42. Johnson (1980), p. 66.

43. Johnson (1980), p. 66.

44. Johnson (1980), p. 67.

45. Coates (1988).

46. Johnson (1980).

47. Johnson (1980), p. 71.

48. Johnson (1980), p. 71.

49. Johnson (1980), p. 72.

50. Freed (1994). At one end of the continuum, questions seek factual, public information; at the other end, they seek no information and may con-

vey information (e.g., rhetorical questions or humorous questions where the speaker knows the answer or no answer is expected).

51. Fishman (1978, 1980, 1983).

52. Unfortunately, Fishman does not report differences between the total amount of speech by men and by women in her sample as a baseline. If men dominated the conversations, the effect is quite strong; if women dominated the conversations, the gender difference is small in magnitude.

53. Simkins-Bullock & Wildman (1991).

54. McMillan et al. (1977).

55. Swacker (1976).

56. Swacker (1976), p. 156.

57. Expert power is one of six sources of social power identified by French & Raven (1959). The six forms of power are expert power, reward power, coercive power, referent power, legitimate power, and informational power.

58. Johnson (1976).

59. Holmes (1984).

60. Holmes (1984, 1985, 1986).

61. Holmes (1985), p. 33.

62. Holmes (1985), p. 33.

63. Sayers & Sherblom (1987).

64. Carli (1990), Coates (1987), Fishman (1980), Hartman (1976), Preisler (1986).

65. Baumann (1976), Holmes (1985), Martin & Craig (1983), McMillan et al. (1977), Sayers & Sherblom (1987).

66. Holmes (1985).

67. Holmes (1985), p. 33.

68. Hartman (1976).

69. Hartman (1976), p. 87.

70. Coates (1987).

71. Holmes (1986).

72. Holmes (1986).

73. Holmes (1986), p. 6.

74. Holmes (1986), p. 8.

75. Holmes (1986), p. 11.

76. Holmes (1986), p. 8.

77. Holmes (1986), p. 9.

78. Holmes (1986), p. 15.

79. Fishman (1980).

80. See, for example, McMillan et al. (1977).

81. See, for example, Martin & Craig (1983).

82. McMillan et al. (1977), p. 555.

83. Carli (1990).

84. Carli (1990), p. 945.

85. Duncan (1974).

86. See, for example, Bilous & Krauss (1988), Carli (1990), Crosby, Jose & Wong-McCarthy (1981), Hirschman (1973), Roger & Schumacher (1983), and Roger & Nesshoever (1987).

87. Bilous & Krauss (1988), Carli (1990).

88. McLachlan (1991).

89. See, for example, Fishman (1983) and Zimmerman & West (1975).

90. Zimmerman & West (1975).

91. Fishman (1983).

92. Trimboli & Walker (1984).

93. Carli (1990), Hirschman (1973).

94. Coates (1988).

95. See, for example, Kollock et al. (1985) and Woods (1988).

96. Kollock et al. (1985).

97. Woods (1988).

98. Leet-Pellegrini (1980).

99. Roger & Schumacher (1983), Roger & Nesshoever (1987).

100. Key (1972), p. 19.

101. Carli (1990), Lapadat & Seesahai (1978), McMillan et al. (1977), Mulac & Lundell (1986), Mulac et al. (1986), Mulac et al. (1988).

102. Carli (1990), Lapadat & Seesahai (1978), McMillan et al. (1977), Mulac et al. (1988).

103. Mulac & Lundell (1986).

104. Mulac et al. (1986).

105. Lakoff (1975), p. 55.

106. Carli (1990).

107. Aries (1976), Gleser, Gottschalk & Watkins (1959), Hirschman (1973), Mulac & Lundell (1986), Mulac et al. (1988), Poole (1979), Swacker (1976).

108. Aries (1976).

109. Hirschman (1973).

110. Mulac et al. (1988).

111. Mulac & Lundell (1986).

112. Gleser et al. (1959).

113. Poole (1979).

114. Swacker (1976).

115. Mulac et al. (1986).

116. Mulac & Lundell (1986).

117. Swacker (1976), p. 157.

118. Carli (1990).

119. Fishman (1978, 1983).

120. West & Garcia (1988).

121. Murphy (1989).

122. Carli (1990).

123. O'Barr & Atkins (1980).

124. Preisler (1986).

125. Preisler (1986), p. 75.

126. Preisler (1986), p. 289.

127. Carli (1990), Hagen & Kahn (1975), Meeker & Weitzel-O'Neill (1977), Ridgeway (1982).

128. Crosby & Nyquist (1977).

129. Brouwer, Gerritsen & De Haan (1979).

130. Mulac et al. (1986).

131. Males used more present tense and progressive verbs, more active voice verbs, more syllables per word, more definite/demonstrative noun phrases, more judgmental adjectives, and more syllables per word.

132. See, for example, Frances (1979) and Poole (1979).

133. Other predictors for females were action verbs, rhetorical questions, adverbials beginning a sentence, oppositions, negations, prepositional phrases, and greater mean sentence length.

134. Mulac & Lundell (1986).

135. The speech characteristics for men included references to pictures, geographical references, elliptical sentences (that lack subject or predicate), spacial references, impersonals (e.g., *it, there are*), justifiers, and more units (words or vocalized pauses).

136. The language features in common were mean sentence length, intensive adverbs, negations, and oppositions.

137. The other 3 markers of female speech were verbs of cognition, dependent clauses with subordinating conjunctions understood, and pauses.

138. Mulac & Lundell (1986), p. 96.

139. Mulac & Lundell (1986), p. 96.

140. Mulac et al. (1988).

141. See critique by Ragan (1989).

142. Brouwer et al. (1979).

143. Crosby & Nyquist (1977).

144. Soskin & John (1963).

145. McLachlan (1991).

146. Baxter (1984), Johnson (1976), Sagrestano (1992), Steil & Hillman (1993).

147. Linde (1988).

148. Jones (1992).

149. Crosby & Nyquist (1977).

150. O'Barr & Atkins (1980).

151. Johnson (1994).

152. Moore, Shaffer, Goodsell & Baringoldz (1983).

153. Sagrestano (1992).

154. Woods (1988).

155. Leet-Pellegrini (1980).

156. Meeker & Weitzel-O'Neill (1977), Ridgeway (1982).

157. Cameron et al. (1988).

158. See, for example, Preisler (1986) and Mulac et al. (1988).

159. Carli (1990), McMillan et al. (1977).

160. Giles, Mulac, Bradac & Johnson (1987).

161. See, for example, Frank (1978), Key (1972) and Kramer (1974).

162. Thorne & Henley (1975), p. 30.

163. See, for example, reviews by Aries (1987), Cameron (1992), Coates (1986), Giles et al. (1980), Haas (1979), Kramarae (1982), Martin & Craig (1983), Pearson (1985), Philips (1980), Poynton (1989), Ragan (1989) and Smythe & Schlueter (1989).

164. Mary-Jeanette Smythe and David Schlueter (1989) carried out a meta-analysis on gender and language aggregating results from studies of different language forms. Unfortunately, their research report indicates that effect size analyses had not been completed. Initial analyses revealed no consistent gender differences in language use.

165. Tannen (1990a) provides a good example of this position. Janis Bohan provides an excellent discussion and critique of the essentialist position (Bohan, 1993). See also Hare-Mustin & Marecek (1990).

166. Maltz & Borker (1982).

167. Henley & Kramarae (1991).

168. Hecht, Collier & Ribeau (1993).

169. Tracy & Eisenberg (1990/1991).

170. Thorne (1993), p. 97.

171. Fiske & Stevens (1993).

172. Henley (1977), Kramarae (1981), Lakoff (1990), MacKinnon (1987), Spender (1980), Thorne & Henley (1975), Torres (1992).

173. Thorne & Henley (1975), p. 15.

174. Fishman (1983).

175. Fishman (1983), p. 405.

176. Kramarae (1990), p. 350.

177. Hauser, Powers, Weiss-Perry, Follansbee, Rajapark & Green (1987).

178. Maccoby (1990), p. 517.

179. Bakan (1966).

180. Bakan (1966), p. 152.

181. See Smith (1979).

182. See methodological critiques by Grady (1981), Parlee (1981), Putnam (1982), Ragan (1989), and Wallston (1981).

183. See discussion of this issue by Wallston (1981).

Chapter 6. The Content of Conversation

1. Kramer (1977).

2. See, for example, Johnson & Aries (1983a), Jones (1980), and Tiger & Luria (1978).

3. Jones (1980), p. 197.

4. See, for example, Baxter & Wilmot (1986), Caldwell & Peplau (1982), Douvan & Adelson (1966), Haas & Sherman (1982), and Johnson & Aries (1983a).

5. Caldwell & Peplau (1982).

6. Caldwell and Peplau do not report the actual mean scores but only the results of a *t*-test, so the size of this difference is impossible to determine from the research report.

7. Baxter & Wilmot (1986).

8. Douvan & Adelson (1966).

9. Haas & Sherman (1982).

10. Johnson & Aries (1983a).

11. See, for example, Aries (1976), Aries & Johnson (1983), Ayres (1980), Baxter & Wilmot (1986), Caldwell & Peplau (1982), Davidson & Duberman (1982), Derlega, Durham, Gockel & Sholis (1981), Douvan & Adelson (1966), Gitter & Black (1976), Haas & Sherman (1982), Johnson & Aries (1983a), Levin & Arluke (1985), Morgan (1976), Reis, Senchak & Solomon (1985), Rubin & Shenker (1978), Stokes, Fuehrer & Childs (1980), Tannen (1990b), Tschann (1988), Wheeler & Nezlek (1977), Williams (1985), and Youniss & Smollar (1985).

12. Aries (1976), Ayres (1980), Derlega et al. (1981), Tannen (1990b).

13. Davidson & Duberman (1982), Douvan & Adelson (1966), Tschann (1988), Youniss & Smollar (1985).

14. Aries & Johnson (1983), Caldwell & Peplau (1982), Gitter & Black (1976), Johnson & Aries (1983a), Morgan (1976), Rubin & Shenker (1978), Stokes et al. (1980), Williams (1985).

15. Levin & Arluke (1985).

16. Baxter & Wilmot (1986), Reis et al. (1985), Wheeler & Nezlek (1977).

17. Dindia & Allen (1992), p. 118.

18. Jourard & Lasakow (1958).

19. Jourard & Richman (1963).

20. Jourard (1971), p. 35.

21. See, for example, Cozby (1973), Dindia & Allen (1992), Goodstein & Reinecker (1974), Hill & Stull (1987), Rosenfeld, Civikly & Herron (1979).

22. Hill & Stull (1987).

23. Hill & Stull (1987), p. 94.

24. Morgan (1976).

25. Gitter & Black (1976).

26. Derlega et al. (1981), Kraft & Vraa (1975).

27. Davidson & Duberman (1982), Tschann (1988).

28. Lavine & Lombardo (1984), Lombardo & Lavine (1981).

29. Altman & Taylor (1973).

30. Sollie & Fischer (1985).

31. Dindia & Allen (1992).

32. Caldwell & Peplau (1982).

33. Johnson & Aries (1983b), Mulcahy (1973), Stokes et al. (1980), Williams (1985).
34. Douvan & Adelson (1966).
35. Johnson & Aries (1983b).
36. Youniss & Smollar (1985).
37. Davidson & Duberman (1982).
38. Tschann (1988).
39. Aries & Johnson (1983).
40. Fitzpatrick & Dindia (1986), Markel et al. (1976).
41. Aries (1976).
42. Aries (1976).
43. Komarovsky (1974).
44. Derlega et al. (1981).
45. Derlega et al. (1981), p. 437.
46. Derlega, Winstead, Wong & Hunter (1985).
47. Reis, Senchak & Solomon (1985).
48. Shimanoff (1983).
49. Findings are inconsistent when willingness to self-disclose to a counselor has been assessed. In one study, men reported they were more willing to self-disclose to males they don't know well than to females (Stokes et al., 1980). In another study, their willingness to disclose to male or female counselors depended on the type of information to be disclosed (Snell, Hampton & McManus, 1992). Findings based on subjects' reports of willingness to disclose are not consistent with findings based on subjects self-reports of actual self-disclosure.
50. Hacker (1981).
51. See, for example, Derlega et al. (1981), Shimanoff (1983), and Reis et al. (1985).
52. Sollie & Fischer (1985).
53. Tschann (1988).
54. Reis et al. (1985).
55. See, for example, Johnson & Aries (1983a) and Komarovsky (1962).
56. Mulcahy (1973).
57. Hendrick (1981).
58. Antill & Cotton (1987), Tschann (1988).
59. Hacker (1981).
60. Hill & Stull (1987).
61. Rubin, Hill, Peplau & Dunkel-Schetter (1980). For example, subjects have been found to disclose more to a high-disclosing than a low-disclosing confederate (Erlich & Graeven, 1971).
62. The other popular measure for the assessment of masculinity and femininity is the Personal Attributes Questionnaire (PAQ) (Spence, Helmreich & Stapp, 1968). This measure has not been frequently used in studies of self-disclosure.
63. Sandra Bem (Bem, 1976) argued that androgynous individuals are

more flexible and situationally adaptive than sex-typed individuals, since they are less constrained and can draw on the capacities of either orientation.

64. Sandra Bem shifted her attention to a new concept—gender schemas—focusing on the ways individuals impose a gender-based classification on social reality and see reality as carved into gender polarized categories (Bem, 1981, 1985, 1993). Janet Spence moved toward thinking about gender as a multidimensional phenomenon, finding at best a loose connection between an individual's thoughts and feelings about sex and gender (Spence, 1985; Spence & Sawin, 1985).

65. Stokes, Childs & Fuehrer (1981).

66. See, for example, Antill & Cotton (1987), Greenblatt, Hasenauer & Freimuth (1980), Lavine & Lombardo (1984), Lombardo & Lavine (1981), Narus & Fischer (1982), Sollie & Fischer (1985), and Stokes et al. (1981).

67. See review by Hill & Stull (1987).

68. Sollie & Fischer (1985).

69. Stokes et al. (1981). High self-disclosure does not necessarily mean intimate self-disclosure. Topics varied a great deal in degree of intimacy.

70. Winstead, Derlega & Wong (1984).

71. Antill & Cotton (1987), Bender, Davis, Glover & Stapp (1976).

72. Reis et al. (1985).

73. Sherrod (1989) found that androgynous or feminine women reported being no more self-disclosing to their best woman friend than androgynous men were to their best male friend.

74. See, for example, Aries (1976), Aries & Johnson (1983), Ayres (1980), Haas & Sherman (1982), Johnson & Aries (1983a), Kipers (1987), and Levin & Arluke (1985).

75. Aries & Johnson (1983).

76. Hill & Stull (1987).

77. Harding (1975).

78. Research by Lillian Rubin (1976) in the 1970s on white, working-class men and women revealed clear role differentiation. Women placed marriage and motherhood at the center of their lives regardless of whether they worked outside the home. Research has shown that the lives of working-class couples were marked by sex segregation, with husbands and wives forming separate social networks (Bott, 1971; Fallding, 1961; Young & Willmott, 1957).

79. Hacker (1981).

80. Caldwell & Peplau (1982), Douvan & Adelson (1966), Swain (1989).

81. Jones (1980), p. 195.

Chapter 7. Gender Stereotypes and the Perception and Evaluation of Participants in Interaction

1. This issue was raised early on by Grady (1979).

2. Broverman, Vogel, Broverman, Clarkson & Rosenkrantz (1972).

3. Bakan (1966).

4. Kramer (1977).

5. Burgoon, Dillard & Doran (1983).

6. Johnson (1976). Johnson used Raven's (1965) six bases of power for her analysis (see discussion in chapter 5).

7. Siegler & Siegler (1976).

8. Hawkins (1988).

9. Zimmerman & West (1975). For a discussion of this study, see chapter 4.

10. Orcutt & Harvey (1985).

11. Orcutt and Harvey found a great deal of variability in responses from one sample to another.

12. Edelsky (1976, 1977).

13. Fillmer & Haswell (1977).

14. Andersen (1984, 1986).

15. Werner & LaRussa (1985).

16. Bergen & Williams (1991).

17. Fecteau et al. (1992).

18. Bem (1974).

19. Spence et al. (1974).

20. Smith (1979).

21. Swim (1994).

22. The assessment of stereotype accuracy is considerably complex and has been well addressed by Judd & Park (1993).

23. Smith (1979).

24. Geis (1993).

25. Smith (1980, 1985).

26. Thakerar & Giles (1981).

27. Newcombe & Arnkoff (1979).

28. Cutler & Scott (1990).

29. Street & Hopper (1982).

30. Werner & LaRussa (1985).

31. Broverman et al. (1972); Rosenkrantz et al. (1968).

32. Werner & LaRussa (1985).

33. Eagly & Mladinic (1989).

34. Eagly & Mladinic (1989), p. 555.

35. The presence of gender differences depends on the situational context of the interaction.

36. Lamude & Daniels (1990).

37. Mulac, Incontro & James (1985).

38. It is interesting to note that subjects were unable to accurately guess the sex of the speaker when speaker sex was not identified.

39. Where speech was incorrectly assigned to a member of the opposite sex, the gender differences were smaller than when language or stereotype effects operated alone.

40. Zahn (1989).

41. Lawrence, Stucky & Hopper (1990).

42. See, for example, Bradac, Schneider, Hemphill & Tardy (1980), Carli (1990), Liska, Mechling & Stathas (1981), Miller & McReynolds (1973), Newcombe & Arnkoff (1979), Quina, Wingard & Bates (1987), and Wiley & Woolley (1988).

43. See, for example, Newcombe & Arnkoff (1979) and Quina et al. (1987).

44. See, for example, Bradac et al. (1980), Carli (1990), Liska et al. (1981), Miller & McReynolds (1973), and Wiley & Woolley (1988).

45. Carli (1990) .

46. Erickson, Lind, Johnson & O'Barr (1978).

47. The case involved a collision between an ambulance and an automobile in which the critically ill patient in the ambulance died shortly after the accident. The patient's family was suing to recover damages for the loss of the patient. The witness was a friend and neighbor of the patient.

48. O'Barr & Atkins (1980).

49. Carli (1990).

50. Cynthia Berryman (Berryman, 1980; see also Berryman-Fink & Wilcox, 1983) found different results, but she used a measure of "female language" that was discrepant with the previous studies. She defined female language by correct pronunciation of *-ing* word endings, paralinguistic behavior like pitch and tone, lack of interruptions, and social-emotional behaviors. Female speech forms were associated with greater credibility; male speech forms with greater extroversion.

51. Bradac, Hemphill & Tardy (1981). In this study, ratings of speech are based only on male speakers.

52. Wiley & Eskilson (1985).

53. Bradac & Mulac (1984a).

54. Liska et al. (1981).

55. Quina et al. (1987).

56. Warfel (1984).

57. Mulac & Lundell (1986).

58. In multiple regression analyses, a combination of linguistic variables predicted socio-intellectual ratings with 53% accuracy (however, five of these variables predicted attributional judgments in a manner inconsistent with expectation), aesthetic quality with 43% accuracy, and dynamism with 33% accuracy.

59. Siegler & Siegler (1976).

60. Newcombe & Arnkoff (1979).

61. Bradac & Mulac (1984b).

62. Wright & Hosman (1983).

63. Wiley & Woolley (1988).

64. Robinson & Reis (1989).

65. Bradley (1981).

66. Bradley (1981).

67. Wright & Hosman (1983).

68. Lawrence et al. (1990).

69. Wiley & Eskilson (1985).

70. Carli (1990).

71. Wiley & Woolley (1988).

72. Wiley & Eskilson (1985).

73. Eagly et al. (1992).

74. Eagly et al. (1992), p. 18.

75. Burgoon et al. (1983).

76. Snyder, Tanke & Berscheid (1977).

77. Zanna & Pack (1975).

78. Rice, Bender & Vitters (1980).

79. Spence & Helmreich (1972).

80. Lott (1987).

81. Bradley (1980).

82. Ralph Wahrman and Meredith Pugh (1974) found that a competent female who deviated from the procedural rules in a group (e.g., interrupted, talked out of turn, suggested she get a larger share of winnings) had much less influence than a male showing the same behavior.

83. Giles, Scherer & Taylor (1979).

84. Giles & Ryan (1982).

85. Brehm & Kassin (1993).

86. Fiske & Taylor (1991).

87. Fiske & Stevens (1993).

88. Fiske & Stevens (1993), p. 179.

89. Ruble & Ruble (1982).

90. Giles & Ryan (1982), Kramarae (1982).

Chapter 8. Conclusions, Explanations, and Implications

1. Pugh & Vasquez-Nutall (1983) cited in Comas-Diaz (1994).

2. Binion (1990).

3. McCullough (1987), cited in Kramarae (1990).

4. An example of this type of critique can be found in Poynton (1989).

5. Gray (1992).

6. Eagly (1987), pp. 18–19.

7. Cohen (1977).

8. Grady (1979).

9. Eagly & Wood (1982), Eagly (1987).

10. See Williams (1993) for research that is now being conducted on men in traditionally female occupations.

11. These three levels of analysis are pointed out by Unger & Crawford (1992).

12. A recent discussion of the different theoretical perspectives on the childhood socialization of gender can be found in Beall & Sternberg (1993).

13. Maltz & Borker (1982).

14. See review by Maccoby (1990).

15. Maltz & Borker (1982), p. 203.

16. Maltz & Borker (1982), p. 212.

17. Tannen (1990a).

18. My thinking has been influenced by Henley and Kramarae (1991), among others.

19. Berk (1985).

20. Graddol & Swann (1989).

21. Fitzpatrick (1988).

22. See research cited in Fitzpatrick (1988), p. 38.

23. Fiske & Stevens (1992).

24. Thorne (1993).

25. For an excellent discussion of individual variability in the gender identity, see Ashmore (1990).

26. Harris (1994).

27. Comas-Diaz (1994).

28. Recent psychoanalytic accounts of development, although quite varied, fall within the personality perspective. They postulate that mothers' differential treatment of sons and daughters leads women to develop a "self-in-relation"—to acquire the personality traits of empathy, connectedness, and an identity characterized by interpersonal involvement. It leads men to repress their relational capacities and to develop autonomy and independence (e.g., Chodorow, 1978; Jordan, 1986; Miller, 1976; Surrey, 1985).

29. Basow (1992), p. 55.

30. See, for example, Henley (1973–1974, 1977), Kramarae (1981), Thorne & Henley (1975), and Unger (1976, 1979).

31. Kramarae (1989).

32. Kramarae (1981), p. 119.

33. See, for example, Bohan (1992), Hare-Mustin & Marecek (1990), and Unger (1983, 1990).

34. Eagly (1987).

35. Deaux & Major (1987).

36. Eagly (1987), p. 19.

37. Berger et al. (1977).

38. Broverman et al. (1972), Rosenkrantz et al. (1968).

39. Broverman, Broverman, Clarkson, Rosenkrantz & Vogel (1970).

40. Graddol & Swann (1989).

41. Deaux & Major (1987).

42. Deaux & Major (1987), p. 382.

43. West & Zimmerman (1987), p. 140.

44. West & Zimmerman, (1987), p. 126.

45. Cameron (1992).

46. Spender (1985), p. 3.

47. Johnson & Aries (1983a).

48. Coates (1986), Holmes (1984).

49. Hoffman & Hurst (1990), p. 199.

50. Eagly (1987).

51. Rubin (1994).

52. See, for example, Berk (1985). Recent research shows that husbands are more likely to do more of the housework traditionally done by women if they are employed fewer hours during the times that their wives are employed (Presser, 1994). This study provides further evidence that greater equality is achieved in the household when social roles are changed.

53. See, for example, Grady (1979, 1981), Hare-Mustin & Marecek (1990), Parlee (1981), Unger (1976, 1979, 1990), and Wallston (1981).

54. Unger (1990), p. 136.

55. See, for example, Epstein (1988), Grady (1981), Parlee (1981), Putnam (1982), Ragan (1989), Unger (1979), Unger & Denmark (1975), and Wallston (1981).

56. An early discussion of the importance of situational influences on behavior can be found, for example, in Unger (1979), and Wallston (1981).

57. Examples include McClelland's work on achievement motivation (McClelland, Atkinson, Clark & Lowell, 1953) and Kohlberg's work on moral development (Kohlberg, 1981).

58. See, for example, Brown & Gilligan (1992), Gilligan (1982), Gilligan, Lyons & Hanmer (1989), Gilligan, Rogers & Tolman (1991), Jordan (1986), and Surrey (1985).

59. In his early work on all-male groups, Bales (Bales & Slater, 1955) found groups tended to have two complementary leaders, a task leader and a social-emotional leader. In all-male groups, men assume the role of social-emotional leader.

60. Spence & Sawin (1985).

61. Spence & Sawin (1985), p. 57.

62. Dimen (1991).

63. Dimen (1991), p. 338.

64. Goldner (1991).

65. Hall (1984, 1987), Henley (1973–1974, 1977), Mayo & Henley (1981).

66. Henley & Harmon (1985).

References

Abelson, R. P. (1985). A variance explanation paradox: When a little is a lot. *Psychological Bulletin, 97*(1), 129–133.

Altman, I., & Taylor, D. (1973). *Social penetration: The development of interpersonal relationships.* New York: Holt, Rinehart & Winston.

Andersen, E. S. (1984). The acquisition of sociolinguistic knowledge: Some evidence from children's verbal role-play. *Western Journal of Speech Communication, 48,* 125–144.

Andersen, E. S. (1986). The acquisition of register variation by Anglo-American children. In B. B. Schieffelin & E. Ochs (Eds.), *Language socialization across cultures* (pp. 153–161). Cambridge: Cambridge University Press.

Anderson, L. R., & Blanchard, P. N. (1982). Sex differences in task and social-emotional behavior. *Basic and Applied Social Psychology, 3*(2), 109–139.

Andrews, P. H. (1984). Performance-self-esteem and perceptions of leadership emergence: A comparative study of men and women. *Western Journal of Speech Communication, 48,* 1–13.

Antill, J. K., & Cotton, S. (1987). Self-disclosure between husbands and wives: Its relationship to sex roles and marital happiness. *Australian Journal of Psychology, 39*(1), 11–24.

Aries, E. (1973). *Interaction patterns and themes of male, female and mixed groups.* Unpublished doctoral dissertation, Harvard University.

Aries, E. (1976). Interaction patterns and themes of male, female, and mixed groups. *Small Group Behavior, 7*(1), 7–18.

Aries, E. (1982). Verbal and nonverbal behavior in single-sex and mixed-sex groups: Are traditional sex roles changing? *Psychological Reports, 51,* 127–134.

Aries, E. (1987). Gender and communication. In P. Shaver & C. Hendrick

(Eds.), *Sex and gender* (pp. 149–176). Newbury Park, CA: Sage Publications.

Aries, E. J., Gold, C., & Weigel, R. H. (1983). Dispositional and situational influences on dominance behavior in small groups. *Journal of Personality and Social Psychology, 44* (4), 779–786.

Aries, E., & Johnson, F. (1983). Close friendship in adulthood: Conversational content between same-sex freinds. *Sex Roles, 9,* 1183–1196.

Ashmore, R. D. (1990). Sex, gender, and the individual. In L. A. Pervin (Ed.), *Handbook of personality: Theory and research* (pp. 486–526). New York: Guilford.

Ayres, J. (1980). Relationship stages and sex and factors in topic dwell time. *Western Journal of Speech Communication, 44,* 253–260.

Baird, J. E., & Bradley, P. H. (1979). Styles of management and communication: A comparative study of men and women. *Communication Monographs, 46,* 101–111.

Bakan, D. (1966). *The duality of human existence.* Chicago: Rand McNally.

Bales, R. F. (1950). *Interaction process analysis: A method for the study of small groups.* Reading, MA: Addison-Wesley.

Bales, R. F. (1958). Task roles and social roles in problem-solving groups. In E. E. Maccoby, T. M. Newcomb, & E. L. Hartley (Eds.), *Readings in Social Psychology* (pp. 437–447). New York: Holt, Rinehart and Winston.

Bales, R. F. (1970). *Personality and interpersonal behavior.* New York: Holt, Rinehart and Winston.

Bales, R. F., & Slater, P. E. (1955). Role differentiation in small decision-making groups. In T. Parsons & R. F. Bales (Eds.), *Family, socialization, and interaction process* (pp. 259–306). New York: Free Press.

Barnett, R. C., Marshall, N. L., Raudenbush, S. W., & Brennan, R. T. (1993). Gender and the relationship between job experiences and psychological distress: A study of dual-earner couples. *Journal of Personality and Social Psychology, 64*(5), 794–806.

Bartol, K. M., & Butterfield, D. A. (1976). Sex effects in evaluating leaders. *Journal of Applied Psychology, 61*(4), 446–454.

Bartol, K. M., & Wortman, M. S. (1979). Sex of leader and subordinate role stress: A field study. *Sex Roles, 5*(4), 513–518.

Basow, S. A. (1992). *Gender: Stereotypes and roles* (3rd ed.). Pacific Grove, CA: Brooks/Cole.

Baumann, M. (1976). Two features of "women's speech"? In B. L. Dubois & I. Crouch (Eds.), *Proceedings of the Conference on the Sociology of the Languages of American Women* (pp. 33–40). San Antonio, TX: Trinity University Press.

Baxter, L. A. (1984). An investigation of compliance-gaining as politeness. *Human Communication Research, 10*(3), 427–456.

Baxter, L. A., & Wilmot, W. W. (1986). Interaction characteristics of disengaging, stable and growing relationships. In R. Gilmour & S. W. Duck

(Eds.), *The emerging field of personal relationships* (pp. 145–159). Hillsdale, NJ: Lawrence Erlbaum.

Bayes, K., Bohman, J., & McCarthy, T. (Eds.). (1978). *After philosophy: End or transformation*. Cambridge, MA: MIT Press.

Beall, A. E. (1993). A social constructionist view of gender. In A. E. Beall & R. J. Sternberg (Eds.), *The psychology of gender* (pp. 127–147). New York: Guilford.

Beall, A. E., & Sternberg, R. J. (1993). *The psychology of gender*. New York: Guilford.

Beattie, G. W. (1981). Interruption in conversational interaction, and its relation to the sex and status of the interactants. *Linguistics, 19*, 15–35.

Bell, A. P., & Weinberg, M. (1978). *Homosexualities: A study of diversity among men and women*. New York: Simon & Schuster.

Bem, S. L. (1974). The measurement of psychological androgyny. *Journal of Consulting and Clinical Psychology, 42*, 155–162.

Bem, S. L. (1976). Probing the promise of androgyny. In A. G. Kaplan & J. P. Bean (Eds.), *Beyond sex-role stereotypes: Readings toward a psychology of androgyny* (pp. 47–62). Boston: Little, Brown and Co.

Bem, S. L. (1981). Gender schema theory: A cognitive account of sex typing. *Psychological Review, 88*, 354–364.

Bem, S. L. (1985). Androgyny and gender schema theory: A conceptual and empirical integration. In T. B. Sonderegger, (Ed.), *Nebraska Symposium on Motivation* (Vol. 32, pp. 179–226). Lincoln: University of Nebraska Press.

Bem, S. L. (1993). *The lenses of gender: Transforming the debate on sexual inequality*. New Haven: Yale University Press.

Bender, V. L., Davis, Y., Glover, O., & Stapp, J. (1976). Patterns of self-disclosure in homosexual and heterosexual college students. *Sex Roles, 2*(2), 149–160.

Bergen, D. J., & Williams, J. E. (1991). Sex stereotypes in the United States revisited: 1972–1988. *Sex Roles, 24* (7/8), 413–423.

Berger, J., Cohen, B. P., & Zelditch, M. (1972). Status characteristics and social interaction. *American Sociological Review, 37*, 241–255.

Berger, J., Fisek, M. H., Norman, R. Z., & Zelditch, M. (1977). *Status characteristics and social interaction*. New York: Elsevier.

Berk, S. F. (1985). *The gender factory: The apportionment of work in American households*. New York: Plenum.

Berryman, C. L. (1980). Attitudes toward male and female sex-appropriate and sex-inappropriate language. In C. L. Berryman & V. A. Eman (Eds.), *Communication, language and sex* (pp. 195–216). Rowley, MA: Newbury House Publishers.

Berryman-Fink, C. L., & Wilcox, J. R. (1983). A multivariate investigation of perceptual attributions concerning gender appropriateness in language. *Sex Roles, 9*(6), 663–681.

Bilous, F. R., & Krauss, R. M. (1988). Dominance and accom- modation in the conversational behaviors of same- and mixed-gender dyads. *Language and Communication, 8*(3/4), 183–194.

Binion, V. J. (1990). Psychological androgyny: A black female perspective. *Sex Roles, 22*(7/8), 487–507.

Bodine, A. (1975). Sex differentiation in language. In B. Thorne & N. Henley (Eds.), *Language and sex: Difference and dominance* (pp. 130–151). Rowley, MA: Newbury House.

Bohan, J. S. (Ed.). (1992). *Seldom seen, rarely heard: Women's place in psychology.* Boulder: Westview Press.

Bohan, J. S. (1993). Regarding gender: Essentialism, constructionism, and feminist psychology. *Psychology of Women Quarterly, 17*, 5–21.

Bohn, E., & Stutman, R. (1983). Sex-role differences in the relational control dimension of dyadic interaction. *Women's Studies in Communication, 6*, 96–104.

Bonacich, P., & Lewis, G. H. (1973). Function specialization and sociometric judgment. *Sociometry, 36*, 31–41.

Bott, E. (1971). *Family and social networks: Roles, norms and external relationships in ordinary urban families* (2nd ed.). London: Tavistock.

Bradac, J. J., Hemphill, M. R., & Tardy, C. H. (1981). Language style on trial: Effects of "powerful" and "powerless" speech upon judgments of victims and villains. *Western Journal of Speech Communication, 45*, 327–341.

Bradac, J. J., & Mulac, A. (1984a). Attributional consequences of powerful and powerless speech styles in a crisis-intervention context. *Journal of Language and Social Psychology, 3*, 1–19.

Bradac, J. J., & Mulac, A. (1984b). A molecular view of powerful and powerless speech styles: Attributional consequences of specific language features and communicator intentions. *Communication Monographs, 51*, 307–319.

Bradac, J. J., Schneider, M. J., Hemphill, M. R., & Tardy, C. H. (1980). Consequences of language intensity and compliance-gaining strategies in an initial heterosexual encounter. In H. Giles, W. P. Robinson & P. M. Smith (Eds.), *Language: Social psychological perspectives* (pp. 71–75). Oxford, England: Pergamon Press.

Bradley, P. H. (1980). Sex, competence and opinion deviation: An expectation states approach. *Communication Monographs, 47*(2), 101–110.

Bradley, P. H. (1981). The folk-linguistics of women's speech: An empirical examination. *Communication Monographs, 48*, 73–90.

Brehm, S., & Kassin, S. M. (1993). *Social Psychology* (2nd ed.). Boston: Houghton Mifflin.

Brouwer, D., Gerritsen, M. M., & De Haan, D. (1979). Speech differences between women and men: On the wrong track? *Language in Society, 8*, 33–50.

Broverman, I. K., Broverman, D. M., Clarkson, F. E., Rosenkrantz, P. S., &

Vogel, S. R. (1970). Sex-role stereotypes and clinical judgments of mental health. *Journal of Consulting and Clinical Psychology, 34*(1), 1–7.

Broverman, I. K., Vogel, S. R., Broverman, D. M., Clarkson, F. E., & Rosenkrantz, P. S. (1972). Sex-role stereotypes: A current appraisal. *Journal of Social Issues, 28*, 59–78.

Brown, L. M., & Gilligan, C. (1992). *Meeting at the crossroads: Women's psychology and girls' development.* Cambridge: Harvard University Press.

Brown, P. (1980). How and why are women more polite: Some evidence from a Mayan community. In S. McConnell-Ginet, R. Borker, & N. Furman (Eds.), *Women and language in literature and society* (pp. 111–136). New York: Praeger.

Brown, P. & Levinson, S. (1978). Universals in language usage: Politeness phenomena. In E. N. Goody (Ed.), *Questions and politeness: Strategies in social interaction* (pp. 56–310). Cambridge: Cambridge University Press.

Brown, S. M. (1979). Male versus female leaders: A comparison of empirical studies. *Sex Roles, 5*(5), 595–611.

Bunyi, J. M., & Andrews, P. H. (1985). Gender and leadership emergence: An experimental study. *Southern Speech Communication Journal, 50*, 246–260.

Burgoon, M., Dillard, J. P., & Doran, N. E. (1983). Friendly or unfriendly persuasion: The effects of violations of expectations by males and females. *Human Communication Research, 10*(2), 283–294.

Caldwell, M. A., & Peplau, L. A. (1982). Sex differences in same-sex friendship. *Sex Roles, 8*(7), 721–732.

Cameron, D. (1992). *Feminism and linguistic theory.* New York: St. Martin's Press.

Cameron, D., McAlinden, F., & O'Leary, K. (1988). Lakoff in context: The social and linguistic functions of tag questions. In J. Coates & D. Cameron (Eds.), *Women in their speech communities: New perspectives on language and sex* (pp. 74–93). New York: Longman.

Carbonell, J. L. (1984). Sex roles and leadership revisited. *Journal of Applied Psychology, 69*, 44–49.

Carli, L. L. (1982). *Are women more social and men more task oriented? A meta-analytic review of sex differences in group interaction, reward allocation, coalition formation and cooperation in the Prisoners' Dilemma game.* Unpublished paper, University of Massachusetts.

Carli, L. L. (1989). Gender differences in interaction style and influence. *Journal of Personality and Social Psychology, 56*(4), 565–576.

Carli, L. (1990). Gender, language, and influence. *Journal of Personality and Social Psychology, 59*(5), 941–951.

Chapman, J. B. (1975). Comparison of male and female leadership styles. *Academy of Management Journal, 18*, 645–650.

Chodorow, N. (1978). *The reproduction of mothering: Psychoanalysis and the sociology of gender.* Berkeley: University of California Press.

Coates, J. (1986). *Women, men and language: A sociolinguistic account of sex differences in language.* London: Longman.

Coates, J. (1987). Epistemic modality and spoken discourse. *Transactions of the Philological Society,* 110–131.

Coates, J. (1988). Gossip revisited: Language in all-female groups. In J. Coates & D. Cameron (Eds.), *Women in their speech communities: New perspectives on language and sex* (pp. 94–122). New York: Longman.

Cohen, E. G., & Roper, S. S. (1972). Modification of interracial interaction disability: An application of status characteristics theory. *American Sociological Review, 37,* 643–657.

Cohen, J. (1977). *Statistical power analysis for the behavioral sciences.* New York: Academic Press.

Comas-Diaz, L. (1994). An integrative approach. In L. Comas-Diaz & B. Green (Eds.), *Women of Color: Integrating ethnic and gender identities in psychotherapy* (pp. 287–318). New York: Guilford.

Cozby, P. C. (1973). Self-disclosure: A literature review. *Psychological Bulletin, 79,* 73–91.

Craig, J. M., & Sherif, C. W. (1986). The effectiveness of men and women in problem-solving groups as a function of group gender composition. *Sex Roles, 14*(7/8), 453–466.

Crocker, J., & McGraw, K. M. (1984). What's good for the goose is not good for the gander: Solo status as an obstacle to occupational achievement for males and females. *American Behavioral Scientist, 27*(3), 357–369.

Crosby, F., Jose, P., & Wong-McCarthy, W. (1981). Gender, androgyny and conversational assertiveness. In C. Mayo & N. Henley (Eds.), *Gender and nonverbal behavior* (pp. 151–169). New York: Springer-Verlag.

Crosby, F., & Nyquist, L. (1977). The female register: An empirical study of Lakoff's hypotheses. *Language in Society, 6,* 313–322.

Cross, S. E., & Markus, H. R. (1993). Gender in thought, belief and action: A cognitive approach. In A. E. Beall & R. J. Sternberg (Eds.), *The psychology of gender* (pp. 55–98). New York: Guilford.

Culler, J. (1982). *On deconstruction: Theory and criticism after structuralism.* Ithaca, NY: Cornell University Press.

Cutler, A., & Scott, D. R. (1990). Speaker sex and perceived apportionment of talk. *Applied Psycholinguistics, 11*(3), 253–272.

Dabbs, J. M., & Ruback, R. B. (1984). Vocal patterns in male and female groups. *Personality and Social Psychology Bulletin, 10*(4), 518–525.

Davidson, L. R., & Duberman, L. (1982). Friendship: Communication and interactional patterns in same-sex dyads. *Sex Roles, 8*(8), 809–822.

Davis, B. M., & Gilbert, L. A. (1989). Effect of dispositional and situational influences on women's dominance expression in mixed-sex dyads. *Journal of Personality and Social Psychology, 57*(2), 294–300.

Day, D. R., & Stogdill, R. M. (1972). Leader behavior of male and female supervisors: A comparative study. *Personnel Psychology, 25,* 353–360.

Deaux, K., & Major, B. (1987). Putting gender into context: An interactive model of gender-related behavior. *Psychological Bulletin, 94*, 369–389.

Denmark, F. L. (1977). Styles of leadership. *Psychology of Women Quarterly, 2*(2), 99–113.

Derlega, V. J., Durham, B., Gockel, B., & Sholis, D. (1981). Sex differences in self-disclosure: Effects of topic content, friendship, and partner's sex. *Sex Roles, 7*(4), 433–447.

Derlega, V. J., Winstead, B. A., Wong, P. T. P., & Hunter, S. (1985). Gender effects in an initial encounter: A case where men exceed women in disclosure. *Journal of Social and Personal Relationships, 2*, 25–44.

Derrida, J. (1981). *Positions*. Chicago: University of Chicago Press.

Dimen, M. (1991). Deconstructing difference: Gender, splitting, and transitional space. *Psychoanalytic Dialogues, 1*(3), 335–352.

Dindia, K. (1987). The effects of sex of subject and sex of partner on interruptions. *Human Communication Research, 13*(3), 345–371.

Dindia, K., & Allen, M. (1992). Sex differences in self-disclosure: A meta-analysis. *Psychological Bulletin, 112*(1), 106–124.

Dobbins, G. H., & Platz, S. J. (1986). Sex differences in leadership: How real are they? *Academy of Management Review, 11*(1), 118–127.

Douvan, E., & Adelson, J. (1966). *The adolescent experience*. New York: John Wiley.

Dovidio, J. F., Brown, C. E., Heltman, K., Ellyson, S. L., & Keating, C. F. (1988). Power displays between women and men in discussions of gender-linked tasks: A multichannel study. *Journal of Personality and Social Psychology, 55*(4), 580–587.

Drass, K. A. (1986). The effect of gender identity on conversation. *Social Psychology Quarterly, 49*(4), 294–301.

Dubois, B. L., & Crouch, I. (1975). The question of tag questions in women's speech: They don't really use more of them, do they? *Language in Society, 4*, 289–294.

Duncan, S. (1974). On the structure of speaker-auditor interaction during speaking turns. *Language in Society, 2*, 161–180.

Duncan, S., & Fiske, D. (1977). *Face-to-face interaction: Research, methods and theory*. Hillsdale, NJ: Lawrence Erlbaum.

Eagly, A. H. (1987). *Sex differences in social behavior: A social-role interpretation*. Hillsdale, NJ: Lawrence Erlbaum.

Eagly, A. H., & Johnson, B. T. (1990). Gender and leadership style: A meta-analysis. *Psychological Bulletin, 108*(2), 233–256.

Eagly, A. H., & Karau, S. J. (1991). Gender and the emergence of leaders: A meta-analysis. *Journal of Personality and Social Psychology, 60*(5), 685–710.

Eagly, A. H., Makhijani, M. G., & Klonsky, B. G. (1992). Gender and the evaluation of leaders: A meta-analysis. *Psychological Bulletin, 111*(1), 3–22.

Eagly, A. H., & Mladinic, A. (1989). Gender stereotypes and attitudes toward women and men. *Personality and Social Psychology Bulletin, 15*, 543–588.

Eagly, A. H., & Wood, W. (1982). Inferred sex differences in status as a determinant of gender stereotypes about social influence. *Journal of Personality and Social Psychology, 43*(5), 915–928.

Eagly, A. H., & Wood, W. (1991). Explaining sex differences in social behavior: A meta-analytic perspective. *Personality and Social Psychology Bulletin, 17*, 306–315.

Eakins, B., & Eakins, R. G. (1983). Verbal turn-taking and exchanges in faculty dialogue. In B. L. Dubois and I. Crouch (Eds.), *Proceedings of the Conference on the Sociology of the Languages of American Women* (pp. 53–62). San Antonio, TX: Trinity University Press.

Edelsky, C. (1976). The acquisition of communicative competence: Recognition of linguistic correlates of sex roles. *Merrill-Palmer Quarterly, 22*, 47–59.

Edelsky, C. (1977). Acquisition of an aspect of communicative competence: Learning what it means to talk like a lady. In S. Ervin-Tripp & C. Mitchell-Kernan (Eds.), *Child Discourse* (pp. 225–243). New York: Academic Press.

Edelsky, C. (1981). Who's got the floor? *Language in Society, 10*, 383–421.

Ellis, D. G. (1982). Relational stability and change in women's consciousness-raising groups. *Women's Studies in Communication, 5*, 77–87.

Ellis, D. G., & McCallister, L. (1980). Relational control sequences in sex-typed and androgynous groups. *Western Journal of Speech Communication, 44*, 35–49.

Engle, M. (1980). Language and play: A comparative analysis of parental initiatives. In H. Giles, W. R. Robinson, & P. M. Smith (Eds.), *Language: Social psychological perspectives* (pp. 29–34). Oxford: Pergamon Press.

Epstein, C. F. (1988). *Deceptive distinctions: Sex, gender and the social order.* New Haven: Yale University Press & N.Y. Russel Sage Foundation.

Erickson, B., Lind, E. A., Johnson, B. C., & O'Barr, W. M. (1978). Speech style and impression formation in a court setting: The effects of "powerful" and "powerless" speech. *Journal of Experimental Social Psychology, 14*, 266–279.

Erlich, H. J., & Graeven, D. B. (1971). Reciprocal self-disclosure in a dyad. *Journal of Experimental Social Psychology, 7*, 389–400.

Fallding, H. (1961). The family and the ideal of a cardinal role. *Human Relations, 14*, 329–350.

Fecteau, T. J., Jackson, J., & Dindia, K. (1992). Gender orientation scales: An empirical assessment of content validity. In L. A. M. Perry, L. H. Turner, & H. M. Sterk (Eds.), *Constructing and reconstructing gender: Links among communication, language, and gender* (pp. 17–34). Albany: State University of New York Press.

Fennell, M. L., Barchas, P. R., Cohen, E. G., McMahon, A. M., & Hildebrand, P. (1978). An alternative perspective on sex differences in organizational settings: The process of legitimation. *Sex Roles, 4*(4), 589–604.

Ferguson, N. (1977). Simultaneous speech, interruptions and dominance. *British Journal of Social and Clinical Psychology, 16,* 295–302.

Fillmer, H. T., & Haswell, L. (1977). Sex-role stereotyping in English usage. *Sex Roles, 3*(3), 257–263.

Fishman, P. M. (1978). Interaction: The work women do. *Social Problems, 25*(4), 397–406.

Fishman, P. M. (1980). Conversational insecurity. In H. Giles, W. P. Robinson, & P. M. Smith (Eds.), *Language: Social psychological perspectives* (pp. 127–132). Oxford: Pergamon.

Fishman, P. M. (1983). Interaction: The work women do. In B. Thorne, C. Kramarae, & N. Henley (Eds.), *Language, gender and society* (pp. 89–101). Rowley, MA: Newbury House.

Fiske, S. T. (1993). Controlling other people: The impact of power on stereotyping. *American Psychologist, 48*(6), 621–628.

Fiske, S. T. & Stevens, L. E. (1993). What's so special about sex? Gender stereotyping and discrimination. In S. Oskamp & M. Costanzo (Eds.), *Gender issues in contemporary society* (pp. 173–196). Newbury Park, CA: Sage Publications.

Fiske, S., & Taylor, S. (1991). *Social cognition* (2nd ed.). New York: McGraw-Hill.

Fitzpatrick, M. A. (1988). *Between husbands and wives: Communication in marriage.* Newbury Park, CA: Sage.

Fitzpatrick, M. A., & Dindia, K. (1986). Couples and other strangers: Talk time in spouse-stranger interaction. *Communication Research, 13*(4), 625–652.

Flax, J. (1990). *Thinking fragments.* Berkeley: University of California Press.

Fleischer, R. A., & Chertkoff, J. M. (1986). Effects of dominance and sex on leader selection in dyadic work groups. *Journal of Personality and Social Psychology, 50*(1), 94–99.

Foschi, M. (1992). Gender and double standards for competence. In C. L. Ridgeway (Ed.), *Gender, interaction, and inequality* (pp. 181–207). New York: Springer-Verlag.

Foss, K. A., & Foss, S. K. (1983). The status of research on women and communication. *Communication Quarterly, 31*(3), 195–204.

Foucault, M. (1973). *The order of things.* New York: Vintage.

Frances, S. J. (1979). Sex differences in nonverbal behavior. *Sex Roles, 5*(4), 519–535.

Frank, F. W. (1978). Women's language in America: Myth and reality. In D. Butturff & E. Epstein (Eds.), *Women's language and style* (pp. 47–61). Akron, OH: L & S Books.

Freed, A. (1994). The form and function of questions in informal dyadic conversation. *Journal of Pragmatics, 21,* 621–644.

French, J. R. P., & Raven, B. H. (1959). The bases of social power. In D. Cartwright (Ed.), *Studies in social power* (pp. 150–167). Ann Arbor: University of Michigan Press.

Frieze, I. H., Sales, E., & Smith, C. (1991). Considering the social context in gender research: The impact of college students' life stage. *Psychology of Women Quarterly, 15*(3), 371–392.

Geis, F. L. (1993). Self-fulfilling prophecies: A social psychological view of gender. In A. E. Beall & R. J. Sternberg (Eds.), *The psychology of gender* (pp. 9–54). New York: Guilford.

Geis, F. L., Boston, M. B., & Hoffman, N. (1985). Sex of authority role models and achievement by men and women: Leadership performance and recognition. *Journal of Personality and Social Psychology, 49*(3), 636–653.

Gergen, K. J. (1985). The social constructionist movement in modern psychology. *American Psychologist, 40*(3), 266–275.

Giles, H., Mulac, A., Bradac, J. J., & Johnson, P. (1987). Speech accommodation theory: The first decade and beyond. In M. L. McLaughlin (Ed.), *Communication yearbook 10* (pp. 13–48). Newbury Park, CA: Sage Publications.

Giles, H., & Ryan, E. B. (1982). Prolegomena for developing a social psychological theory of language attitudes. In E. B. Ryan & H. Giles (Eds.), *Attitudes towards language variation: Social and applied contexts* (pp. 208–223). London: Edward Arnold.

Giles, H., Scherer, K., & Taylor, D. M. (1979). Speech markers in social interaction. In K. R. Scherer & H. Giles (Eds.), *Social markers in speech* (pp. 343–381). Cambridge: Cambridge University Press.

Giles, H., Smith, P. M., Ford, B., Condor, S., & Thakerar, J. N. (1980). Speech style and the fluctuating salience of sex. *Language Sciences, 2,* 260–282.

Gilligan, C. (1982). *In a different voice.* Cambridge, MA: Harvard University Press.

Gilligan, C., Lyons, N., & Hanmer, J. (Eds.). (1989). *Making connections.* Troy, NY: Emma Willard School.

Gilligan, C., Rogers, A. G., & Tolman, D. L. (Eds.). (1991).*Women, girls and psychotherapy: Reframing resistance.* New York: Haworth Press.

Gitter, A. G., & Black, H. (1976). Is self-disclosure self-revealing? *Journal of Counseling Psychology, 23*(4), 327–332.

Gleason, J. B. (1987). Sex differences in parent-child interaction. In S. U. Philips, S. Steele, & C. Tanz (Eds.), *Language, gender, and sex in comparative perspective* (pp. 189–199). Cambridge: Cambridge University Press.

Gleser, G. C., Gottschalk, L. A., & Watkins, J. (1959). The relationship of sex and intelligence to choice of words: A normative study of verbal behavior. *Journal of Clinical Psychology, 15,* 182–191.

Goldberg, J. (1990). Interrupting the discourse on interruptions: An analysis in terms of relationally neutral, power- and rapport-oriented acts. *Journal of Pragmatics, 14,* 883–903.

Goldner, V. (1991). Toward a critical relational theory. *Psychoanalytic Dialogues, 1*(3), 249–272.

Goodstein, L. D., & Reinecker, V. M. (1974). Factors affecting self-disclosure: A review of the literature. In B. A. Maher (Ed.), *Progress in experimental personality research* (Vol. 7, pp. 49–77). New York: Academic Press.

Graddol, D., & Swann, J. (1989). *Gender voices*. Oxford: Basil Blackwell.

Grady, K. E. (1979). Androgyny reconsidered. In J. H. Williams (Ed.), *Psychology of women: Selected readings* (pp. 172–177). New York: Norton.

Grady, K. E. (1981). Sex bias in research design. *Psychology of Women Quarterly, 5,* 628–636.

Gray, J. (1992). *Men are from Mars, women are from Venus.* New York: Harper Collins.

Greenblatt, L., Hasenauer, J. E., & Freimuth, V. S. (1980). Psychological sex type and androgyny in the study of communication variables: Self-disclosure and communication apprehension. *Human Communication Research, 6,* 117–129.

Greif, E. B. (1980). Sex differences in parent-child conversations. *Women's Studies International Quarterly, 3,* 253–258.

Haas, A. (1979). Male and female spoken language differences: Stereotypes and evidence. *Psychological Bulletin, 86,* 616–626.

Haas, A., & Sherman, M. A. (1982). Reported topics of conversation among same-sex adults. *Communication Quarterly, 30*(4), 332–342.

Hacker, H. M. (1981). Blabbermouths and clams: Sex differences in self-disclosure in same-sex and cross-sex friendship dyads. *Psychology of Women Quarterly, 5*(3), 385–401.

Hagen, R. L., & Kahn, A. (1975). Discrimination against competent women. *Journal of Applied Social Psychology, 5*(4), 362–376.

Hall, J. (1984). *Nonverbal sex differences: Communication accuracy and expressive style.* Baltimore: Johns Hopkins University Press.

Hall, J. A. (1987). On explaining gender differences: The case of nonverbal communication. In P. Shaver & C. Hendrick (Eds.), *Sex and gender* (pp. 177–200). Newbury Park, CA: Sage Publications.

Hans, V. P., & Eisenberg, N. (1985). The effects of sex-role attitudes and group composition on men and women in groups. *Sex Roles, 12*(5/6), 477–490.

Harding, S. (1975) Women and words in a Spanish village. In R. Reiter (Ed.), *Toward an anthropology of women* (pp. 283–308). New York: Monthly Review Press.

Hare-Mustin, R. T., & Marecek, J. (1988). The meaning of difference: Gender theory, postmodernism, and psychology. *American Psychologist, 43*(6), 455–464.

Hare-Mustin, R. T., & Marecek, J. (1990). *Making a difference: Psychology and the construction of gender.* New Haven: Yale University Press.

Harris, A. (1994). Ethnicity as a determinant of sex role identity: A replic tion study of item selection for the Bem Sex Role Inventory. *Sex Roles, 31* (3/4), 241–273.

Hartman, M. (1976). A descriptive study of the language of men and women born in Maine around 1900 as it reflects the Lakoff hypotheses in "Language and women's place." In B. L. Dubois & I. Crouch (Eds.), *Proceedings of the Conference on the Sociology of the Languages of American Women* (pp. 81–90). San Antonio, TX: Trinity University Press.

Hauser, S. T., Powers, S. I., Weiss-Perry, B., Follansbee, D. J., Rajapark, D., & Green, W. M. (1987). *The constraining and enabling coding system manual.* Unpublished manuscript.

Hawkins, K. (1988). Interruptions in task-oriented conversations: Effects of violations of expectations by males and females. *Women's Studies in Communication,* 11(2), 1–20.

Hecht, M. L., Collier, M. J., & Ribeau, S. A. (1993). *African American communication: Ethnic identity and cultural interpretation.* Newbury Park, CA: Sage Publications.

Heiss, J. S. (1962). Degree of intimacy and male-female interaction. *Sociometry, 25,* 197–208.

Hendrick, S. S. (1981). Self-disclosure and marital satisfaction. *Journal of Personality and Social Psychology, 40*(6), 1150–1159

Henley, N. (1973–1974). Power, sex, and nonverbal communication. *Berkeley Journal of Sociology, 18,* 1–26. Reprinted in B. Thorne & N. Henley (Eds.). (1975). *Language and sex: Difference and dominance* (pp. 184–203). Rowley, MA: Newbury House.

Henley, N. M. (1977). *Body politics: Power, sex, and nonverbal communication.* Englewood Cliffs, NJ: Prentice Hall.

Henley, N. M., & Harmon, S. (1985). The nonverbal semantics of power and gender: A perceptual study. In S. L. Ellyson & J. F. Dovidio (Eds.), *Power, dominance, and nonverbal behavior* (pp. 151–164). New York: Springer-Verlag.

Henley, N. & Kramarae, C. (1991). Gender, power, and miscommunication. In N. Coupland, H. Giles, & J. M. Wiemann, (Eds.), *"Miscommunication" and problematic talk* (pp. 18–43). Newbury Park, CA: Sage Publications.

Hershey, S., & Werner, E. (1975). Dominance in marital decision making in women's liberation and non-women's liberation families. *Family Process, 14,* 223–233.

Hill, C. T., & Stull, D. E. (1987). Gender and self-disclosure: Strategies for exploring the issues. In V. J. Derlega & J. H. Berg (Eds.), *Self-disclosure: Theory, research, and therapy* (pp. 81–100). New York: Plenum Press.

Hilpert, F. P., Kramer, C., & Clark, R. A. (1975). Participants' perceptions of self and partner in mixed-sex dyads. *Central States Speech Journal, 26,* 52–56.

Hirschman, L. (1973). *Female-male difference in conversational interaction.* Paper given at the meeting of the Linguistic Society of America, San Diego, CA.

Hoffman, C., & Hurst, N. (1990). Gender stereotypes: Perception or rationalization? *Journal of Personality and Social Psychology, 58*(2), 197–208.

Hollander, E. P., & Yoder, J. (1980). Some issues in comparing women and men as leaders. *Basic and Applied Social Psychology, 1*(3), 267–280.

Holmes, J. (1984). Women's language': A functional approach. *General Linguistics, 24*(3), 149–178.

Holmes, J. (1985). Sex differences and mis-communication: Some data from New Zealand. In J. B. Pride (Ed.), *Cross-cultural encounters: Communication and miscommunication* (pp. 24–43). Melbourne, Australia: River Seine Publications.

Holmes, J. (1986). Functions of *you know* in women's and men's speech. *Language in Society, 15*(1), 1–21.

Holmes, J. (1989). Sex differences and apologies: One aspect of communicative competence. *Applied Linguistics, 10*(2), 194–213.

Horner, M. (1972). Toward an understanding of achievement-related conflicts in women. *Journal of Social Issues, 28*(2), 157–175.

Hyde, J. S., & Linn, M. C. (Eds.). (1986). *The psychology of gender: Advances through meta-analysis.* Baltimore: Johns Hopkins.

Irish, J. T., & Hall, J. A. (in press). Interruptive patterns in medical visits: The effects of role, status, and gender. *Social Science and Medicine*

Izraeli, D. N. (1983). Sex effects or structural effects? An empirical test of Kanter's theory of proportions. *Social Forces, 62*, 153–165.

Jacobson, M. B., & Effertz, J. (1974). Sex roles and leadership: Perceptions of the leaders and the led. *Organizational Behavior and Human Performance, 12*, 383–396.

Jago, A. G., & Vroom, V. H. (1982). Sex differences in the incidence and evaluation of participative leader behavior. *Journal of Applied Psychology, 67*(6), 776–783.

James, D., & Clarke, S. (1993). Women, men, and interruptions: A critical review. In D. Tannen (Ed.) *Gender and conversational interaction* (pp. 231–280). New York: Oxford University Press.

James, D., & Drakich, J. (1993). Understanding gender differences in amount of talk: A critical review. In D. Tannen (Ed.), *Gender and conversational interaction* (pp. 281–312). New York: Oxford University Press.

John, B. A., & Sussman, L. E. (1984–1985). Initiative taking as a determinant of role-reciprocal organization. *Imagination, Cognition and Personality, 4*(3), 277–291.

Johnson, C. (1994). Gender, legitimate authority, and leader-subordinate conversations. *American Sociological Review, 59*, 122–135.

Johnson, F., & Aries, E. (1983a). The talk of women friends. *Women's Studies International Forum, 6*, 353–361.

Johnson, F., & Aries, E. (1983b). Conversational patterns among same-sex pairs of late adolescent close friends. *Journal of Genetic Psychology, 142*, 225–238.

Johnson, J. L. (1980). Questions and role responsibility in four professional meetings. *Anthropological Linguistics, 22*, 66–76.

Johnson, P. (1976). Women and power: Toward a theory of effectiveness. *Journal of Social Issues, 32*(3), 99–110.

Johnson, R. A., & Schulman, G. I. (1989). Gender-role composition and role entrapment in decision-making groups. *Gender and Society, 3*(3), 355–372.

Jones, D. (1980). Gossip: Notes on women's oral culture. *Women's Studies International Quarterly, 3*, 193–198.

Jones, K. (1992). A question of context: Directive use at a morris team meeting. *Language in Society, 21*, 427–445.

Jordan, J. V. (1986). The meaning of mutuality. *Work in Progress* (No. 23). Wellesley, MA: Stone Center for Developmental Services and Studies.

Jose, P. E., Crosby, F., & Wong-McCarthy, W. J. (1980). Androgyny, dyadic compatibility and conversational behaviour. In H. Giles, W. P. Robinson, & P. M. Smith (Eds.), *Language: Social psychological perspectives* (pp. 115–119). Oxford: Pergamon Press.

Jourard, S. M. (1971). *Self-disclosure: An experimental analysis of the transparent self*. New York: Wiley.

Jourard, S. M., & Lasakow, P. (1958). Some factors in self-disclosure. *Journal of Abnormal and Social Psychology, 56*, 91–98.

Jourard, S. M., & Richman, P. (1963). Factors in the self-disclosure inputs of college students. *Merrill Palmer Quarterly, 9*, 141–148.

Judd, C. M., & Park, B. (1993). Definition and assessment of accuracy in social stereotypes. *Psychological Review, 100*, 109–128.

Kaess, W. A., Witryol, S. L., & Nolan, R. E. (1961). Reliability, sex differences and validity in the leaderless group discussion technique. *Journal of Applied Psychology, 45*(5), 345–350.

Kanter, R. M. (1977a). Some effects of proportions on group life: Skewed sex ratios and responses to token women. *American Journal of Sociology, 82*(5), 965–990.

Kanter, R. M. (1977b). *Men and women of the corporation*. New York: Basic Books.

Kenkel, W. F. (1963). Observational studies of husband-wife interaction in family decision-making. In M. B. Sussman (Ed.), *Sourcebook in marriage and the family* (pp. 144–156). Boston: Houghton Mifflin.

Kennedy, C. W., & Camden, C. T. (1983). A new look at interruptions. *Western Journal of Speech Communication, 47*, 45–58.

Kenny, D. A., & Zaccaro, S. J. (1983). An estimate of variance due to traits in leadership. *Journal of Applied Psychology, 68*, 678–685.

Key, M. R. (1972). Linguistic behavior of male and female. *Linguistics, 88*, 15–31.

Kimble, C. E., & Musgrove, J. I. (1988). Dominance in arguing mixed-sex dyads: Visual dominance patterns, talking time, and speech loudness. *Journal of Research in Personality, 22*, 1–16.

Kimble, C. E., Yoshikawa, J. C., & Zehr, H. D. (1981). Vocal and verbal assertiveness in same-sex and mixed-sex groups. *Journal of Personality and Social Psychology, 40*(6), 1047–1054.

Kipers, P. S. (1987). Gender and topic. *Language in Society, 16*(4), 543–557.

Klein, H. M., & Willerman, L. (1979). Psychological masculinity and femininity and typical and maximal dominance expression in women. *Journal of Personality and Social Psychology, 37,* 2059–2070.

Kohlberg, L. (1981). *The philosophy of moral development: Essays on moral development* (Vol. 1). San Francisco: Harper & Row.

Kollock, P., Blumstein, P., & Schwartz, P. (1985). Sex and power in interaction: Conversational privileges and duties. *American Sociological Review, 50,* 34–46.

Komarovsky, M. (1962). *Blue-collar marriage.* New York: Random House.

Komarovsky, M. (1974). Patterns of self-disclosure of male undergraduates. *Journal of Marriage and the Family, 36,* 677–686.

Kraft, L. W., & Vraa, C. W. (1975). Sex composition of groups and pattern of self-disclosure by high school females. *Psychological Reports, 37,* 733–734.

Kramarae, C. (1981). *Men and women speaking.* Rowley, MA: Newbury House.

Kramarae, C. (1982). Gender: How she speaks. In E. B. Ryan & H. Giles (Eds.), *Attitudes towards language variation: Social and applied contexts* (pp. 84–98). London: Edward Arnold.

Kramarae, C. (1989). Redefining gender, class and race. In C. M. Lont & S. A. Friedley (Eds.), *Beyond boundaries: Sex and gender diversity in communication* (pp. 317–329). Fairfax, VA: George Mason University Press.

Kramarae, C. (1990). Changing the complexion of gender in language research. In H. Giles & W. P. Robinson (Eds.), *Handbook of language and social psychology* (pp. 345–361). Chichester, England: John Wiley & Sons.

Kramer, C. (1974). Women's speech: Separate but unequal? *Quarterly Journal of Speech, 60,* 14–24.

Kramer, C. (1977). Perceptions of female and male speech. *Language and Speech, 20,* 151–161.

LaFrance, M. (1981). Gender gestures: Sex, sex-role and nonverbal communication. In C. Mayo & N. M. Henley (Eds.), *Gender and nonverbal behavior* (pp. 129–150). New York: Springer-Verlag.

LaFrance, M., & Carmen, B. (1980). The nonverbal display of psychological androgyny. *Journal of Personality and Social Psychology, 38,* 36–49.

Lakoff, R. (1973). Language and woman's place. *Language in Society, 2,* 45–79.

Lakoff, R. (1975). *Language and woman's place.* New York: Harper and Row.

Lakoff, R. (1977). Women's language. *Language and Style, 10,* 222–247.

Lakoff, R. J. (1990). *Talking power: The politics of language in our lives.* New York: Basic Books.

Lamude, K. G., & Daniels, T. D. (1984). Perceived managerial communicator style as a function of subordinate and manager gender. *Communication Research Reports, 1*(1), 91–96.

Lamude, K. G., & Daniels, T. D. (1990). Mutual evaluations of communication competence in superior-subordinate relationships: Sex role incongruency and pro-male bias. *Women's Studies in Communication, 13*(2), 39–56.

Lapadat, J. & Seesahai, M. (1978). Male versus female codes in informal contexts. *Sociolinguistic Newsletter, 8*, 7–8.

Larrabee, M. J. (Ed.). (1993). *An ethic of care: Feminist and interdisciplinary perspectives.* New York: Routledge.

Lavine, L. O., & Lombardo, J. P. (1984). Self-disclosure: Intimate and nonintimate disclosures to parents and best friends as a function of Bem Sex-Role category. *Sex Roles, 11*, 735–744.

Lawrence, S. G., Stucky, N. P., & Hopper, R. (1990). The effects of sex dialects and sex stereotypes on speech evaluations. *Journal of Language and Social Psychology, 9*(3), 209–224.

Leet-Pellegrini, H. M. (1980). Conversational dominance as a function of gender and expertise. In H. Giles, W. P. Robinson, & P. M. Smith (Eds.), *Language: Social psychological perspectives* (pp. 97–104). Oxford: Pergamon Press.

Leik, R. K. (1963). Instrumentality and emotionality in family interaction. *Sociometry, 26*, 131–145.

Levin, J., & Arluke, A. (1985). An exploratory analysis of sex differences in gossip. *Sex Roles, 12*, 281–286.

Levinger, G. (1964). Task and social behavior in marriage. *Sociometry, 27*, 433–448.

Lewis, G. H. (1972). Role differentiation. *American Sociological Review, 37*, 424–434.

Linde, C. (1988). The quantitative study of communicative success: Politeness and accidents in aviation discourse. *Language in Society, 17*, 375–399.

Linn, M. C., & Petersen, A. C. (1986). A meta-analysis of gender differences in spacial ability: Implications for mathematics and science achievement. In J. S. Hyde & M. C. Linn (Eds.), *The psychology of gender: Advances through meta-analyses* (pp. 67–101) Baltimore: Johns Hopkins University Press.

Liska, J., Mechling, E. W., & Stathas, S. (1981). Differences in subjects' perceptions of gender and believability between users of deferential and nondeferential language. *Communication Quarterly, 29*, 40–48.

Lockheed, M. E. (1985). Sex and social influence: A meta-analysis guided by theory. In J. Berger & M. Zelditch (Eds.), *Status, rewards and influence* (pp. 406–429). San Francisco: Jossey-Bass.

Lockheed, M. E., & Hall, K. P. (1976). Conceptualizing sex as a status characteristic: Applications to leadership training   strategies. *Journal of Social Issues, 32*(3), 111–124.

Lombardo, J. P., & Lavine, L. O. (1981). Sex-role stereotyping and patterns of self-disclosure. *Sex Roles, 7*(4), 403–411.

Lott, B. (1987). Sexist discrimination as distancing behavior: I. A laboratory demonstration. *Psychology of Women Quarterly, 11*(1), 47–58.

Mabry, E. A. (1985). The effects of gender composition and task structure on small group interaction. *Small Group Behavior, 16*(1), 75–96.

Maccoby, E. E. (1990). Gender and relationships: A developmental account. *American Psychologist, 45*(4), 513–520.

Maccoby, E. E. & Jacklin, C. N. (1974). *The psychology of sex differences.* Stanford: Stanford University Press.

MacKinnon, C. (1987). *Feminism unmodified: Discourses on life and law.* Cambridge: Harvard University Press.

Maier, N. R. F. (1970). Male versus female discussion leaders. *Personnel Psychology, 23*, 455–461.

Maltz, D. N,. & Borker, R. A. (1982). A cultural approach to male-female miscommunication. In J. J. Gumperz (Ed.), *Language and social identity* (pp. 196–216). Cambridge: Cambridge University Press.

Mann, R. D. (1959). A review of the relationships between personality and performance in small groups. *Psychological Bulletin, 56*(4), 241–270.

Marche, T., & Peterson, C. (1993). The development and sex-related use of interruption behavior. *Human Communication Research, 19*(3), 388–408.

Markel, N. N., Long, J. F., & Saine, T. J. (1976). Sex effects in conversational interaction: Another look at male dominance. *Human Communication Research, 2*(4), 356–364.

Martin, C. R. (1972). Support for women's lib: Management performance. *Southern Journal of Business, 7,* 19–28.

Martin, J. N., & Craig, R. T. (1983). Selected linguistic sex differences during initial social interactions of same-sex and mixed-sex student dyads. *Western Journal of Speech Communication, 47,* 16–28.

Martin, P. Y., & Shanahan, K. A. (1983). Transcending the effects of sex composition in small groups. *Social Work With Groups, 6*(3/4), 19–32.

Mayo, C. & Henley, N. (Eds.). (1981). *Gender and nonverbal behavior.* New York: Springer-Verlag.

McCarrick, A. K., Manderscheid, R. W., & Silbergeld, S. (1981). Gender differences in competition and dominance during married-couples group therapy. *Social Psychology Quarterly, 44*(3), 164–177.

McClelland, D. C., Atkinson, J. W., Clark, R. A., & Lowell, E. L. (1953). *The achievement motive.* Englewood Cliffs, NJ: Prentice-Hall.

McCullough, M. (1987, November). *Women's friendships across cultures: Black and white friends speaking.* Paper presented at the Speech Communication Association Meeting, Boston, MA.

McGuire, W. J., McGuire, C. V., & Winton, W. (1979). Effects of household sex composition on the salience of one's gender in the spontaneous self-concept. *Journal of Experimental Social Psychology, 15,* 77–90.

McLachlan, A. (1991). The effects of agreement, disagreement, gender and familiarity on patterns of dyadic interaction. *Journal of Language and Social Psychology, 10*(3), 205–212.

McMillan, J. R., Clifton, A. K., McGrath, D., & Gale, W. S. (1977). Women's language: Uncertainty or interpersonal sensitivity and emotionality? *Sex Roles, 3*(6), 545–559.

Mednick, M. T. (1989). On the politics of psychological constructs: Stop the bandwagon, I want to get off. *American Psychologist, 44*(8), 1118–1123.

Meeker, B. F., & Weitzel-O'Neill, P. A. (1977). Sex roles and interpersonal behavior in task-oriented groups. *American Sociological Review, 42*, 91–105.

Megargee, E. I. (1969). Influence of sex roles on the manifestation of leadership. *Journal of Applied Psychology, 53*(5), 377–382.

Miller, G. R., & McReynolds, M. (1973). Male chauvinism and source competence: A research note. *Speech Monographs, 40*, 154–155.

Miller, J. B. (1976). *Toward a new psychology of women*. Boston: Beacon Press.

Miller, J. B. (1985). Patterns of control in same-sex conversations: Differences between women and men. *Women's Studies in Communication, 8*, 62–69.

Mischel, W. (1968). *Personality and assessment*. New York: Wiley.

Moore, S. F., Shaffer, L., Goodsell, D. A., & Baringoldz, G. (1983). Gender or situationally determined spoken language differences? The case of the leadership situation. *International Journal of Women's Studies, 6*(1), 44–53.

Morgan, B. S. (1976). Intimacy of disclosure topics and sex differences in self-disclosure. *Sex Roles, 2*, 161–166.

Moskowitz, D. S., Jung Suh, E., & Desaulniers, J. (1994). Situational influences on gender differences in agency and communion. *Journal of Personality and Social Psychology, 66*(4), 753–761.

Mulac, A. (1989). Men's and women's talk in same-gender and mixed-gender dyads: Power or polemic? *Journal of Language and Social Psychology, 8*(3-4), 249–270.

Mulac, A., Incontro, C. R., & James, M. R. (1985). Comparison of the gender-linked language effect and sex role stereotypes. *Journal of Personality and Social Psychology, 49*(4), 1098–1109.

Mulac, A., & Lundell, T. L. (1986). Linguistic contributors to the gender-linked language effect. *Journal of Language and Social Psychology, 5*(2), 81–101.

Mulac, A., Lundell, T. L., & Bradac, J. J. (1986). Male/female language differences and attributional consequences in a public speaking situation: Toward an explanation of the gender-linked language effect. *Communication Monographs, 53*, 115–129.

Mulac, A., Wiemann, J. M., Widenmann, S. J., & Gibson, T. W. (1988). Male/female language differences and effects in same-sex and mixed-sex dyads: The gender-linked language effect. *Communication Monographs, 55*(4), 315–335.

Mulcahy, G. A. (1973). Sex differences in patterns of self-disclosure among adolescents: A developmental perspective. *Journal of Youth and Adolescence, 2*(4), 343–356.

Mullen, B., Salas, E., & Driskell, J. E. (1989). Salience, motivation, and artifact as contributions to the relation between participation rate and leadership. *Journal of Experimental Social Psychology, 25*, 545–559.

Murphy, S. K. (1989). Influences of sex composition and topic management in initial interactions. In C. M. Lont & S. A. Friedley (Eds.), *Beyond boundaries: Sex and gender diversity in communication* (pp. 75–94). Fairfax, VA: George Mason University Press.

Murray, S. O. (1985). Toward a model of members' methods for recognizing interruptions. *Language in Society, 14*, 31–40.

Murray, S. O., & Covelli, L. H. (1988). Women and men speaking at the same time. *Journal of Pragmatics, 12*, 103–111.

Narus, L. R., & Fischer, J. L. (1982). Strong but not silent: A reexamination of expressivity in the relationships of men. *Sex Roles, 8*(2), 159–168.

Natale, M., Entin, E., & Jaffe, J. (1979). Vocal interruptions in dyadic communication as a function of speech and social anxiety. *Journal of Personality and Social Psychology, 37*(6), 865–878.

Nemeth, C., Endicott, J., & Wachtler, J. (1976). From the '50s to the '70s: Women in jury deliberations. *Sociometry, 39*(4), 293–304.

Newcombe, N., & Arnkoff, D. B. (1979). Effects of speech style and sex of speaker on person perception. *Journal of Personality and Social Psychology, 37*(8), 1293–1303.

Nohara, M. (1992). Sex differences in interruption: An experimental reevaluation. *Journal of Psycholinguistic Research, 21*(2), 127–146.

Nyquist, L., & Spence, J. T. (1986). Effects of dispositional dominance and sex role expectations on leadership behaviors. *Journal of Personality and Social Psychology, 50*(1), 87–93.

O'Barr, W. M., & Atkins, B. K. (1980). "Women's language" or "powerless language"? In S. McConnell-Ginet, R. Borker, & N. Furman (Eds.), *Women and language in literature and society* (pp. 93–110). New York: Praeger.

Octigan, M., & Niederman, S. (1979). Male dominance in conversations. *Frontiers, 4*(1), 50–54.

O'Leary, V. E., Unger, R. K., Wallston, B. S. (Eds.). (1985). *Women, gender, and social psychology*. Hillsdale, NJ: Lawrence Erlbaum.

Oliver, M. B., & Hyde, J. S. (1993). Gender differences in sexuality: A meta-analysis. *Psychological Bulletin, 114*, 29–51.

Orcutt, J. D., & Harvey, L. K. (1985). Deviance, rule-breaking and male dominance in conversation. *Symbolic Interaction, 8*(1), 15–32.

Parlee, M. B. (1981). Appropriate control groups in feminist research. *Psychology of Women Quarterly, 5*(4), 637–644.

Parsons, T. (1955). The American family: Its relations to personality and to the social structure. In T. Parsons & R. F. Bales (Eds.), *Family, socialization and interaction process* (pp. 3–33). Glencoe, IL: Free Press.

Pearson, J. C. (1985). *Gender and communication*. Dubuque, IA: William C. Brown.

Pedersen, T. B. (1980). Sex and communication: A brief presentation of an experimental approach. In H. Giles, W. P. Robinson, & P. M. Smith (Eds.), *Language: Social psychological perspectives* (pp. 105–114). New York: Pergamon.

Petzel, T. P., Johnson, J. E., & Bresolin, L. (1990). Peer nominations for leadership and likability in problem-solving groups as a function of gender and task. *Journal of Social Psychology, 130*(5), 641–648.

Philips, S. U. (1980). Sex differences and language. *Annual Review of Anthropology, 9*, 523–544.

Piliavin, J. A., & Martin, R. R. (1978). The effects of the sex composition of groups on style of social interaction. *Sex Roles, 4*(2), 281–296.

Poole, M. E. (1979). Social class, sex and linguistic coding. *Language and Speech, 22*, 49–67.

Poynton, C. (1989). *Language and gender: Making the difference*. Oxford: Oxford University Press.

Preisler, B. (1986). *Linguistic sex roles in conversation*. Berlin: Mouton de Gruyter.

Prentice, D. A., & Miller, D. T. (1992). When small effects are impressive. *Psychological Bulletin, 112*(1), 160–164.

Presser, H.B. (1994). Employment schedules among dual-earner spouses and the division of household labor by gender. *American Sociological Review, 59*, 348–364.

Pugh, C. & Vasquez-Nutall, E. (1983, April). *Are all women alike? Reports of white, Hispanic and Black women*. Paper presented at the meeting of the American Personnel and Guidance Association, Washington, DC.

Pugh, M. D., & Wahrman, R. (1983). Neutralizing sexism in mixed-sex groups: Do women have to be better than men? *American Journal of Sociology, 88*(4), 746–762.

Pugh, M. D., & Wahrman, R. (1985). Inequality of influence in mixed-sex groups. In J. Berger & M. Zelditch (Eds.), *Status, rewards, and influence* (pp. 142–162). San Francisco: Jossey-Bass.

Putnam, L. L. (1982). In search of gender: A critique of communication and sex-roles research. *Women's Studies in Communication, 5*, 1–9.

Quina, K., Wingard, J. A., & Bates, H. G. (1987). Language style and gender stereotypes in person perception. *Psychology of Women Quarterly, 11*(1), 111–122.

Ragan, S. L. (1989). Communication between the sexes: A consideration of sex differences in adult communication. In J. F. Nussbaum (Ed.), *Life-span communication: Normative processes* (pp. 179–193). Hillsdale, NJ: Lawrence Erlbaum Associates.

Ragins, B. R. (1992). Power and subordinate evaluations of male and female leaders. In L. A. M. Perry, L. H. Turner, & H. M. Sterk (Eds.), *Constructing and reconstructing gender: The links among communication, language, and gender* (pp. 163–174). Albany, NY: State University of New York Press.

Rakow, L. F. (1986). Rethinking gender research in communication. *Journal of Communication, 36*(4), 11–26.

Rapp, R. (1992). Family and class in contemporary America: Notes towards an understanding of ideology. In B. Thorne & M. Yalom (Eds.), *Rethinking the family: Some feminist questions* (pp. 168–187). New York: Longman.

Raven, B. H. (1965). Social influence and power. In I. D. Steiner & M. Fishbein (Eds.), *Current studies in social psychology* (pp. 371–382). New York: Holt.

Reis, H. T., Senchak, M., & Solomon, B. (1985). Sex differences in the intimacy of social interaction: Further examination of potential explanations. *Journal of Personality and Social Psychology, 48*(5), 1204–1217.

Rice, R. W., Bender, L. R., & Vitters, A. G. (1980). Leader sex, follower attitudes toward women, and leadership effectiveness: A laboratory experiment. *Organizational Behavior and Human Performance, 25*, 46–78.

Rice, R. W., Instone, D., & Adams, J. (1984). Leader sex, leader success, and leadership process: Two field studies. *Journal of Applied Psychology, 69*, 12–31.

Ridgeway, C. L. (1982). Status in groups: The importance of motivation. *American Sociological Review, 47*, 76–88.

Ridgeway, C. L. (1988). Gender differences in task groups: A status and legitimacy account. In M. Webster, Jr., & M. Foschi (Eds.), *Status generalization: New theory and research* (pp. 188–206). Stanford, CA: Stanford University Press.

Ridgeway, C. L., & Diekema, D. (1989). Dominance and collective hierarchy formation in male and female task groups. *American Sociological Review, 54*, 79–93.

Ridgeway, C. L., & Diekema, D. (1992) Are gender difference status differences? In C. L. Ridgeway (Ed.), *Gender, interaction, and inequality* (pp. 157–180). New York: Springer-Verlag.

Ridgeway, C. L., & Johnson, C. (1990). What is the relationship between socioemotional behavior and status in task groups? *American Journal of Sociology, 95*, 1189–1212.

Risman, B. J. (1987). Intimate relationships from a micro-structural perspective: Men who mother. *Gender and Society, 1*, 6–32.

Robinson, L. F., & Reis, H. T. (1989). The effects of interruption, gender, and status on interpersonal perceptions. *Journal of Nonverbal Behavior, 13*(3), 141–153.

Roger, D., & Nesshoever, W. (1987). Individual differences in dyadic conversational strategies: A further study. *British Journal of Social Psychology, 26*(3), 247–255.

Roger, D. B., & Schumacher, A. (1983). Effects of individual differences on dyadic conversational strategies. *Journal of Personality and Social Psychology, 45*, 700–705.

Rogers, W. T., & Jones, S. E. (1975). Effects of dominance tendencies on floor holding and interruption behavior in dyadic interaction. *Human Communication Research, 1*, 113–122.

Rorty, R. (1979). *Philosophy and the mirror of nature.* Princeton, NJ: Princeton University Press.

Rosenfeld, L. B., Civikly, J. M., & Herron, J. R. (1979). Anatomical and psychological sex differences. In G. J. Chelune & Associates (Eds.), *Self-disclosure: Origins, patterns and implications of openness in interpersonal relationships* (pp. 80–109). San Francisco: Jossey-Bass.

Rosenkrantz, P., Vogel, S. R., Bee, H., Broverman, I. K., & Broverman, D. M. (1968). Sex role stereotypes and self-concepts in college students. *Journal of Consulting and Clinical Psychology, 32*, 287–295.

Rosenthal, R. & Rubin, D. B. (1979). A note on percent variance explained as a measure of the importance of effects. *Journal of Applied Social Psychology, 9*, 395–396.

Rosnow, R. L., & Rosenthal, R. (1989). Statistical procedures and the justification of knowledge in psychological science. *American Psychologist, 44*(10), 1276–1284.

Ross, L. (1977). The intuitive psychologist and his shortcomings: Distortions in the attribution process. In L. Berkowitz (Ed.), *Advances in experimental social psychology* (Vol. 10, pp. 174–221). New York: Academic Press.

Rubin, L. (1976). *Worlds of pain: Life in the working-class family.* New York: Basic.

Rubin, L. (1994). *Families on the fault line.* New York: Harper Collins Publishers.

Rubin, Z., Hill, C. T., Peplau, L. A., & Dunkel-Schetter, C. (1980). Self-disclosure in dating couples: Sex roles and the ethic of openness. *Journal of Marriage and the Family, 42*, 305–317.

Rubin, Z., & Shenker, S. (1978). Friendship, proximity, and self-disclosure. *Journal of Personality, 46*, 1–11.

Ruble, D. N., & Ruble, T. L. (1982). Sex stereotypes. In A. G. Miller (Ed.), *In the eye of the beholder: Contemporary issues in stereotyping* (pp. 188–252). New York: Praeger.

Sacks, H., Schegloff, E. A., & Jefferson, G. (1974). A simplest systematics for the organization of turn-taking for conversation. *Language, 50*, 696–735.

Sagrestano, L. (1992). Power strategies in interpersonal relationships. *Psychology of Women Quarterly, 16*, 481–495.

Sayers, F., & Sherblom, J. (1987). Qualification in male language as influenced by age and gender of conversational partner. *Communication Research Reports, 4*(1), 88–92.

Schneier, C. E., & Bartol, K. M. (1980). Sex effects in emergent leadership. *Journal of Applied Psychology, 65*(3), 341–345.

Shaw, M. E., & Sadler, O. (1965). Interaction patterns in heterosexual dyads varying in degree of intimacy. *Journal of Social Psychology, 66*, 345–351.

Sherrod, D. (1989). The influence of gender on same-sex friendships. In C. Hendrick (Ed.), *Close relationships* (pp. 164–186). Newbury Park, CA: Sage Publications.

Shimanoff, S. B. (1983). The role of gender in linguistic references to emotive states. *Communication Quarterly, 31*, 174–179.

Shockley-Zalabak, P. S., & Morley, D. D. (1984). Sex differences in conflict style preferences. *Communication Research Reports, 1*(1), 28–32.

Siderits, M. A., Johannsen, W. J., & Fadden, T. F. (1985). Gender, role, and power: A content analysis of speech. *Psychology of Women Quarterly, 9*, 439–450.

Siegler, D. M., & Siegler, R. S. (1976). Stereotypes of males' and females' speech. *Psychological Reports, 39*, 167–170.

Simkins-Bullock, J. A., & Wildman, B. G. (1991). An investigation into the relationships between gender and language. *Sex Roles, 24*(3/4), 149–160.

Smith, P. M. (1979). Sex markers in speech. In K. R. Scherer & H. Giles (Eds.), *Social markers in speech* (pp. 109–146). Cambridge: Cambridge University Press.

Smith, P. M. (1980). Judging masculine and feminine social identities from content-controlled speech. In H. Giles, W. P. Robinson, & P. M. Smith (Eds.), *Language: Social psychological perspectives* (pp. 121–126). New York: Pergamon.

Smith, P. M. (1985). *Language, the sexes and society.* Oxford: Basil Blackwell.

Smith-Lovin, L. & Brody, C. (1989). Interruptions in group discussions: The effects of gender and group composition. *American Sociological Review, 54*, 424–435.

Smith-Lovin, L., & Robinson, D. T. (1992). Gender and conversational dynamics. In C. L. Ridgeway (Ed.), *Gender, interaction, and inequality* (pp. 122–156). New York: Springer-Verlag.

Smythe, M., & Huddleston, B. (1992). Competition and collaboration: Male and female communication patterns during dyadic interactions. In L. A. M. Perry, L. H. Turner & H. M. Sterk (Eds.), *Constructing and reconstructing gender: The links among communication, language, and gender* (pp. 251–260). Albany, NY: State University of New York Press.

Smythe, M., & Schlueter, D. W. (1989). Can we talk?? A meta-analytic review of the sex differences in language literature. In C. M. Lont & S. A. Friedley (Eds.), *Beyond boundaries: Sex and gender diversity in communication* (pp. 31–48). Fairfax, VA: George Mason University Press.

Snell, W. E., Hampton, B. R., & McManus, P. (1992). The impact of counselor and participant gender on willingness to discuss relational topics: Development of the Relationship Disclosure Scale. *Journal of Counseling and Development, 70*(3), 409–416.

Snodgrass, S. E. (1985). Women's intuition: The effect of subordinate role on interpersonal sensitivity. *Journal of Personality and Social Psychology, 49*(1), 146–155.

Snodgrass, S. E. (1992). Further effects of role versus gender on interpersonal sensitivity. *Journal of Personality and Social Psychology, 62*(1), 154–158.

Snodgrass, S. E., & Rosenthal, R. (1984). Females in charge: Effects of sex of subordinate and romantic attachment status upon self-ratings of dominance. *Journal of Personality, 52*(4), 355–371.

Snyder, M., Tanke, E. D., & Berscheid, E. (1977). Social perception and interpersonal behavior: On the self-fulfilling nature of social stereotypes. *Journal of Personality and Social Psychology, 35*(9), 656–666.

Sollie, D. L., & Fischer, J. L. (1985). Sex-role orientation, intimacy of topic, and target person differences in self-disclosure among women. *Sex Roles, 12*(9/10), 917–929.

Soskin, W. F., & John, V. P. (1963). The study of spontaneous talk. In R. Barker (Ed.), *The stream of behavior* (pp. 228–281). New York: Appleton-Century-Crofts.

Spence, J. T. (1985). Gender identity and its implications for the concepts of masculinity and femininity. In T. B. Sonderegger (Ed.), *Nebraska Symposium on Motivation* (Vol. 32, pp. 59–96). Lincoln: University of Nebraska Press.

Spence, J. T., & Helmreich, R. (1972). Who likes competent women? Competence, sex-role congruence of interests and subjects' attitude toward women as determinants of interpersonal attraction. *Journal of Applied Social Psychology, 2,* 197–213.

Spence, J. T., Helmreich, R., & Stapp, J. (1974). The Personal Attributes Questionnaire: A measure of sex-role stereotypes and masculinity/femininity. *Journal Supplement Abstract Service Catalog of Selected Documents in Psychology, 4,* 43–44 (Ms. No. 617)

Spence, J., & Sawin, L. L. (1985). Images of masculinity and femininity: A reconceptualization. In V. E. O'Leary, R. K. Unger, & B. S. Wallston (Eds.), *Women, gender, and social psychology* (pp. 35–66). Hillsdale, NJ: Lawrence Erlbaum.

Spender, D. (1980). *Man made language.* London: Routledge and Kegan Paul.

Spender, D. (1985). *Man made language* (2nd ed.). London: Routledge and Kegan Paul.

Spillman, B., Spillman, R., & Reinking, K. (1981). Leadership emergence: Dynamic analysis of the effects of sex and androgyny. *Small Group Behavior, 12*(2), 139–157.

Stack, C. (1986). The culture of gender: Women and men of color. *Signs, 11*(2), (Winter), 321–324.

Stake, J. E. (1978). The Ability/Performance dimension of self-esteem: Implications for women's achievement behavior. *Psychology of Women Quarterly, 3,* 364–377.

Stake, J. E. (1981). Promoting leadership behaviors in low performance-self-esteem women in task-oriented mixed-sex dyads. *Journal of Personality, 49*(4), 401–414.

Stake, J. E., & Stake, M. N. (1979). Performance-self-esteem and dominance behavior in mixed-sex dyads. *Journal of Personality, 47*(1), 71–84.

Steil, J. M., & Hillman, J. L. (1993). The perceived value of direct and indirect influence strategies: A cross-cultural comparison. *Psychology of Women Quarterly, 17*, 457–462.

Stein, R. T., & Heller, T. (1979). An empirical analysis of the correlations between leadership status and participation rates reported in the literature. *Journal of Personality and Social Psychology, 37*(11), 1993–2002.

Stitt, C., Schmidt, S., Price, K., & Kipnis, D. (1983). Sex of leader, leader behavior and subordinate satisfaction. *Sex Roles, 9*(1), 31–42.

Stokes, J., Childs, L., & Fuehrer, A. (1981). Gender and sex roles as predictors of self-disclosure. *Journal of Counseling Psychology, 28*(6), 510–514.

Stokes, J., Fuehrer, A., & Childs, L. (1980). Gender differences in self-disclosure to various target persons. *Journal of Counseling Psychology, 27*(2), 192–198.

Street, R. L., & Hopper, R. (1982). A model of speech style evaluation. In E. B. Ryan & H. Giles (Eds.), *Attitudes towards language variation: Social and applied contexts* (pp. 175–188). London: Edward Arnold.

Strodtbeck, F. L. (1951). Husband-wife interaction over revealed differences. *American Sociological Review, 16*, 468–473.

Strodtbeck, F. L., & Mann, R. D. (1956). Sex role differentiation in jury deliberations. *Sociometry, 19*, 3–11.

Surrey, J. (1985). Self-in-relation: A theory of women's development. *Work in Progress*. Wellesley, MA: Stone Center for Developmental Services and Studies.

Swacker, M. (1976). Women's verbal behavior at learned and professional conferences. In B. L. Dubois & I. Crouch (Eds.), *Proceedings of the Conference on the Sociology of the Languages of American Women* (pp. 155–160). San Antonio, TX: Trinity University Press.

Swain, S. (1989). Covert intimacy in men's friendships: Closeness in men's friendships. In B. J. Risman & P. Schwartz (Eds.), *Gender in intimate relationships: A microstructural approach* (pp. 71–86). Belmont, CA: Wadsworth.

Swim, J. K. (1994). Perceived versus meta-analytic effect sizes: An assessment of the accuracy of gender stereotypes. *Journal of Personality and Social Psychology, 66*(1), 21–36.

Tannen, D. (1983). When is an overlap not an interruption? One component of conversational style. In R. DiPietro, W. Frawley, & A. Wedel (Eds.), *The First Delaware Symposium on Language Studies* (pp. 119–129). Newark: University of Delaware Press.

Tannen, D. (1990a). *You just don't understand: Women and men in conversation*. New York: William Morrow.

Tannen, D. (1990b). Gender differences in conversational coherence: Physical alignment and topical cohesion. In B. Dorval (Ed.), *Conversational organization and its development. Advances in discourse processes* (Vol. 38, pp. 167–206). Norwood, NJ: Ablex Publishing Corp.

Thakerar, J., & Giles, H. (1981). They are-so they spoke: Noncontent speech stereotypes. *Language and Communication, 1*(2/3), 255–261.

Thomas, J. R., & French, K. E. (1985). Gender differences across age in motor performance: A meta-analysis. *Psychological Bulletin, 98,* 260–282.

Thorne, B. (1993). *Gender play: Girls and boys in school.* New Brunswick, NJ: Rutgers University Press.

Thorne, B., & Henley, N. (1975). Difference and dominance: An overview of language, gender and society. In B. Thorne & N. Henley (Eds.), *Language and sex: Difference and dominance* (pp. 5–42). Rowley, MA: Newbury House.

Tiger, V., & Luria, G. (1978). Inlaws outlaws: The language of women. In D. Butturff & E. Epstein (Eds.), *Women's language and style* (pp. 1–10). Akron, OH: L & S Books, University of Akron.

Torres, L. (1992). Women and language: From sex differences to power dynamics. In C. Kramarae & D. Spender (Eds.), *The knowledge explosion: Generations of feminist scholarship.* (pp. 281–290). New York: Teacher's College Press.

Tracy, K., & Eisenberg, E. (1990–1991). Giving criticism: A multiple goals case study. *Research on Language and Social Interaction, 24,* 37–70.

Tresemer, D. W. (1977). *Fear of success.* New York: Plenum.

Trimboli, C., & Walker, M. B. (1984). Switching pauses in cooperative and competitive conversations. *Journal of Experimental Social Psychology, 20,* 297–311.

Tschann, J. M. (1988). Self-disclosure in adult friendship: Gender and marital status differences. *Journal of Social and Personal Relationships, 5*(1), 65–81.

Unger, R. K. (1976). Male is greater than female: The socialization of status inequality. *Counseling Psychologist, 6*(2), 2–9.

Unger, R. K. (1979). *Female and male: Psychological perspectives.* New York: Harper & Row.

Unger, R. K. (1983). Through the looking glass: No wonderland yet! (The reciprocal relationship between methodology and models of reality). *Psychology of Women Quarterly, 8,* 9–32.

Unger, R. (1990). Imperfect reflections of reality: Psychology constructs gender. In R. T. Hare-Mustin & J. Marecek (Eds.), *Making a difference: Psychology and the construction of gender* (pp. 102–149). New Haven: Yale University Press.

Unger, R., & Crawford, M. (1992). *Women and gender: A feminist psychology.* New York: McGraw–Hill.

Unger, R. K. & Denmark, F. L. (1975). *Woman: Dependent or independent variable?* New York: Harper & Row.

Wagner, D. G. (1988). Gender inequalities in groups: A situational approach.

In M. Webster, Jr., & M. Foschi (Eds.), *Status generalization: New theory and research* (pp. 55–68). Stanford, CA: Stanford University Press.

Wagner, D. G., Ford, R. S., & Ford, T. W. (1986). Can gender inequalities be reduced? *American Sociological Review, 51*, 47–61.

Wahrman, R., & Pugh, M. D. (1974). Sex, nonconformity and influence. *Sociometry, 37*(1), 137–147.

Wallston, B. S. (1981). What are the questions in psychology of women? A feminist approach to research. *Psychology of Women Quarterly, 5*(4), 597–617.

Warfel, K. A. (1984). Gender schemas and perceptions of speech style. *Communication Monographs, 51*, 253–267.

Wentworth, D. K., & Anderson, L. R. (1984). Emergent leadership as a function of sex and task type. *Sex Roles, 11*(5/6), 513–524.

Werner, P. D., & LaRussa, G. W. (1985). Persistence and change in sex role stereotypes. *Sex Roles, 12*, 1089–1100.

West, C. (1979). Against our will: Male interruptions of females in cross-sex conversation. In J. Orasanu, M. K. Slater, & L. L. Adler (Eds.), *Language, sex and gender: Does la difference make a difference?* (pp. 81–97). New York: The New York Academy of Sciences.

West, C., & Garcia, A. (1988). Conversational shift work: A study of topical transitions between women and men. *Social Problems, 35*(5), 551–575.

West, C., & Zimmerman, D. H. (1977). Women's place in everyday talk: Reflections on parent-child interaction. *Social Problems, 24*, 521–529.

West, C., & Zimmerman, D. H. (1983). Small insults: A study of interruptions in cross-sex conversations between unacquainted persons. In B. Thorne, C. Kramarae, & N. Henley (Eds.), *Language, gender and society* (pp. 102–117). Rowley, MA: Newbury House.

West, C., & Zimmerman, D. H. (1987). Doing gender. *Gender and Society, 1*(2), 125–151.

Wheelan, S. A., & Verdi, A. F. (1992). Differences in male and female patterns of communication in groups: A methodological artifact? *Sex Roles, 27*(1/2), 1–15.

Wheeler, L., & Nezlek, J. (1977). Sex differences in social participation. *Journal of Personality and Social Psychology, 35*, 742–754.

Wiley, M. G., & Eskilson, A. (1985). Speech style, gender stereotypes, and corporate success: What if women talk more like men? *Sex Roles, 12*(9/10), 993–1007.

Wiley, M. G., & Woolley, D. E. (1988). Interruptions among equals: Power plays that fail. *Gender and Society, 2*(1), 90–102.

Williams, C. (1993). *Doing "women's work": Men in nontraditional occupations*. Newbury Park, CA: Sage Publications.

Williams, D. G. (1985). Gender, masculinity-femininity, and emotional intimacy in same-sex friendship. *Sex Roles, 12*, 587–600.

Willis, F. N., & Williams, S. J. (1976). Simultaneous talking in conversation and sex of speakers. *Perceptual and Motor Skills, 43*(3), 1067–1070.

Winstead, B. A., Derlega, V. J., & Wong, P. T. P. (1984). Effects of sex-role orientation on behavioral self-disclosure. *Journal of Research in Personality, 18*, 541–553.

Wolman, C., & Frank, H. (1975). The solo woman in a professional peer group. *American Journal of Orthopsychiatry, 45*(1), 164–171.

Wood, J. (1994). *Gendered lives: Communication, gender and culture.* Belmont, CA: Wadsworth Publishing.

Wood, W., & Karten, S. J. (1986). Sex differences in interaction style as a product of perceived sex differences in competence. *Journal of Personality and Social Psychology, 50*(2), 341–347.

Wood, W., & Rhodes, N. (1992). Sex differences in interaction style in task groups. In C. L. Ridgeway (Ed.), *Gender, interaction, and inequality* (pp. 97–121). New York: Springer-Verlag.

Woods, N. (1988). Talking shop: Sex and status as determinants of floor apportionment in a work setting. In J. Coates & D. Cameron (Eds.), *Women in their speech communities: New perspectives on language and sex* (pp. 141–157). New York: Longman.

Wright, J. W., & Hosman, L. A. (1983). Language style and sex bias in the courtroom: The effects of male and female use of hedges and intensifiers on impression information. *Southern Speech Communication Journal, 48*, 137–152.

Wyatt, N. (1988). Shared leadership in the weaver's guild. In B. Bate & A. Taylor (Eds.), *Women communicating: Studies of women's talk* (pp. 147–175). Norwood, NJ: Ablex Publishing Corp.

Yamada, E. M., Tjosvold, D., & Draguns, J. G. (1983). Effects of sex-linked situations and sex composition on cooperation and style of interaction. *Sex Roles, 9*(4), 541–553.

Young, M., & Willmott, P. (1957). *Family and kinship in East London.* Baltimore: Penguin.

Youniss, J., & Smollar, J. (1985). *Adolescent relations with mothers, fathers, and friends.* Chicago: University of Chicago Press.

Zahn, C. J. (1989). The bases for differing evaluations of male and female speech: Evidence from ratings of transcribed conversation. *Communication Monographs, 56*(1), 59–74.

Zanna, M. P., & Pack, S. J. (1975). On the self-fulfilling nature of apparent sex differences in behavior. *Journal of Experimental Social Psychology, 11*, 583–591.

Zimmerman, D. H., & West, C. (1975). Sex roles, interruptions and silences in conversation. In B. Thorne & N. Henley (Eds.), *Language and sex: Difference and dominance* (pp. 105–129). Rowley, MA: Newbury House.

Author Index

Subject Index